Education Studies in Ireland
Key Disciplines

Education Studies in Ireland

Key Disciplines

Edited by
BRENDAN WALSH

GILL & MACMILLAN

Gill & Macmillan Ltd
Hume Avenue
Park West
Dublin 12
with associated companies throughout the world *www.gillmacmillan.ie*

© Brendan Walsh, Aidan Seery, Rose Malone, James O'Higgins-Norman
and Geraldine Scanlon 2011

Front cover main images © Shane Phelan/Alamy
Front cover inset images courtesy of Thad Zajdowicz, USA; Enric S., Barcelona;
Sanja Gjenero, Croatia; iStockphoto.com

978 07171 4766 3
Index compiled by Cover to Cover
Print origination in Ireland by TypeIT, Dublin
Printed by GraphyCems, Spain

A CIP catalogue record for this book is available from the British Library.

Contents

Foreword Sheelagh Drudy, University College Dublin   ix

Introduction Brendan Walsh, Dublin City University   1

Chapter One: Philosophy of Education
Aidan Seery, Trinity College Dublin

Introduction and definitions	5
A working 'concept' of education	7
Philosophy of education and the subject areas	11
Understanding learners-models of self	15
The purposes of education in actions and agency	18
The ethics of teaching and learning and the professional code	26
Summing up	29
Recommended reading	29

Chapter Two: History of Education in Ireland
Brendan Walsh, Dublin City University

Education in ancient and medieval Ireland	34
Schooling in 16th-century Ireland	36
The17th century	37
The 18th century	39
The 19th century	40
Moulding the system: the role of the Catholic Church	45
Intermediate (secondary) education	49
Schooling in independent Ireland	52
The Investment in Education report	55
The Programme for Action in Education 1984–1987	58
The green paper Education for a Changing World	60

The National Education Convention   61
The white paper Charting our Education Future   62
The Teaching Council   65
Recommended reading   66

Chapter Three: Curriculum Studies
Rose Malone, National University of Ireland, Maynooth

What is curriculum?   72
Curriculum in Ireland: the Junior Certificate   74
The Junior Certificate in the future   89
The curriculum in Ireland at senior cycle   90
Recommended reading   102

Chapter Four: Sociology of Education
James O'Higgins-Norman, Dublin City University

Introduction   107
Education and social cohesion   108
Education as meritocracy   111
Education as cultural capital   114
Education and religion   117
Education, gender and sexuality   122
Recommended reading   125

Chapter Five: Psychology of Education
Geraldine Scanlon, Dublin City University

What is Psychology?   132
Research in psychology and its application to education   133
Theoretical perspectives on development   136
School-wide positive behaviour support   138
Social learning theory   139
Cognitive theories   139
Developmental perspectives on cognitive development   140
Additional factors for consideration in cognition   144
Individual differences   147

The context of adolescence   154
Psychosocial development   154
Recommended reading   161

Index   171

Foreword

The chapters in this book, *Education Studies in Ireland: Key Disciplines*, provide most useful analyses and overviews of the key theories and findings relevant to teacher education in the fields of philosophy, history, curriculum studies, sociology and psychology. The relevance of these to professional practice is clear and each chapter provides a guide to further reading. Each forms part of the building blocks for what is now generally accepted as the aim of teacher education programmes, i.e. the development of the reflective practitioner.

The quality of teaching is fundamental to the future of Irish society, especially to social cohesion, to citizenship, to competitiveness and to economic recovery. High-quality teaching is inextricably linked to teacher education – initial, induction and in-career. The nature and content of teacher education have been the subject of intense discussion and debate at both national and international levels for the past decade. Indeed, a number of key policy documents at European level have put teacher education at the heart of the development of the knowledge economy. Inevitably, there has been a variety of policy positions in different jurisdictions concerning what should comprise the content and approaches within teacher education programmes. One of the issues which has been intensely debated is whether the 'foundation disciplines' (sometimes referred to as the 'education sciences') should continue to have an important place in teacher education. Europe-wide studies of teacher education programmes illustrate that the foundation disciplines form an essential component of study.

In Ireland, since the establishment of the Registration Council in 1926, the foundation disciplines of philosophy of education, psychology of education, sociology of education, history of education and curriculum studies have come to form core and mandatory elements of all recognised teacher education programmes. The Teaching Council which was established in 2006 has a statutory role in the accreditation and review of teacher education programmes. As one of its early tasks, the council set about a review and revision of the regulations for initial teacher education. The revised regulations built upon those of the Registration Council. In addition to the foundation disciplines mentioned above, the new regulations also include meeting the diverse needs of pupils, including children with special educational needs, disadvantaged pupils and intercultural education, as well as ICT. As will be seen in the various chapters of this book, the diverse needs of pupils have traditionally been explored in research in the sociology and psychology of education. They are also integrated in the other foundation disciplines, as well as in the professional and practicum elements of programmes.

Why have the foundation disciplines been so highly valued by Irish teacher education? Part of the answer to this lies in the rationale provided by both the Registration and Teaching Councils. This rationale is that the foundation disciplines enable the student teacher to build a conceptual framework, which would help her/him to develop an informed and coherent theory of education for practical teaching and future professional work. The affirmation of the importance of the foundation disciplines has also been evident in the comments of external examiners (mainly from universities outside Ireland) on initial teacher education programmes.

The position of many of those who argue in favour of the importance of the foundation disciplines in teacher education is two-fold. Firstly, it is based on a philosophy of education that asserts the value of a critical and democratic professionalism in which teacher education would provide students with relevant teaching competences/capabilities and skills, but would also enable them to have the professional and theoretical insights, and the flexibility, to adapt their practice to changing pupil and educational contexts. Secondly, the position is based on an approach to professional practice that is research and evidence based. For this, the teacher, as a professional, requires a familiarity with the findings of research and with educational theory in order to inform professional practice. Furthermore, this approach envisages that the teacher can be actively engaged in interrogating and researching her/his own practice in order to develop and meet the needs of pupils more fully in rapidly changing circumstances.

Dr Brendan Walsh, the editor, and all of the contributors are to be commended for this very useful volume on the foundation disciplines of education. It will be a valuable resource for student teachers, in-career teachers, policy-makers and the general public.

Sheelagh Drudy
Emeritus Professor of Education
University College Dublin
December 2010

Introduction

The purpose of this book is to provide students, beginning teachers and educational professionals engaged in non-school settings with a comprehensive, critical overview of the foundation disciplines of education. All educational practice is informed by a large body of theory, some of which has its origins in the work of educators who lived many centuries ago. Because educational practice is always evolving, the theory informing it is always being examined and updated, resulting in the constant creation of new knowledge. Yet, despite the ever-widening scope of educational practice, a number of key concepts and bodies of knowledge remain that inform and enrich the endeavour. Any meaningful engagement with the study of education requires critical immersion in these disciplines. To deny this is to declare that educational practice is devoid of theoretical foundation. The chapters that follow, then, introduce the reader to the key foundational bodies of knowledge that inform the study of education; in doing so, they provide a clear, comprehensive, critical and engaging overview of the five key disciplines.

In Chapter One, Aidan Seery notes that, in recent years, the foundation studies of education have increasingly come under pressure. This is largely due to policy-makers and so-called interested parties (such as industrialists and business leaders) becoming frustrated with educators' insistence upon the importance not only of education as a practice, but of the theoretical foundations that underpin it. Education is not, educators insist, simply a process of 'doing', rather one of 'becoming' or 'flourishing', of, to paraphrase Michael Oakeshott, 'becoming human'. Such understandings are perhaps under threat as never before as official rhetoric concerning the value of education, not as a worthwhile human endeavour but as an economic imperative, almost drown out profounder concerns founded upon centuries of reflection, experience and professional commitment. It should be remembered, argues Seery, that education has intrinsic values and characteristics and that these may be quite at variance with the values that a society or economy might suggest for it. In other words, education, like law or medicine, has its own integrity, its own theory and practice aside from any social, economic or political requirements that others may wish to foist upon it. This means that teachers (and what they do) have their own professional integrity *as educators*, first and foremost. Reflecting upon this, Seery suggests that, as educators, we should be vigilant.

As Walsh indicates in Chapter Two, education has been the ideological battlefield of religion, nationalism, economics and a plethora of 'isms' over the centuries. Indeed, outside parties are, historically, unsympathetic to the claim that education is characterised by its own intrinsic aims and purposes. This is, we suggest, worth reflecting on, as the student or beginning teacher seeks to develop and articulate a defence of his/her practice.

By becoming immersed in the theory of education, student teachers not only acquire its vernacular, the language educationalists employ to speak specifically about our profession, but come to understand the particular culture of education as a practice. In common with other disciplines, education has its own history, its theoretical antecedents and culture that have developed over millennia. In choosing to teach, we take part in a conversation that stretches to the beginning of human history. There is, therefore, a vital and often brilliant body of theoretical knowledge informing what we do. Anything less than willing engagement with that body of knowledge will impoverish our practice and mean, ultimately, that our students get less than they deserve.

The philosophy of education, as with philosophy generally, is a key, foundational discipline. Many students approach it with trepidation, perhaps, because of a misunderstanding of the nature of philosophy. In this book, Aidan Seery (School of Education, TCD) provides a comprehensive, analytical and accessible introduction to philosophy as a body of knowledge and its particular application to education. Engaging with this discipline is crucial for those seeking a genuine encounter with educational thought and practice. Philosophical enquiry tends to promote critical questioning: why, for example do we educate? Surely it is incumbent upon education professionals to be able to articulate a defensible response to this question; to be able to explain their choice of profession. 'Who should we educate?' 'What should we teach?' 'Why should we teach one discipline, or parts of it, and not another?' Reflecting upon these questions may help to clarify certain moral, political or pedagogical principles at which we had not previously even guessed. While guiding the reader through the most important concepts, Seery also writes of education as a practice and its implications for the human family. Returning to Aristotle's notion of education as *eudaimonia* ('flourishing'), the reader is invited to think seriously about the purposes of education; is it, after all, simply a technical engagement, a matter of 'getting' children to learn prescribed knowledge or is it something more, something to do with becoming more human? If so, then we are involved in a momentous engagement with far-reaching consequences.

In surveying the evolution of schooling in Ireland, Brendan Walsh (School of Education Studies, DCU) details how our present system was shaped by the events of previous centuries. History is a complex and contested discipline and the version presented here is but one telling of the story. For example, a text such as this cannot hope to deal with the personal or oral history of pupils or teachers, nor can it do justice to the various readings of history, such as feminist, colonial, class and so forth. Indeed, the version presented here is largely concerned with policy and structure; it presents the macro version of the evolution of schooling and serves as a clear, complete overview of the key stages in that development, setting it in its contemporaneous social and religious context. The evolution of the system after independence is traced and the major policy decisions and their consequences detailed and explained. A critical awareness is crucial here. For example, while a policy document may be a historic fact, the aspirations articulated within may not; in other words, 'saying it, doesn't make it so'! Chapter Two, then, accounts for the development of the school system in Ireland from its earliest articulation in ancient Ireland to the advent of the Teaching Council Act of 2001.

Chapter Three examines curriculum content as an aspect of education that has profound pedagogical and political consequences. Rose Malone (School of Education, NUI Maynooth) examines the pedagogical implications of curriculum content and theory. As Malone points out, understandings of what constitutes the curriculum are contested. Chapter Three provides a survey of the curriculum in Ireland, including recent developments, particularly those from the 1990s that resulted in significant changes. Malone also explains the complexities of curriculum, including the 'hidden' curriculum and the relationship between it and assessment. Finally, Malone provides a comprehensive survey of the junior- and senior-level curriculum in Ireland and provides fictional case studies, enabling the reader to see, at first hand, the various inflexions and challenges presented by students and teachers from different backgrounds and dispositions.

In Chapter Four, James O'Higgins-Norman (School of Education Studies, DCU) provides a comprehensive account of both the development of the sociology of education and of recent developments in education in Ireland. O'Higgins-Norman explains the work of pioneering sociologists, such as Durkheim and Weber, showing how their early work influenced and shaped contemporary sociological thought. Key concepts, such as social cohesion, meritocracy and education as social capital are explained and critiqued. O'Higgins-Norman also provides a thought-provoking section on the present state of religion in education in Ireland and discusses the relationship between Churches, state and curriculum in terms of contemporary realities rather than ideological assumptions. Finally, O'Higgins-Norman provides an overview of the contested role of sexuality within educational discourse.

In Chapter Five, Geraldine Scanlon (School of Education Studies, DCU) examines the contemporary implications of developments in educational psychology and explains how these enhance and inform our understanding of the nature of learning. Educational psychology has also contributed enormously to our understanding of adolescence which, since the early twentieth century at least, has proven to be a challenging time for young people. Of increasing relevance to beginning teachers are the definitions, characteristics and remediation associated with special educational needs. Chapter Five also explains the concepts of intelligence, motivation, individual differences and their application to classroom practice. The emergence of the adolescent and adult self are explained and the relevance of this to teaching and life in the classroom are examined.

Dr Brendan Walsh
School of Education Studies
Dublin City University
July 2010

Chapter One
Philosophy of Education
Aidan Seery, Trinity College Dublin

INTRODUCTION AND DEFINITIONS

The philosophy of education, along with the sociology, history and psychology of education (the 'foundation subjects'), has been regarded traditionally, by policy-makers and educationalists at least, as an important study in the preparation of teachers. This tradition of the foundation subjects, while still part of initial teacher education in Ireland, is currently the subject of critical scrutiny, if not explicit threat, in many countries. In the United Kingdom, for instance, the philosophy of education, and to a lesser extent the other 'informing disciplines', has almost completely disappeared from initial teacher education. In the United States, there is no particular requirement for studies in the philosophy of education to qualify for certification. On the European mainland, courses that introduce the academic analysis and critique of the purposes and practices of education are part of the preparation of most teachers (in Germany, for instance, this takes place under the rubric of 'Kritische Pedagogik'). In Ireland then, we hold to the belief that it is necessary and worthwhile to invite student teachers to engage with the particular sets of questions and methods of analysis that we find in the informing disciplines. The way in which students of education regard these studies may not reflect the sense of importance given to them by the profession and the academy, nor may they see their immediate relevance to teaching, but with a little effort and passion, these rich bodies of knowledge can perhaps provide exciting, challenging and fruitful ways of thinking about the practice of education.

This 'informing' rather than 'foundational' view, is the one this chapter, about the role of the philosophy of education in teaching, assumes.

Sometimes, the traditional three pillars in Irish teacher education – theory, methodologies and teaching practice – have been interpreted so that theory dictates methodology which, in turn, dictates classroom practice. But this linear and pseudo-scientific view is one that does not fit well with teachers' experiences and so, rightly, has been widely rejected. Far from providing clear blueprints about how to teach, the informing disciplines can serve the practice of education by providing languages and interpretative frameworks that can help a teacher reflect, analyse and understand more deeply what it is that they do and why they do it.

The philosophy of education differs in a number of ways from the other two informing disciplines. It has different methods and approaches and uses different languages. Perhaps most importantly, the disciplines of educational psychology and sociology can be viewed for the most part as descriptive sciences. They attempt to describe, for instance, how cognition occurs in the brain or how groups form and act in societies. In the philosophy of education, by contrast, the concern is with what are called 'normative' questions, that is, questions about the intentions, plans and purposes of human activity. It tries to tackle questions about what education *should* be about, what it *should* look like and how it *should* be conducted.

Approaching the philosophy of education for the first time can be daunting, or at least strange. Without a background in this way of thinking, the language and methods of the subject are new to most students and necessitate a little time to acquire. An additional difficulty for some is that the philosophy of education does not possess well-defined thematic boundaries nor does it have an agreed set of approaches or methodologies. It is much more the case that there are a number, and types, of questions that arise in educational theorising that are broadly philosophical in nature (however 'philosophical' might be construed here) or that lend themselves to philosophical analysis.

In this short introduction, it will be possible to sketch only a small number of themes and engage in only one or two methodological approaches, focusing on some ideas that seem relevant for initial teacher education, and the reflection of the beginning teacher or anyone intending to work in education. From the beginning, it is important to point out that the philosophy of education begins with educational questions rather than with philosophical ones; that is, they are fundamentally practical in nature rather than speculative. In their most general form, these questions are sometimes grouped around the enquiry into 'Who do we educate?', 'Why do we educate?', 'How do we educate?', 'When do we educate?' and 'What should we teach/learn?' We will be able to give tentative answers to only some of these questions. Not only would the space here not suffice to answer all of them, there is the much more acute problem that there are no agreed answers! The message that goes out from the philosophy of education is that thinking about these questions and some of the theorising that others have done around these questions can be useful, enlightening, rich and enjoyable.

The rest of this chapter is structured as an extended reflection under five headings based on a suggested description of education. You may find that the proposed notion fits or does not fit with your own understanding of education. If it does, at least in part, then hopefully what follows will help deepen that understanding. If it does not, then by struggling with the differences, by articulating your objections and formulating your own philosophy of education, you are, perhaps more radically, 'doing' philosophy of education.

A WORKING 'CONCEPT' OF EDUCATION

One methodological approach used in philosophy is that of conceptual analysis and we might begin, as some texts do (see Walsh) with an examination of the 'concept' of education. However, even the most elementary examination must heed the Foucaultian warning that all concepts are historically and socially constructed with inherent power relations, making the task a difficult and extended one. Therefore, there is no natural, objective, eternal concept of education – instead every notion of education is shaped by histories, societies and powerful bodies. This is also true of the following broad description which is offered as a starting point for the rest of our discussion. For our purposes, then, we will work with the notion that education is the intentional, personal, social and political process through which human beings come to meanings and understandings of themselves and the world and its demands, and also develop abilities and skills through their engagement with knowledge, which leads ultimately to action and agency.

This is a dense and compact description and, as indicated, we will examine some of its features in more depth below. Before that, it is perhaps worthwhile to comment briefly on a number of important themes and tensions.

Firstly, education is concerned not just about the meeting of individual needs, even in its most informal settings or uniquely personal pursuits. All education takes place in cultural and social contexts and against a background of traditions of thought and language that shape even the most personal of learning experiences. More than this, societies and cultures can and do make legitimate demands on education that may not always tally with personal, psychological needs.

Secondly, education has a bi-directional dynamic. To paraphrase one curriculum theorist, education should provide 'windows on the world' and a 'mirror to the self'. The bodies of knowledge into which children are inducted in formal schooling are each a language and way of looking at the world. Science, history, literature and mathematics offer important access routes to understanding the world in different ways and for different purposes. Equally, the same bodies of knowledge, though perhaps some more than others, offer ways in which human beings can understand themselves in new ways and with different vocabularies, thus enriching their construction of self in the world.

Thirdly, educational encounters are three-way relationships. The explicit relationship to knowledge, as well as the human relationship between teacher and pupil or student, is characteristic of education and distinguishes educational activity from forms of engagement associated with social work, counselling, caring and even parenting. So, while teachers may often find themselves in the roles of social engineer, counsellor and carer, the particular role of the teacher is concerned with how learners grapple with knowledge in all of its aspects.

Finally, and perhaps most importantly, education, as understood here, finds its expression and fulfilment only in action and particularly in agency, where the latter term refers to self-directed, moral action. This idea has its roots in the Aristotelian notion of the aim of education being 'right action'. Beyond the rhetoric of 'competencies and skills' and 'generic entrepreneurial learning' lies the responsibility of a society and culture for the aims, uses and consequences of the education it promotes. As Pring (2004) indicates in his anecdote about the letter written by a school principal who survived a concentration camp, it was educated doctors and nurses who carried out atrocious experiments and learned engineers who constructed gas chambers. Instrumental learning alone and the now common reduction of education to techniques of 'teaching and learning' neither guarantee a favourable outcome nor release a society from the responsibility, through education, to endeavour to build a more humane world. Education is fundamentally a value-laden, moral activity and the philosophy of education has a unique role in foregrounding and analysing this aspect of the phenomenon. Against this background, let us now examine some particular themes that emerge from this conception of education.

A teacher's knowledge of knowledge

As indicated, one of the defining characteristics of education is its fundamental orientation towards knowledge and one of the guiding questions concerns what it is that should be taught and learned. As Nel Noddings points out, a teacher might have an interest in questions of knowledge for a number of reasons. Firstly, for most teachers, it is important that what they teach is the 'truth', knowledge that they can engage with, confident of its integrity and reliability. This is possible only if a teacher has some critical understanding of the presuppositions and limitations of a particular body of knowledge. Secondly, some knowledge of 'knowledge' is required if a teacher is to be in a position to decide when a student has actually gained or achieved knowledge or what counts as knowledge in a particular subject area? Thirdly, teachers also make important decisions about whether all kinds of knowledge or just some kinds are presented to pupils. For this reason, it is worthwhile to have a brief look at the nature and status of knowledge as it appears in contemporary educational theory and philosophy.

Each of the bodies of knowledge that make up the curriculum of most formal education has a theory of knowledge out of which it constructs its particular view of the world. Each theory of knowledge contains some fundamental understandings concerning objectivity, truth, certainty and the manner in which knowledge is gained and developed in the field. While it is obviously not possible to discuss these concepts in any depth here, and even though almost any discussion of them is missing from contemporary educational theory, a strong case can be made, as Hogan points out, that all educational endeavour is meaningless if no consideration is given to the ideas of truth and integrity in knowledge. The formal induction of children to the ways of knowing that are manifest in the school curriculum and in the practices of teaching and learning must assume that there is at least something meaningful and useful about knowing certain things. Some of these things may have only local application and validity, most of them may have only provisional and model-like status, but none, it would seem, can do without some normative direction given by a notion of truth.

Truth and truth theories

The concept of truth employed in contemporary bodies of knowledge and in modern philosophy is neither singular nor universally agreed. However, a short excursion into this fundamental idea as it finds expression in the bodies of knowledge of school subjects does seem appropriate.

The classical theory that truth is the correspondence of assertions or claims with reality is the oldest and best-known explanation. Its origins are to be found in the Aristotelian tradition and it finds its most concise formulation in the scholastic formula 'veritas est adaequatio rei et intellectus' but there are a number of ways in which the terms of this formula are understood. The relation is sometimes referred to as conformity, fitting agreement or the more technical term, 'adequation'. The two terms of the formula are variously given as 'consciousness-world', 'thinking-being', 'knowledge-reality', 'language-world' and 'conviction-fact'. One metaphor that has been influential is Ludwig Wittgenstein's idea that knowledge claims mirror or picture reality but that the variety of interpretations and the difficulties that are encountered when attempts are made at making this metaphor more precise are substantial. For our purposes at least, the core message from this theory is its suggestion that the claims of texts and teachers have their validity and legitimacy because what is being taught is indeed the result of seeing how the world really is.

Philosophers occupy themselves with the important technical details and consequences of decidability, processes and measurability of this correspondence. For the educator, it would seem important that, without engaging in these debates, there is a realisation that the correspondence claim, and its difficulties, throws light on the heart of the educational process. If it were not the case that we had agreed criteria for the conditions, processes and validity of the correspondence relation between what is taught and the way the world is, then the task of educating could be reduced to the simple transmission of fixed and certain claims about the world that have been either discovered or constructed over the course of our cultural and intellectual tradition and history. The fact that there remain real difficulties surrounding this notion of truth indicates that education, teaching and learning cannot be understood in this way, and that, in turn, demands a different view of the practice of teaching.

The correspondence theory of truth, however, is not the only one that has been proposed. A list of even the important theories could, in fact, serve as marking posts of almost the whole landscape of modern philosophy. This list would include: the semantic theory of Tarski; the linguistic theories of Ayer, Strawson and Davidson; the intersubjective theories of Pierce and Habermas; the coherence theory of Hempel and Rescher; the classical-pragmatic theory of James and Dewey; the existential-ethical theory of Jaspers; and the phenomenological-hermeneutical theory of Husserl, Heidegger and Gadamer. A number of these theories have found their way into the philosophy of education and have generated rich fields of research. Although these cannot all be discussed adequately here, three, in particular, are worthy of a brief mention.

The notion of intersubjectivity is central to the tradition of idealism and, in particular, to what is known as the transcendental idealism of Immanuel Kant. Pierce develops from this, the idea that truth is a regulative principle in the dynamic of conviction and consensus within a boundless community of researchers. Knowledge claims are approximations to an ideal boundary value that lies at the culmination of scientific enquiry. They are those claims which survive when every possible experiment, test and trial has been conducted and all objections have been refuted. This is obviously an ideal notion of knowledge that can never be fully realised. Knowledge, as it exists at any point in history, is tentative, may not be exact and is provisional on further investigation.

Habermas places the notion of truth in a communicative discourse in which the validity of claims is tried and tested by argumentation and, ultimately, accepted or not. This notion of truth has entered educational theory to some degree in the guise of 'constructivism' which, in its social form, holds that learners construct their knowledge of the world in discursive action in classrooms, through their interaction with texts, and in the general discourse with the scientific and wider community. This results in an approach to knowledge generation, and teaching and learning that is characterised by enquiry, discussion and the communal evaluation of evidence and argument. In this approach, teachers are not simply the repositories of static, naturalistic knowledge engaged in cultural and social transmission, but the leaders and guides of enquiry and active democratic negotiators of evidence and convictions.

If for no other reason than the dominant position of John Dewey in the philosophy of education of the 20th century, the classical-pragmatic notion of truth and knowledge is worthy of noting here. While it is sometimes argued that neither Dewey nor William James construct a theory of truth in the strict sense, their ideas have a recognised history and have found expression in a number of modern educational theories. In brief, the pragmatic approach claims that many questions traditionally concerned with truth can be put aside and that the principal criteria for knowledge is not whether it corresponds with some reality, or even if it can gain the approval of either a scientific or discursive community. The most important criterion is whether or not that which is claimed to be knowledge is *useful*. Knowledge, according to the pragmatic tradition, is naturally connected to human intentions, interests and purposes rather than being abstract formulations of seemingly objective states of affairs. Two questions which arise immediately but cannot be addressed here are: 'Who decides which things are in the interest of human beings?' and 'How do we go about the process of deciding?' Dewey, in particular has tried to answer these two points and some of his ideas appear later in this section.

Finally, the hermeneutical view of truth, as developed in the work of Hans-Georg Gadamer, has attracted the attention and engaged the work of a number of philosophers of education, particularly in Ireland. Both Dunne and Hogan have written extensively on the notion of education as the dialogue between generations in which truth and knowledge unfold in a historical play or game. In this view, truth is an event in *understanding*. It emerges, or is uncovered, in an infinite dialogue with historical tradition and is not the product of an autonomous, egological consciousness. The learning, or understanding, subject is not an objective, remote spectator on the world who forms abstract judgments. On the contrary, far from constructing meanings about the world for themselves, an individual learner is actually constituted by the historical meanings contained in the cultural and historical tradition. The learner comes into existence, so to speak, only in the process of understanding the meanings of the world which pre-figure any individual.

This view has provided for a radical and rich interpretation of education as the formal and informal manifestations of this dialogue with culture and history. As such, it seems to support the view that education is the process by which we actually *become* the individuals we are at any point in our life histories. The consequences of this interpretation are far-reaching, including the important assertion that education has a legitimacy and inherent characteristics all of its own without recourse to any external, social or political factors. This point will be taken up later when we consider the aims and purposes of education. This view also opens up a way of thinking about teaching and learning events and how they are constructed and understood. Once again, it is clear that this understanding of education is far removed from the transmission or 'skills and competencies' models of education that seem to have gained so much influence in recent debate.

PHILOSOPHY OF EDUCATION AND THE SUBJECT AREAS

In addition to some general ideas and conceptions of knowledge and truth in the ways of knowing represented in the curriculum, teachers can also benefit from an introduction to the theories of knowledge in school subject areas. For some in initial teacher education, such an introduction may have been part of an academic degree, for others, however, their only encounter with, say, the philosophy of science, mathematics, the arts and so on, occurs within a course in the philosophy of education. It is not possible to look at all subject areas (apologies to all primary educators!), so we will look briefly at a few areas of the curriculum to illustrate the contribution that an understanding of the philosophy of a subject can make to how teachers think about their own and other subject areas. The subjects have been chosen to show the contrasting notions of what counts as knowledge, truth and objectivity in different subject areas and, as a consequence, to illustrate some of the demands that are made of learners, particularly in formal schooling, when presented, often daily, with a number of subject approaches.

History: a little philosophy

In Dickens' *Hard Times*, Mr Gradgrind declares that the only things that should be taught to children are facts: 'Facts alone are wanted in life.' This same call was echoed at the end of the nineteenth century by historians as a result of a new understanding of history. The movement in the nineteenth century to construct history on the basis of fact is, however, not a chance event. It can be seen as part of a larger project in many branches of knowledge to model all knowledge on that of the physical sciences. The successes of empirical knowledge in the advances of engineering and technology were regarded as an indication that only this kind of knowledge was capable of certainty and securing the progress of humanity. History was not the only body of knowledge to move in this direction. Modern psychology, with its origins in the work of Wilhelm Wundt in the 1870s, and later sociology have both, to greater and lesser extents in the course of their history, modelled their assumptions and methodologies on those of the empirical sciences. Even philosophy was not immune to this cultural influence and the positivists of the Vienna Circle in particular set out to develop a clear and unequivocal set of symbols and sentences that described the data of the world accurately.

While this approach might seem naive and reductionist to contemporary thought, there are still residual common attitudes that the physical sciences represent the apotheosis of knowledge as they provide objectivity and certainty independent of the 'messiness' of consciousness. For the educator, this approach promises a certain clarity for teaching and learning. According to this approach, education can proceed as a neutral, impersonal activity that is untainted by prejudice or bias.

However, the ensuing debate about the nature and status of the empirical and human sciences holds an important lesson about the difficulties associated with, or even the desirability of, viewing knowledge as a cumulative set of facts about the world uncovered by a reliable and uncontested method. In the case of history, Dilthey and Croce were perhaps the first to challenge the autonomy and primacy of fact. The event of Caesar crossing the Rubicon may be a fact, but it is not necessarily a historical fact. It becomes a historical fact by virtue of being selected by historians as historically significant in the project of trying to understand the past. Historical facts, not discovered facts, are selected and historical knowledge comes about when these are written about. As Oakeshott put it: 'History is made by nobody save the historian: to write history is the only way of making it.' This view immediately introduces the difficulty, and pedagogically interesting challenge, that the position and intentions of the author become an unavoidable factor in the construction of historical knowledge. As Collingwood points out, Augustine of Hippo looked at history from the point of view of the early Christian and Gibbon from that of an eighteenth-century Englishman. There is no point in asking which the right point of view was; each was the only point of view possible for the author who adopted it.

However, this does not mean that history is condemned to a relativism in which all possible interpretations are equally valid and equally meaningful. History can claim a methodological stringency that can achieve warrantable assertibilty.

An examination of even a simple model of how history is written is useful for what it tells us about the nature of knowledge in the field. It is also useful with a view to the pedagogy of history and the teaching of history. In a first stage, both the historian and the learner engage in a gathering and interpretation of sources. These sources are sometimes classified as primary and secondary evidence of events which, even as primary sources, are already refracted through the eyes and experiences of the original authors. A second stage involves the critical assessment of the records selected to question the perspectives and purposes of their origins and to evaluate their significance in context. In a third and crucial move, the historian engages her informed imagination in what has been termed an act of 'imaginative re-construction'. This involves the attempt to understand events with the mind of a contemporary of the event but also, and inevitably, from the viewpoint of the present. Finally, the constructed narrative is placed and evaluated in the light of the larger context of other writings and interpretations and is placed in the public domain where it is subject to peer and general review and scrutiny.

The lesson here suggests that learning in history, as in all other subjects of the curriculum, can and perhaps should be more than an exercise in accumulating traditional and authoritative narratives of the world. The learning of history provides an important pedagogical opportunity to examine the nature of knowledge itself and how it comes about. Questions of the nature of fact, objectivity and truth can be considered reflectively, and perhaps even in the light of theories of truth as outlined earlier. At the very least, there is the opportunity to learn of the complexity and richness of knowledge, the challenges of repeated interpretation, and the cultural and social power relations that can be at play in how human beings know about the world.

Science: the model of all knowledge?

As a second example of a body of knowledge or subject area, the physical sciences also offer an insight into the nature and status of contemporary knowledge. As indicated, this field of knowing is often regarded as the pre-eminent example of how human beings have been able to use observation, reason and experimentation to explain, and ultimately control, their environment through knowledge. Its conclusions are generally considered to be unbiased, objective and certain, and its methodology, the so-called 'scientific method', is held up to be the model of all knowledge generation. Only in the very recent past have questions and doubts emerged about the exceptional status of the physical sciences and these have been mostly with regard to ethical rather than epistemological or methodological considerations. However, it is worth noting that an objection to the over-reaching claim sometimes made by science to be the only kind of knowledge worth pursuing or having validity has been voiced throughout its history by people of faith who claim that legitimate knowledge can be achieved in other ways, including illumination and introspection. Nonetheless, there is little denying the elevated position that science holds, particularly in Western societies where it is regarded as a triumph of what human reason can achieve by natural means. We consider it here because some introductory knowledge of scientific knowledge would seem important to all teachers, since no matter what their subject area, they are likely to be confronted by the impressive claims of the natural sciences.

The commonplace or traditional view of science has its foundations in the idea of inductive reasoning, that is, the formulation of generalisations on the basis of repeated, specific examples. The observation that all of the swans on the canal are white can lead to the generalisation that all swans are white. But there are some obvious difficulties, well known in the philosophy of science, with arguing in this manner. Firstly, the conclusion is only secure if all swans, both past and present, could be observed. Even if this was possible, it would still not permit the prediction that all swans in the future would be white and all it takes to demolish a claim based on induction is a single counter-example. So inductive reasoning is hardly a candidate as the foundation for scientific knowledge. The problem of induction has led philosophers of science to consider how a reliable foundation can be found for this important body of knowledge and, once again as with the example of history, these efforts illuminate both the nature of scientific knowledge and have significant pedagogical consequences.

Karl Popper is regarded as one of the most important early thinkers who assumed the project of constructing a philosophy of science that does not depend on inductive reasoning. In his influential work *The Logic of Scientific Discovery*, he presents an interesting argument. Rather than science being based on the collection of data and then generalising, he proposes that science begins with intuition and conjecture, leading to a hypothesis that might explain the observed phenomenon. In a way, then, science *begins with theory* rather than ending with it and facts are always, in some way, theory-laden. Hypotheses are tested deductively, taking the hypothesis to be provisionally true and then designing experiments that show either that the hypothesis is acceptable, or needs to be revised or rejected. This approach is known as the hypothetico-deductive method. Hypotheses are retained as good or best models until such time as they are falsified, but they are never proven true.

Further important contributions to our understanding of the nature of science have been made particular by Thomas Kuhn with his influential *The Structure of Scientific Revolutions* and Feyerabend's *Against Method*. A number of significant conclusions can be drawn from these works that include the idea that science is not necessarily concerned with progressing towards an ever more true representation of nature, and that science is a human activity that is driven by human concerns and the result of creative imagination and reasoning. For the educator, some knowledge of the philosophy of science can bring awareness that even scientific knowledge, while enormously powerful and useful, is not independent of minds, history and society. Scientific meanings and understandings are constructed in communities of practising scientists operating within the current 'normal paradigm' but open to the possibility that paradigms can change.

These two examples, history and science, of ways of knowing in the curriculum seem to suggest to the teacher a particular relationship with knowledge that we wish to develop in students. It is characterised by an openness to imagination and creativity, and a critique that is informed by a view of often changing human purposes. This is significantly different from a view that education provides certain knowledge and straightforward induction into predefined ways of seeing the world. Educational activity, on this view, derives life and energy precisely from the uncertainty of knowledge and the invitation to every generation to review and renew its focus. As Hogan (1995) aptly points out, uncertainty is the great educational value, not certainty.

UNDERSTANDING LEARNERS-MODELS OF SELF

Continuing with the extended reflection on our working description above, the philosophy of education can also serve the educational project by reflecting on the other two parties in the three-way relationship: the teacher and the student. The purpose of such a reflection is to come to an understanding of how teachers see students and how teachers see themselves in the educational relationship. Taking the teacher first, much has been written recently, and much could be said, about teacher 'self' and teacher identity. However, we will not consider this theme here. Because of the confines of this overview and its focus on the beginning teacher who is faced with the immediate demand of trying to understand their students, we will examine some models of self that can provide a theoretical background to ways of conceptualising and understanding the nature of the learner and the ways in which these views might influence a teacher's understanding of her students and her practice.

Student selves as mind/body/soul

The classical or scholastic model regards the human learner as composed of body, mind and soul, with education serving as a formative and/or disciplining process of each of these components. This model has a long history and is still found at the core of much faith-based educational thought. In its two classical forms, the model is associated with Plato and Aristotle. In the case of Plato, human beings are made up of two independent substances: soul and body. The soul is the superior entity and is the seat of knowledge, while the body is inferior, subject as it is to decay and death. Knowledge is an illuminated mental state, it belongs to the eternal realm of light outside 'the cave' and education consists of bringing pupils into the light of certain knowledge out of the world of shadow and mere opinion.

Aristotle's so called *hylomorphism* proposes that everything, including human beings, is a combination of matter (*hyle*) and form (*eidos* or *morphe*). Applied to the learner, the Aristotelian 'soul' (psyche) is the form of the matter that is the body. It is the form (soul) of a thing that gives it its life, its individuality and its uniqueness (and is therefore a broader concept than our modern 'mind' or 'consciousness') but the two are inextricably linked which has led to Aristotle being regarded the father of 'holism', the idea that an integrated, self-conscious, living, concrete, empirical human being takes precedence over abstractions of what it is to be human. Aristotle's picture of the human being still has currency and his psychological analysis of the faculties of the psyche – nutrition, reproduction, sensation, perception, locomotion, imagination, and rational, self-conscious thought – has had a lasting influence in educational thought.

Our more modern views of self owe their origins to the thought of Descartes, who, like Plato before him, proposes a strict two-substance *dualism* of mind and body. Mind, for Descartes, is the conscious, rational, immaterial part of human nature and that which distinguishes human beings from animals. The body is substantially connected to the mind but being material falls for the most part under the remit of the new, empirical sciences, that is, it can be considered as a machine. However, in light of the failure of Descartes' explanation of the connection between mind and body (through the pituitary gland), the Cartesian model suffers from almost insurmountable problems. Nevertheless, this model of self is of particular consequence to educators and educationalists since it still provides the *conceptual* framework for cognitive and other branches of psychology that have been so influential in education in the past century. However, it is regarded by many, not only in education, to be a reductive model that neglects educationally important aspects of being human.

Attempts to construct anti- or post-Cartesian models of self fill libraries and it is not possible, or useful, to try to survey all of these. A brief mention should, however, be made to three further approaches that can be identified in educational theory. The first is the *functionalist* model. The position assumed here is that it is not necessary to know or understand how a human learner is constituted ontologically. No matter what is going on in bodies at the level of physiology, we can consider a human being simply in terms of how they function psychologically and structurally. A metaphor used in this connection is that of the computer. We can analyse and understand how a computer works at the level of software without any knowledge of what kind of hardware is realising the program at work. Thus, we can view students as a conglomeration of functions – thinking, desiring, wanting and so on – and seek to engage with them at this level alone. One particular version of this way of thinking that has achieved considerable influence in education is Howard Gardner's theory of 'multiple intelligences'. At a first glance, this seems an attractive solution and a perfectly legitimate way for an educator to view a learner. On the other hand, it disregards the Aristotelian notion that mind or soul and body are so inextricably linked that the learner is always an embodied learner. To neglect consideration of this embodiedness and its consequences for moral agency is, for many educators, to reinforce an overly abstract idea of the learner that has prevailed in educational theory because of the influence of neo-Platonism and Enlightenment thought.

One view that does not make this error is that taken by *existentialism*. Instead of seeing human beings as being made up of different substances, of powers and faculties, of mental states and functions, it claims that human beings can be understood only in terms of their experience of their own existence. And this experience is a particular and paradox one. The existentialist experience is that the world is puzzling and perplexing without any guiding meaning or sensible orientation. The experience of self is also an experience of the world and is in the same degree puzzling and perplexing. The result is that, in contrast to the Enlightenment project of transparency in reason, the human condition is one of being a stranger to oneself and a stranger in the world. This is what defines the individual and this is how learners are present in the educational relationship and why the imperative that they know themselves and use reason to control their own lives might seem an illusory goal. While perhaps few educators would, on enquiry, declare themselves to be existentialist teachers, anyone who has taught and learned with young people and adults might not find this view so strange, even though they may also remark that it is perhaps not a complete picture.

Finally, it is worth mentioning some aspects of contemporary, post-modernist views that have shaken educational thought in the past 20 years and have challenged all previous notions of subjectivity and self-knowledge. For a number of cultural and intellectual reasons, the great foundationalist and logocentric project of certain knowledge of self begun by Descartes was deemed to have run its course or simply to have failed. The hope that certain knowledge of self and the world could be found in the rational structure of the mind or in the certainty of sense data had not, or could not, be fulfilled.

The realisation of the fallibility of all of our knowledge (see Popper, Kuhn and Feyerabend above) together with the appreciation of the role of culture and history in shaping the knowledge that we have of ourselves and the world, led to the claim that there is no such thing as 'universal human nature', or 'the [learning] subject'. These notions, so the post-modernists claim, have all been constructed by a particular culture and at a particular point in history, with power interests promoting them over other, alternative notions. Lyotard, then, can claim the end of all 'meta-narratives' those great systematic theories and views (Christianity, Marxism, science, psychoanalysis and so on) which claim to explain the world and, since there can no longer be any single theory of the subject, Foucault can declare the 'death of the subject'.

The result of this radical scepticism about knowledge and human subjectivity is e emergence of a multiplicity of meanings, a diversity of understandings and, ultimately, a relativism of all canonical claims. Human beings are no longer seen as autonomous subjects but as the result of the unique meshing of the historical, social and cultural factors at work in a person's life. Not surprisingly, perhaps, the post-modernist view enables greater space for a view of human identity constructed on gender, race, ethnicity and sexuality, on the idea that human beings are 'rational animals' (Aristotelianism). If, as post-modernists claim, there is no such thing as 'human nature', then self and identity are not matters of the 'realisation of potentialities' (Aristotle) or of natural development (Rousseau, Fröbel), ideas close to many educators' hearts. It is much more the case that human learners continuously 'self-create' themselves in the process of acculturation that replaces the modernist notion of education as learning freedom and autonomy.

A number of ways of viewing the human learner, or subject, have been presented in the belief that the way in which teachers see their pupils is an important aspect in how teachers construct their understanding of the educational relationship, its purposes and practice. A teacher holding a classical mind/soul/body view of her student will quite likely be a different kind of teacher to a colleague convinced of her student as a 'self-creator'.

Remaining briefly with the post-modernist theme, one of the most potent and challenging consequences of a post-modernist society is the idea that the very possibility of education, in any of its traditional understandings, is no longer possible. In this world, education, at best, becomes simply one more technology of power in which all efforts are focused on more effective and efficient ways of 'learning'. As Wain points out, at the core of this shift is the move away from a normative notion of education (with its ethical, moral and public aims) to a normatively neutral idea of learning. The idea that education cannot, or should not, be reduced to learning suggests a fundamental decision on the part of not only policy-makers but also individual teachers, and leads into the consideration, in the next section, of the possible purposes of education.

THE PURPOSES OF EDUCATION IN ACTIONS AND AGENCY

The working definition offered at the beginning of these reflections is broadly descriptive in nature. However, at least one word in this definition suggests that education is not a purely technical or natural process. Education, it is claimed, is an intentional action, that is, it is directed at explicit or implicit aims or purposes. These aims and purposes can be found at the level of society, policy-makers, curriculum designers, teachers and students and, in each case, there may or may not be a coincidence of positions. In what follows, we examine some of the more common, explicit aims for education that have been articulated and which continue to exert an influence on teacher thinking and activity.

A useful first categorisation of aims is provided by the distinction between intrinsic and extrinsic aims. Intrinsic aims are those either inhering in the very notion of education itself or those inhering in some internal, natural orientation or dynamic in human beings. Extrinsic aims are those that identifiably come from external sources – a community, a social system or an economic order. This distinction is, of course, contestable, since the argument can be made that the boundaries between internal and external are arbitrary or that it may not be possible to identify the source of influencing factors. Nevertheless, in discussing the aims of education in historical context, this distinction can still be of value.

Before presenting the thoughts of a number of philosophers on the specific aims of education, there is one position that deserves mention. This is the important claim that education does not derive its aims and orientation from external sources but is a form of life, a way of being in the world that has an internal dynamic prior to all other considerations about the usefulness or appropriateness of education. One expression of this position is given by John Dewey. Dewey, perhaps the most eminent philosopher of education of the 20th century, refused to give aims for education other than 'growth'. At first glance, this does not seem to contribute much to an understanding of education, however, Dewey was greatly influenced by Darwin, so that his concept of growth is grounded in the ideas of adaptation and change as a result of experience. In as much as every individual life is a series of experiences, education can be understood as neither more nor less than the 'reconstruction or re-organisation of experience' (Dewey). The educational relationship between teacher, student and knowledge is an engagement with this natural, evolving dynamic in human life that enables Hogan to suggest that education can be regarded as the 'courtship of experience', with all of the risks and uncertainties that this undertaking might entail.

A consequence of regarding education as having an inherent integrity in the natural response of the human being to itself and its environment is that education has intrinsic values and characteristics before any values that a society or economy might suggest for it. Educational practices, on this reading, can claim to be 'practices' in the way described by McIntyre and debated with Dunne.

The notion of the reorganisation of experience, as such, is a formal idea that does not imply a particular direction or content. However, the educational literature contains a number of attempts to explicate substantial aims for education. Some of the most influential include the ideas of human flourishing (Aristotle), autonomy (Locke and Kant), democracy (Dewey), liberation (Freire) and happiness (Noddings), but we could perhaps also include other aims, such as those of citizenship, patriotism, salvation and consumerism, indicating that the project of education has been, or can be, employed in the service of many ends.

Aristotle: education and human flourishing

Aristotle claims that human action is always directed by a goal or an end and for Aristotle, as for Plato, the goal of human activity is happiness, or flourishing (*eudaimonia*). The Greek notion is not to be identified with joy, pleasure or fortune as these are often involuntary states that simply happen to people. For Aristotle, flourishing is the result of human action, something that human beings can bring about in themselves. The means to it are right, virtuous action that is learned by habit and is inextricably linked with life in the community of others.

The aim of education is to develop the ability for right or virtuous action. This demands two things: the development of virtues (*areteis*) and ethical insight or practical wisdom (*phronesis*). Both are framed in the rational appreciation and knowledge of the nature of true human fulfilment. Aristotelian education is marked by the cultivation of rationality as the means by which human beings come to an understanding of their own ultimate flourishing and the natural ends of all other things in the world. This demands deep learning of all bodies of knowledge as the precondition for making rational, informed choices. This learning is not adoption and application of abstract theory and concepts but, in keeping with Aristotle's own 'scientific' approach, a careful, inductive reasoning, taking due notice of the particulars of situations and events. A second indispensible element in Aristotelian early education at least is the development of good habits. These, informed by reason, are not to be found naturally in the student, nor can they be learned from instruction or text; they must be practised.

Aristotle presents a very attractive purpose to education in the ultimate fulfilment of human potentialities. As will be familiar to any student of the history of education, Aristotle's views of education and indeed the world, dominated Christian thought at least since the 12th century and provided the foundation for the first 'pedagogical science' of the Jesuit schools of the 16th century and beyond. As a consequence, a residue of this idea can still be found in modern educational policy, curriculum writing and generally in educational discourse even though, as we will see below, the 'realisation of potentialities' notion has, particularly in primary education, taken on a naturalistic flavour that Aristotle would not have subscribed to.

Rousseau and naturalism

One of the most influential texts in educational theory is Jean-Jacques Rousseau's *Émile* (1762). In it, he broaches a number of themes still discussed and still controversial in schooling today: the relationship between the individual and society; the tension between freedom and control; and the conflict between compliance and autonomy. Written in the spirit of Romanticism, *Émile* must be seen in the context of Rousseau's conception of society in what he terms 'the social contract'. The rigid, authoritarian social structures of the early 18th century crushed human nature and growth and a new societal form needed to be constructed. To achieve this, a new education was necessary that protected the early learner from the forces of socialisation inherent in all education. This new education was possible because of the Romantic conviction that the universe and nature (including human nature) were inherently good. If this was the case, then natural growth and development, if not interfered with, would produce goodness and integrity. The role of education, simply, was to permit the free and natural growth and development of the human subject.

Rousseau is therefore associated to the present day with the idea of anti-authoritarian education, or emancipatory education, and with the education of the child as child. However, some of this referencing is based on a distorted, or non-reading, of Rousseau's work. The free, natural growth of the child and the learning from natural experience is just one stage in the education of Émile. Stages two and three consist of the learning of useful knowledge and learning to enquire into the theories and concepts or society, politics and morality, so that the learner develops from a 'natural state' to a 'civilised' or 'public state'. While some of the claims made for Rousseau's education may be exaggerated, a number of consequences remain active. Firstly, there is the rarely contested notion in early education that the development of the child is promoted by 'meeting the natural needs' and acknowledging difference and individuality. Secondly, this natural development confers on the child a right to grow to personhood in its own way, without excessive interference from educational or social forces.

Opponents of Rousseau's theory point to the dangers of associating the moral notion of goodness with natural processes and thus the over-moralising of educational or developmental processes. Also, the idealisation of the natural state can lead to a distorted and illusory view of childhood that denies its conflicting experiences and thus hides what might be the 'real' needs of a child. Nevertheless, Rousseau's naturalistic thinking has left a lasting impression on Western education.

Kant and the primacy of autonomy

Both Rousseau and Immanuel Kant are Enlightenment figures, the era in which human beings were challenged (by Kant) to have the courage to use their own reason and to overcome their 'self-caused dependency' on authority and power for their knowledge of both themselves and the world. This rallying-call provides the motive for the most powerful and enduring idea of a liberal education; that the most important purpose of education is to promote and nurture personal autonomy. Learners, through education, should develop degrees of civic, social and moral autonomy consistent with their developmental stage. Ultimately, they should be enabled to make the important decisions of their lives on their own, free from the tutelage of teachers, family, social groups or sex. They are, of course, responsible to others for their actions and the consequences and civic society is predicated on the idea that autonomy exists only when recognised by others. For these reasons, autonomous agency is the basis of a shared human dignity.

Kant follows the call to engage reason with an unsurpassed analysis of the structure, content and extent of reason in his 'Critiques'. In the *Critique of Pure Reason* (1781), he examines the possibility of knowledge in a way that attempts to overcome the division between empiricism and idealism. The individual human consciousness is the location that brings together the sense data of the phenomenal world with the conceptual structures of reason. Only in a complicated interaction of both is knowledge constructed. In the *Critique of Practical Reason* (1788), he examines the conditions for the possibility of moral judgment and in the *Critique of Judgment* (1790), a careful analysis of aesthetics is undertaken. All of these works have had a lasting influence on the theory of knowledge, moral education and education in the arts. In the case of the theory of knowledge, the currently popular model of learning in the pedagogy of science, constructivism, owes its origins to Kant's *Critique of Pure Reason*.

The influence of Kant and the Enlightenment on educational thought is not always regarded as positive by some educationalists. The criticism is made that Kant's bequest to education is a notion that is excessively rational and cerebral and that this has led to a learner-centred analysis of education that promotes individualism and neglects the social and relational aspects of educational undertakings and the social construction of knowledge. One such set of criticisms can be found in the contribution of feminist thought to education.

Feminist thought: heart and hand as well as head

As Jane Roland Martin points out, not only do women's philosophical works not feature in the classical canon of educational theory, but even texts that dealt with the education of women were excluded. Rousseau's *Émile*, for instance, does contain a section dealing with the 'education' of a young woman, Sophie, as Émile's companion. Interestingly, the same argument from natural dispositions is made for Sophie's education being designed 'to bear constraint from the first, ... to master [her] own fantasies in order to submit to the will of others'. Obviously, even what is 'natural' has been decided by men!

A number of feminist educational authors have sought to reverse this silencing and neglect and, in doing so, have made an important contribution to modern educational theory. Here we will review just a few of these ideas which come from work situated in what is known as 'third wave' feminism that, as Theyer-Bacon points out, is marked by an attempt to avoid the binaries of essentialist notions of male and female in favour of a recognition of diverse realisations of engendered life.

Feminist thinkers point out that, in education, the work, legitimate interests and values associated traditionally with women have been neglected. These fields include practical and creative work in domestic settings, and the interests and values of relationships, nurturing and care. Martin, for instance, points to the value distinction made between 'productive' and 'reproductive' work that is reinforced in education by the valorisation of those subjects that promote preparation for productive work.

The distinction and separation between the rational and emotional domains of life is also considered an undesirable consequence of male-dominated philosophy, together with a number of traditional binaries, such as the juxtapositions of mind and body, abstraction and experience and so on.

In this phase of feminism, it is the nature of theory itself that is under scrutiny and in a way which, intuitively, seems more accommodating to the difficulties that the traditional theory-practice debate has presented to teachers. The dominant view of theory with its notions of detachment, generalisability, neutrality, and reproduceability and transferability has never sat easily with teachers whose experiences tell of the importance of the relational, the particular, the contingent, the finite and the different.

The work of feminist philosophers of education has done much to challenge dominant views in epistemology, ethics, sexuality and ecology and remains a rich area of further research.

Dewey and democracy

John Dewey is the outstanding and still controversial figure of the philosophy of education in the past century. As Noddings has claimed, he is both a revered and reviled figure, whom some claim saved education in the United States, at least from a stale, moribund authoritarianism, and whom others claim is responsible for destroying educational standards with his 'progressive' child-centred education. As with most important debates, there is probably some truth to be found on both sides. On the one hand, there is little doubt that an 'education' based on memorisation, compliance and physical discipline was unsuitable for modern Western societies. On the other hand, the simplistic dichotomy of 'child-centred' versus 'teacher-centred' education with an exclusive emphasis on the child has led in some parts to a marginalisation of the role of the teacher in the educational relationship to that of an overseer, manager or facilitator in a process that barely requires her intervention.

Dewey, above all, is the philosopher of education for democracy. This simple formula conceals, however, an enormous richness of thought that is expressed by Dewey in a vast body of work that spans more than 60 years. Here we can just expand a little on how Dewey viewed democracy and the role of education in it.

One of the most useful metaphors that can be applied to Dewey's thought on both democracy and education is that of growth. Influenced by Darwin's writings, Dewey constructs a view of human life and experience that valorises the empirical and the practical but in a way that emphasises the interaction and inter-relatedness of things that change and develop over time. In his anthropology, Dewey is anti-Cartesian. His learner is an embodied whole not separable into mind and matter and is always connected to others in society and to nature. In his epistemology, he avoids positivist reductionism that claims that all that can be known about states of affairs can be discovered by a single type of enquiry. For Dewey, experience is always more than what can be known about it through the traditional ways of knowing which provide only particular lenses on affairs. For this reason, while a wide range of subjects should be part of school curricula, the experience of learning in face-to-face contact and embodied interaction holds central place before any intellectualising in abstractions.

In his political thinking on the nature of democracy, Dewey also adopts a biological model. In stark contrast to the political philosophy of Locke, who builds a model of society based on individual freedoms, the right to property and the non-interference of state powers, Dewey's democracy is ideal community life. Individuals are not isolated rights-bearers who have to assert themselves in opposition to others; they live in association and are networked with others. Living in association can confer on human beings a freedom that surpasses the freedom of escape and, in an almost Aristotelian sense, flourishing in community gives ultimate freedom. A democracy is akin to a living organism, such as a cell, which is always more than the numerical sum of its parts and in which all parts are connected, have their meaning from the whole and must react to changes in the environment.

Dewey's educational thought follows from his philosophical anthropology and political philosophy. Education is a central mechanism of the continued growth of a society towards ideal democracy. As such, it is a natural expression of adaptive reaction of a living process. For this reason, Dewey can claim that education does not require any aim or purpose outside or beyond itself. As a mechanism of the 'social continuity of life', it makes little sense to speak of fixed aims in a process that is constantly adapting to environmental changes. In Dewey's open system, human beings do not have predefined ends or ultimate states as proposed by Aristotle. Human beings decide these aims themselves in negotiation, debate and responsible decision-making.

Even this brief noting of some key ideas in Dewey makes clear the misplacement of some of the accusations that are brought against him. Dewey is not the source of 'child-centred' education in the sense of the development of individualism. Individuality is a virtue in education but not individualism. Dewey is not a proponent of 'self-development' towards the realisation of a true self or a fixed end, but of the growth of a person in a community of shared and evolving interests.

Dewey, however, *is* the educationalist of experience. It is only in the concrete, lived situations of communities, in its debates about what direction it should go and what should be achieved, that growth occurs and democracy is built. Education, therefore, must include credible activity and engagement in the affairs of the world. It must include the learning of responsibility, since progress is neither natural nor preordained and human beings must decide which life possibilities they wish to see realised. For this reason, curricula should not be over-theoretical or academic but enable physical, practical and social engagement with the real world. Classrooms should also model the larger democratic society and teach the values and the living of a democratic life, developing, in particular, the skills of social enquiry needed to resolve tensions in the conflict of individual interests.

Freire: education as liberation

Critical pedagogy, or emancipatory-critical pedagogy, was an important movement in educational theory in the 20th century. In opposition to the individual-centred cognitivism that holds sway in much of the current discourse on teaching and learning, critical pedagogy argues for an interpretative, hermeneutical paradigm more appropriate to an understanding of education, particularly with regard to the relationship between education and society. This interpretative approach is, however, not simply a matter of methodology. Critical pedagogy has a programmatic aim of teaching and learning for social transformation and change in schooling.

The iconic figure of critical pedagogy is Paolo Freire, the Brazilian educator and educationalist. Reflecting on the situation of the poor, illiterate and oppressed, he concludes that education, if conceived and practised in a new way, can be the key to transforming people's lives. Human freedom is not a static ideal but a practical achievement; it is brought about by the 'praxis' of individuals. (Praxis refers to a cycle of 'knowledge/reflection-action-knowledge/reflection' and leads to transformation that is the conscious synthesis of thought, language and experience.)

Education, for Freire, can assist in the transformation of people's lives in a number of ways. Firstly, it can provide the precondition of literacy. Without language and literacy, the 'oppressed' cannot read the world, cannot articulate perceptions of their situation or enter into critical dialogue with others. Secondly, education and schooling can enable dialogue between the individual and the world. This dialogue has two purposes, to expose the objective political and social situations in which people find themselves and also to explicate the subjective awareness that people have of their situation. These are crucially not the same and the dialogue becomes a dialectic in which not only can reality be transformed but those involved in the change are changed themselves. As Freire points out, oppression dehumanises both the oppressor and the oppressed. An education that liberates both oppressor and oppressed has to question established and favoured kinds of knowledge, values and instrumental procedures wherever they exist. It has to recognise and incorporate the material and emotional experiences of the learner outside the classroom and root itself in community.

Freire's legacy is still strong and has been re-cast to analyse and inform emancipatory education in liberal, capitalist societies on the basis that 'oppression' is not confined to crude political and social subjugation and that 'false consciousness', the inability or reluctance to examine one's perceptions and values critically, is not evident only in the poor. This wider application of the ideas of critical pedagogy places it clearly in the traditions that influenced Freire himself:

Christian existentialism, Marxism, Marcuse and the Frankfurt School. In these traditions, education is open, sometimes conflictual, challenging and disturbing and learners are forced to face their fears of autonomy and responsibility in the loss of inherited securities.

This overview of some of the key ideas that have been formulated on the aims and purposes of education has considered only a small number of the possibilities that have either been proposed, or imposed, at different times. An extended list would have to include the reduction of educational aims and goals to purely economic ends; the misuse of education towards demagogic and propagandist ends to promote patriotism, sexism, nationalism, consumerism and other 'isms' besides. These possibilities for education highlight the importance of vigilance and reflection on the part of teachers and educators that they are not simply teaching and learning 'operatives' engaged in a socially, culturally and politically neutral activity. A second possible consequence of reflection on the aims and purposes of education is the consideration of whether certain pedagogical approaches and methods are more appropriate for the achievement of some aims rather than others. One obvious example is the implications for practice of the Deweyan aim of learning and growing democracy. How do classrooms look when they reflect growing democracy? What kinds of pedagogical knowledge, rather than subject knowledge, do teachers need to enable their classrooms to be places of learned democracy? Or, how does a classroom look that exercises Socratic enquiry, or promotes Aristotle's learning of practical wisdom and good judgment?

The intentional, purposeful and moral nature of educational activity has been an underlying theme of the discussion so far and so, in the final section, we examine in some more detail some approaches to the ethics of teaching and learning.

THE ETHICS OF TEACHING AND LEARNING AND THE PROFESSIONAL CODE

The ethics of teaching, learning and educational practice is another area to which the philosophy of education can make a contribution through teaching and research. Despite all attempts to reduce traditional, liberal ideas of education to the science and technology of efficient delivery, value-neutrality and evidence-based measurables, the view that education is fundamentally an ethical and moral undertaking is still widely held. Taking this as a starting point, it is worthwhile examining the origins and status of ethical demands and the ways in which teachers can articulate an ethical position on the core evaluations that they make of educational activity.

Three schools of thought offer ways in which we can argue rationally for ethical decisions and actions and these will be outlined briefly here. There are, however, also non-rational positions taken on ethical matters. These include different forms of subjective relativism, emotivism, prescriptivism and importantly, cultural relativism. Common to all of these approaches is the claim that it is not possible to defend universal, moral assertions. These relativist positions can pose a particular challenge to teachers in their relations with students and parents. Cultural relativism, for instance, claims that norms and values vary in different cultures and therefore no universal morality can apply to all of humanity with the result that it is impossible to adjudicate between moral claims of students from different cultural backgrounds.

The schools of thought of utilitarianism, deontology and virtue ethics, on the other hand, provide standpoints from which to argue rationally for universal meanings that make demands on behaviour. The notion of rationality employed here is, of course, not the same as scientific rationality which does not allow for purposes, evaluative meanings or intentionality. Ethics and moral judgment are not matters of fact. However, human beings do attach significance and purpose to their actions and these can be analysed.

In utilitarianism, the case is made that all human action is governed by the phenomena of pleasure and pain. Jeremy Bentham formulates the principle of utility as that which approves or disapproves of actions according to their tendency to increase happiness and decrease pain. This seemingly simple principle avoids the difficulties of deciding whether some values are more important than others and reduces the process of ethical decision-making to one of adding up 'utilities'. These features represent both the strengths and weaknesses of the approach. It would seem to be the case that human beings do have a hierarchy of values and that there are even some which do not fit easily with the pleasure-pain binary. Secondly, there is the problem of quantifying utility in order to carry out the calculus. However, despite these difficulties, utilitarianism is widely invoked especially in the English-speaking world.

The tradition of deontology owes its origins to the work of the German idealist philosopher Immanuel Kant. He shifts the debate on the principles behind ethical demands from how to decide what we should do to what we should not do. The categorical imperative dictates that we are to do only that which we could rationally will that everyone else be free to do. This rather abstract approach severs the link between substantial notions of the 'good' from the idea of what is right. The categorical imperative does not have a content, it does not give an inventory of those values and things which are good and therefore to be pursued. However, we do not want people to lie to us or break their promises and therefore it is wrong to do either even if there might be some good to be attained by doing so. Deontic ethics or morality has been particularly important in the construction of public ethics in democracies that are home to many cultural and ethnic groups holding different notions of the good. No particular set of values is valorised in this approach but it is possible to agree on actions that obligatorily must be avoided for the protection of all. Deontic ethics is therefore also referred to as the ethics of obligation or duty.

A third way of rationalising about ethical evaluations and demands is to reason that certain virtues, character traits and dispositions are desirable and therefore worth pursuing. Proponents of this approach argue that there are certain virtues that contribute to the well-being of individuals and societies and the emphasis is on attributes of the person rather than judging acts (as in the case of deontic ethics). This approach is known as the 'aretaic view', after the Greek word for virtue. It is associated with Aristotle's work in ethics but also with his view of education. Because of the lasting influence of Aristotelian thought on education, this view of ethics and morality has held a privileged position in educational ethics. Its difficulty lies in identifying character traits that are desirable in all possible circumstances without consideration of times, cultures and places. Loyalty, for instance, may be a virtue in certain situations but not in others where courage to be disloyal is called for. Nevertheless, for many, the question of what kind of a person do I want myself or my students to be is more important than what a person is morally required to do or not to do.

These sketches are brief outlines of views that are rich in detail and in connections not discussed here. However, they can perhaps serve as a simple scheme to begin reflecting on how a teacher might regard the ethical demands and dimensions of her profession. They can provide a deeper theoretical layer that underpins or illuminates the more performative demands of a code of practice or conduct that is a feature of all modern professional life including teaching.

In Ireland, the Teaching Council, as the statutory regulatory body for first- and second-level teaching, published the 'Codes of Professional Conduct for Teachers' in 2007. The term 'conduct' rather than 'practice' reflects the wording of the relevant legislation and while the council fulfilled the requirement of publishing a code of conduct, it included also a statement of core values and a code of professional practice. This was intended to assert the fundamental ethical nature of educational activity, although a number of the commitments presented are more purely professional than ethical in nature. The code does not espouse a particular ethic of education, nor does it argue for a particular description of educational activity which might have been employed to evoke the ethical and moral responses that find expression in the core values. This perhaps leaves them unconnected to anything but a diffuse assumed sharedness.

The Teaching Council document groups the core values into the three categories of quality of experience, educational outcomes and relationships. In the first, the teacher is viewed as committed to educational experiences that are centred on the child, adaptable and the result of continuous learning on the part of the teacher. Significantly, the second category includes probably the only explicit ethical commitment to social justice, equality and justice. It does this in the context of a view of the learner that acknowledges the socio-historical and cultural nature of embodied existence and flourishing. This commitment to what is commonly termed 'holism' might be better regarded as a commitment to a 'comprehensive' view of education as there is no indication of the inter-connectedness of the listed features. However, the term 'comprehensive' has a particular history in education that disqualifies it from being used in its original sense. Finally, the category of relationships places a commitment to the care of students and then to collaboration and co-operation with three widening circles of educational partners: colleagues, parents and society at large. This commitment to a type of relational view of education is significant despite the impression that the opportunity to say something more about the value of the relationship with the learner in a shared pursuit of knowledge and even truth was missed.

The code of practice, then, expands on the roles, responsibilities and relationships with regard to students, parents, the curriculum, professional development, society and the state. The dominant language of the code is that of 'teaching and learning' rather than, for instance, that of self-formation, transformation or other purposive enterprise, so that the reader could be left with the impression of a 'technicist' approach to teaching and there is some indication of an underlying 'service' model of education. Finally, the actual code of conduct gives concrete shape to some of the implications of the ethical principles and principles of professional practice outlined earlier.

The code as a whole, then, contains the kind of statements about service ideals, the characteristics of the professional, ethical and professional commitments, and rules that are common in most professional codes. It does contain a set of imperatives but, if it is not to be consigned to a forgotten shelf in a staff room, it must be employed as a stimulus to reflection and analysis of dispositions and practices in individuals and schools.

SUMMING UP

This consideration of some of the characteristics of the educational relationship, its purposes and the types of commitment involved concludes this brief overview of some of the ways in which the philosophy of education can inform the practice of education. The languages that we employ to speak about education, the way in which we view knowledge and the educational relationship with students – the big questions about the purpose of the whole enterprise – can be illuminated and critiqued in a powerful way using the methods of philosophical analysis and reflection. Sketching this backdrop at the beginning of teacher education does not provide simple guidelines or rules for practice. That is not its purpose. If an introduction to the philosophy of education can provide a language and way of thinking that helps teachers reflect on and understand more deeply what they are doing and why they are doing it, then it will have served a noble purpose in a noble profession.

RECOMMENDED READING

Anthologies and collections

Blake, N. and Smeyers, P. et. al (eds) (2003). *The Blackwell Guide to the Philosophy of Education*. Oxford: Blackwell.

Carr, W. (2005). *The RoutledgeFalmer Reader in philosophy of education*. London: Routledge.

Chambliss, J. J. (ed.) (1996). *Philosophy of education: an encyclopedia.* London: Garland.

Curren, R. (ed.) (2007). *Philosophy of Education: An Anthology.* Oxford: Blackwell.

Curren, R. (ed.) (2003). *A Companion to the Philosophy of Education.* Oxford: Blackwell.

Hare, W. and Portelli, J. P. (eds) (2001). *Philosophy of Education: introductory readings.* Calgary Alberta: Detselig.

Heyting, F., Lenzen, D. and White, J. (eds) (2001). *Methods in philosophy of education.* London: Routledge.

Hirst, P. and White, P. (1998). *The Philosophy of Education: critical readings.* London: Routledge.

Kohli, W. (1995). *Critical conversations in philosophy of education.* London: Routledge.

Rorty, A. O. (1998). *Philosophers on Education: Historical Perspectives.* London: Routledge.

Siegel, H. (ed.) (2009). *The Oxford Handbook of philosophy of education.* Oxford: Oxford University Press.

Teaching Council (2007). *Codes of Professional Conduct for Teachers.* Maynooth, Teaching Council of Ireland.

Books

Aristotle (1995). *Politics* (trans. E. Barker). Oxford: Oxford University Press.

Barrow, R. and Woods, R. (2006). *An introduction to philosophy of education.* London: Routledge.

Bentham, J. (1983). *Deontology; together with A table of the springs of action; and the Article on utilitarianism.* Oxford: Clarendon Press.

Bruner, J. S. (1960). *The Process of Education.* London: Oxford University Press.

Carr, D. (2003). *Making Sense of Education: An introduction to the philosophy and theory of education and teaching.* Oxford: RoutledgeFalmer.

Carr, W. (1995). *For Education: Towards Critical Educational Inquiry.* Buckingham: Open University Press.

Collingwood, R. G. (1994). *The Idea of History.* New York: Oxford University Press.

Croce, B. (1941). *History as the story of liberty.* London: Allen & Unwin.

Dewey, J. (1900). *The School and Society.* Chicago: University of Chicago Press.

Dewey, J. ([1916] 1966). *Democracy and Education.* New York: Free Press.

Dilthey, W. (2002). *Selected Works Volume II: The Formation of the Historical World in the Social Sciences.* Princeton, NJ: Princeton University Press.

Dunne, J. (1997). *Back to the Rough Ground: Practical Judgment and the Lure of Technique.* Notre Dame, IN: University of Notre Dame Press.

Dunne, J. and Hogan, P. (2004). *Education and Practice: Upholding the Integrity of Teaching and Learning.* Oxford: Blackwell.

Feyerabend, P. (1975). *Against Method.* London: NLB.

Foucault, M. (1977). *Discipline and Punish: The Birth of the Prison.* London: Allen Lane.

Freire, P. (1973). *Pedagogy of the Oppressed.* New York: Seabury Press.

Fröbel, F. (1885). *The Education of Man* (trans. J. Jarvis) New York: A. Lovell and Co.

Gadamer, H.-G. (1975). *Truth and Method*. London: Sheed and Ward.

Gardner, H. (1983). *Frames of Mind: the theory of multiple intelligences*. London: Heinemann.

Giroux, H. (1989). *Schooling for Democracy. Critical Pedagogy in the Modern Age*. London: Routledge.

Greene, M. (1995). *Releasing the Imagination: Essays on Education, the Arts and Social Change*. San Francisco, CA: Jossey Bass.

Habermas, J. (1971). *Knowledge and Human Interests* (trans. J. Shapiro). London: Heinemann Educational.

Hadot, P. (1995). *Philosophy as a Way of Life. Spiritual Exercises from Socrates to Foucault*. Oxford: Blackwell.

Halstead, J. M. and Taylor, M. J. (eds) (1996). *Values in Education and Education in Values*. London: Falmer Press.

Hirst, P. H. and Peters, R. (1970). *The Logic of Education*. London: Routledge and Kegan Paul.

Hogan, P. (1995). *The Custody and Courtship of Experience*. Dublin: Columba Press.

Hogan, P. (2010). *The New Significance of Learning: Imagination's Heartwork*. London: Routledge.

Illich, I. (1971). *Deschooling Society*. London: Calder Boyars.

James, W. ([1899] 1958). *Talks to Teachers on Psychology*. New York: W. W. Norton.

Kuhn, T. (1962). *The Structure of Scientific Revolutions*. Chicago, IL: University of Chicago Press.

Lyotard, J.-F. (1984). *The Postmodern Condition: a report on knowledge* (trans. G. Bennington and B. Massumi). Manchester: Manchester University Press.

Macedo, S. (2000). *Diversity and Distrust: Civic Education in a Multicultural Democracy*. Cambridge, MA: Harvard University Press.

MacIntyre, A. (1999). *Dependent rational animals*. London: Duckworth.

Martin, J. R. (1994). *Changing the Educational Landscape: Philosophy, Women and the Curriculum*. London: Routledge.

Noddings, N. (2007). *The Philosophy of Education*. Boulder, CO: Westview.

Nussbaum, M. (1997). *Cultivating Humanity: A Classical Defence of Reform in Liberal Education*. Cambridge, MA: Harvard University Press.

Oakeshott, M. (1972). 'Education: The Engagement and Its Frustration'. In R. F. Dearden, P. H. Hirst and R. S. Peters (eds), *Education and the Development of Reason* (pp. 19–49). London: Routledge and Kegan Paul.

Peters, M. A. (1996). *Poststructuralism, Politics and Education*. London: Bergin and Garvey.

Pierce, C. S., (1931–58). *The Collected Papers of Charles Sanders Pierce*, C. Hartshorne, P. Weiss (Vols. 1–6) and A. Burks (Vols. 7–8) (eds), Cambridge, MA: Harvard University Press.

Plato (1953). *The Dialogues of Plato* (trans. B. Jowett). Oxford: Clarendon Press.

Popper, K. (1959). *The Logic of Scientific Discovery*. London: Hutchinson.

Pring, R. (2004). *Philosophy of education: aims, theory, common sense and research*. London: Continuum.

Rousseau, J.-J. ([1782] 1961). *Émile* (trans B. Foxley). London: Dent.

Scheffler, I. (1960). *The Language of Education*. Springfield, IL: Thomas.

Siegel, H. (1988). *Educating Reason: Rationality, Critical Thinking and Education*. London: Routledge

Smeyers, P. and Marshall, J. D. (eds) (1995). *Philosophy and Education: Accepting Wittgenstein's Challenge*. Dordrecht, Netherlands: Kluwer.

Tamir, Y. (1995). *Democratic Education in a Multicultural State*. Oxford: Blackwell.

Taylor, C. (1989). *Sources of the Self: The Making of the Modern Identity*. Cambridge, MA: Harvard University Press.

Thayer-Bacon, B. J. and Turner, G. M. (2007). 'What feminist inquiry contributes to philosophy and the philosophy of education: a symposium. *Educational Theory*, 57 (3), 297–306.

Walsh, P. (1993). *Education and Meaning: Philosophy in Practice*. London: Cassell Education.

Winch, C. (1998). *The Philosophy of Human Learning*. London: Routledge.

Winch, C. and Gingell, J. (1999). *Key concepts in the philosophy of education*. London: Routledge.

White, J. (1990). *Educational Aims and the Good Life*. London: Kogan Paul.

Woolman, M. (2006). *Ways of Knowing*. Sydney, Aus: Ibid Press.

Journal articles

It is obviously impossible to construct a comprehensive list of articles published on the themes discussed. What follows is just a very small sample of some recent writing in the main journals. The most influential journals in the philosophy of education are:

> *Journal of Philosophy of Education*
> *Educational Philosophy and Theory*
> *Educational Theory*
> *Studies in Philosophy and Education*
> *Theory and Research in Education*

Biesta, G. (2002). 'How General Can Bildung Be? Reflections on the Future of a Modern Educational Ideal'. *Journal of the Philosophy of Education*, vol. 36, no. 3, 377–90.

Chambliss, J. J. (2009). 'Philosophy of Education Today'. *Educational Theory*, 59 (2), 233–51.

Curran, R. (2009). 'Education as a Social Right in a Diverse Society'. *Journal of Philosophy of Education*, 43 (1), 45–56.

Dall'Alba, G. (2009). 'Phenomenology and Education: an introduction'. *Educational Philosophy and Theory*, 41 (1), 7–10.

Endres, B. (2007). 'The Conflict Between Interpersonal Relations and Abstract Systems in Education'. *Educational Theory*, 57 (2), 171–86.

Garrison, J. (2009). 'Teacher as Prophetic Trickster'. *Educational Theory*, 59 (1), 67–83.

Gary, K. (2006). 'Leisure, Freedom and Liberal Education'. *Educational Theory*, 56 (2), 121–36.

Hammershøj, L. G. (2009). 'Creativity as a Question of Bildung'. *Journal of Philosophy of Education*, 43 (4), 545–58.

Hogan, P. (2005). 'The Integrity of Learning and the Search for Truth', *Educational Theory*, vol. 55, no. 2, 185–200.

Long, F. (2008). 'Protocols of silence in educational discourse'. *Irish Educational Studies*, 27 (2), 121–33.

Mason, M. (2001). 'The Ethics of Integrity: Educational Values Beyond Postmodern Ethics'. *Journal of Philosophy of Education*, 35, (1), 47–69.

Mulcahy, D. G. (2008). 'Newman's Theory of a Liberal Education: A Reassessment and its Implications'. *Journal of Philosophy of Education*, 42 (2), 219–31.

Mulhall, S. (1998). 'Political Liberalism and Civic Education: The Liberal State and its Future Citizens'. *Journal of Philosophy of Education*, 32 (2), 161–76.

Nicholson, C. (1989). 'Postmodernism, Feminism, and Education: The Need for Solidarity'. *Educational Theory*, 39 (3), 197–205.

Pring, R. (2007). 'The Common School'. *Journal of Philosophy of Education*, 34 (3), 325–33.

Seery, A. (2008). 'Zizek's dialectics of ideology and the discourses of Irish education'. *Irish Educational Studies*, vol. 27, no. 2, 133–46.

Smeyers, P. and Burbules, N. C. (2006). 'Education as Initiation into Practices'. *Educational Theory*, 56 (4), 439–49.

Smith, R. (2009). 'Between the Lines: Philosophy, Text and Conversation'. *Journal of Philosophy of Education*, 43 (3), 437–49.

Vandenberg, D. (2009). 'Critical Thinking about Truth in Teaching: The epistemic ethos'. *Educational Philosophy and Theory*, 41 (2), 155–66.

Wain, K. (2008). 'The Future of Education ... and its Philosophy'. *Studies in Philosophy and Education*, 34 (3), 325–33.

White, J. (2007). 'Well-being and Education: Issues of Culture and Authority. *Journal of Philosophy of Education*, 41 (1), 17–28.

Winch, Christopher (2002). 'The Economic Aims of Education'. *Journal of Philosophy of Education*, 36 (1), 101–17.

White, R. (2008). 'Rousseau and the Education of Compassion'. *Journal of Philosophy of Education*, 42 (1), 35–48.

Wringe, C. (2009). 'Teaching, Learning and Discipleship: Education Beyond Knowledge Transfer', *Journal of Philosophy of Education*, 43 (2), 239–51.

Zembylas, M. (2007). 'A Politics of Passion in Education: The Foucauldian Legacy'. *Educational Philosophy and Theory*, 39 (2), 135–50.

Chapter Two

History of Education in Ireland

Brendan Walsh, Dublin City University

EDUCATION IN ANCIENT AND MEDIEVAL IRELAND

The first formal, state-aided system of education in Ireland was founded in 1831. However, even before the 16th century, when King Henry VIII proposed the founding of schools within the Pale, a long tradition of learning had evolved in Ireland, reaching its high point in the great monastic schools of the eighth to 12th centuries. Before the coming of Christianity, there were complex arrangements of tribal communities and from these evolved the tradition of the *filid* – the poets and scholars of the Middle Ages. *Filid* had a number of functions within the community. They acted, for example, as guardians of ancient traditions, they had a profound knowledge of local history, topography and genealogy – particularly important in settling disputes regarding titles and land. They also acted as chroniclers of royal and community events as they were usually attached to the royal court. Hence, long before the monastic age, a particular type of learning, associated with power and respect, existed in Ireland.

Education, as we understand it, did not exist in this early society. However, as in most ancient societies, a strong oral and storytelling tradition evolved, much of it later captured by the monastic scribes. Children learned crafts, agriculture and animal husbandry at home, while boys of higher rank, learned horse riding and girls were taught sewing and embroidery (*Seanchus Mór, Ancient Laws of Ireland*). Collections such as the *Seanchus Mór* provide invaluable information about this period. Those training to become a *file* had to complete a prescribed course of learning that lasted 12 years, disciplines included: grammar, philosophy, tales, law, language of poetry, versification, etymology, composition and oratory. In the final three years, the scholar had to master 350 historical and romantic tales and know the duties of the king. Learning was by rote as books were very rare and writing uncommon, but evidently a detailed, defined and systematic curriculum existed in pre-Christian Ireland. These communities of learning evolved over time into what are generally referred to as 'native schools'. Two sources for these are The *Clanricarde Memoires* (1722) by Thomas Sullivan and the *Account of Edmund Campion* (1572). These are, therefore, rather late sources, but they provide invaluable information regarding the nature of learning in the native schools. The schools emphasised composition, memorisation and the guidance of a master teacher. The development of the *filid* communities and the native schools led to learning taking a prominent place in Irish society, to the development of a tradition of scholarship and, ultimately, a model upon which native monastic learning could be developed.

The impact of Christianity on models of learning cannot be underestimated and much has been written of the great Irish monastic period. An indication of the strength of the tradition which confronted St Patrick upon arrival, however, was his admission that his enemies initially disparaged his 'lack' of learning. He reveals in his *Confession* and *Letter to Coroticus* that he was 'unlearned', that he had 'not studied like the others' and was embarrassed 'to reveal [his] lack of education'. Patrick's mission was the conversion of the native Druidic order. Therefore, he had to demonstrate the intellectual rigour of Christianity in the face of older beliefs that were culturally and intellectually influential. Hence Patrick's eagerness to see centres of learning established at the new monastic settlements, the greatest of which was founded at Armagh between AD 445 and 457.

It is worth pausing to consider the development, spread and influence of the monasteries. The skeletal remains dotted about the Irish landscape testify to the great dissolution under Henry VIII when Catholic monasteries in England and Ireland were closed and their communities dispersed. But between the late fifth century and the mid-16th century, a network of complex institutions spread throughout Ireland, comprising religious communities and ecclesiastical colleges. Between the fifth and seventh centuries, monasteries were founded at Aran, Clonard, Clonmacnoise, Tuam, Clonfert, Derry, Durrow, Cork and Kildare.

These establishments produced the first written information concerning teaching and learning in Ireland. Monasteries produced three significant texts:

- glosses, including the meaning of Irish words and translations, often with commentaries written in the margins;
- grammars, usually copies (in Irish) of Latin grammars; and
- copied books, the most common literary activity.

While the monasteries acted primarily as places of learning for monks, some catered for small numbers of laymen, although usually these were people considering entering religious life. Monasteries also attracted scholars from abroad; in the early eighth century, Aldhelm, Bishop of Malmsburg, complained of the English going to the Irish monasteries in 'fleet loads'.

The Norse Invasions (837–1014) brought the early monastic period to an end. Repeated attacks from the illiterate Norse resulted in the destruction of monastic communities and the loss of manuscripts produced in the *scriptoria*. While some communities along the western seaboard were unmolested, the invasions represented a prolonged and destructive interruption of monastic learning and it was not until the kingship of Brian Ború (1002–1014) and the defeat of the Norse at Clontarf that a period of revival began. The period 1014–1169 was relatively peaceful and witnessed a revival in learning, art and literature; the Cross of Cong (1123), Cormac's Chapel (Cashel, 1134) and the *Book of Leinster* (1160) all date from this era. Many monasteries were rebuilt and new communities founded, such as the Cistercians at Mellifont in 1142. The native schools also began to thrive again which, for them, marked the beginning of the transformation from the oral to written tradition.

The arrival of Richard Fitzgilbert de Clare ('Strongbow') in 1170 is well known to any Irish schoolchild. In 1171, Henry II (who had sent an embassy to Rome shortly after his coronation in 1154 to entreat the Pope's permission to invade Ireland so that he might teach the Christian faith to a 'rude and barbarous people') was declared Lord of Ireland, thus beginning the long, torturous relationship between the two islands. Richard Fitzgilbert de Clare, his followers and a large number of Irish chieftains swore fealty to King Henry and, by the mid-13th century, almost 70 per cent of Ireland was under Norman control. The gradual intermingling of Norse and native Irish led, famously, to the description of the one-time invaders as, 'more Irish than the Irish themselves' by the end of the 14th century. This gaelicisation of the Norse resulted in Ireland's remaining isolated, particularly outside the Pale, from the influence of the English crown, a situation that was untenable after Henry VIII's break with Rome in the mid-1530s. Since the coming of St Patrick, Ireland had, despite differences, remained loyal to the Roman Catholic Church; indeed, the Synod of Cashel (1172) at which the Irish accepted Henry II as monarch, had proclaimed Catholicism as the official religion of Ireland and this was still the position when Henry VIII acceded to the throne in 1509.

SCHOOLING IN 16TH-CENTURY IRELAND

The Tudor break with Rome made it imperative to discover ways of persuading the Irish, if not to embrace the tenets of the Established Church, then at least to weaken its loyalty to Rome. That an administration, seeking to initiate social or ideological change, should choose schooling as the vehicle by which this should be affected is a theme to which we will return below. The Tudor regime understood the importance of education in social engineering and, in 1537, set about establishing a network of parish schools within the Pale. The primary purpose of these was to encourage the use of the English language in the region. They were also intended to replace the native schools, although most of these had been closed under the Act of Suppression a year earlier. There is little evidence that the act had any significant effect. Indeed, in what was to become a long history of subversion, those Irish that could afford the luxury of allowing their sons to attend any form of schooling, simply ignored the few parish schools that had come into existence.

Upon Henry VIII's death in 1547 his young son Edward acceded to the throne, but his life and reign were short and he died in 1553. Edward VI was much influenced by a number of zealous Protestant converts and, in 1552, ordered the translation of the liturgy and prayers of church services in Ireland from Latin to

English, indicating a symbolic break with the language of the universal church. An indication of the ineffectiveness of the plan to establish parish schools may be gleaned from the decision by Elizabeth I, who acceded to the throne in 1558, to establish a network of diocesan schools. These schools, founded to promote the Protestant Reformation and the English language in Ireland, were offered freely to all and were intended to be established throughout the island, not just within the Pale. The Elizabethan administration insisted that the schoolmaster be an Englishman or English by birth. It should be remembered that, with the exception of a very small minority, the population of Ireland at this period was entirely Irish speaking. Further, each school and one third of the master's salary should be provided at local expense. We are not here concerned with what is now commonly understood as popular education. Young men attending the diocesan schools belonged to families that could afford the expense and do without their sharing in the domestic and agricultural work at home. Many such Catholic families responded by sending their sons abroad to receive an education in the Catholic seminaries of France and Spain. The exodus of even a small number of young Catholics to these sympathetic ports encouraged the Elizabethan administration to develop a counter-measure in the form of a university in Ireland. In 1577, the Lord Deputy, Sir Henry Sidney, wrote to Elizabeth that the number of Catholics leaving had trebled since 1570 declaring that the Irish were using the seminaries as a 'pretext' for study. Consequently, in 1592, a proposal to found a university in Dublin to prevent Catholics travelling to 'foreign universities' led to the establishment of the University of Dublin, Trinity College. However, the accession of Charles I in 1625 saw a ban placed upon Catholics attending Trinity and, in 1641, the suppression of Catholic practice in Ireland.

THE 17TH CENTURY

We may, therefore, with some justification, consider the establishment of Trinity College as having more to do with politics than pedagogy; a concept that had little meaning at the time. The purpose of education, particularly at university level, was the propagation of religious belief, particularly within the emerging Protestant model. During this period, the great universities of Oxford and Cambridge, for example, were exercised almost completely in the preparation of young men for religious life. In the same way that we cannot conceive of schooling in the 16th century as remotely similar to contemporary schooling, so our contemporary understanding of the purpose of university education is radically different from that of the Elizabethans.

The monarchy of James I (1603–25) had little impact on education in Ireland. James' administration was concerned with settling the province of Ulster and, to that end, the founding of free schools in the same manner as the Elizabethan diocesan schools was ordered. The schools should be under the control of the Protestant bishops who were to raise funds using the rents from lands allocated to them. Yet between 1612 and 1625 only six schools were established (Cavan, Derry,

Fermanagh, Tyrone, Armagh and Donegal) largely because of the delay in allocating lands to the respective bishops and their reluctance to engage with the proposal. The schools that were established catered for the children of well-to-do settlers and had no impact on the wider community.

The reign of Charles I (1625–49) is, perhaps, most notable for the manner of its end; the monarch's execution and the establishment of the Cromwellian regime. As mentioned above, Charles forbade Catholics from attending Trinity College, ordered the suppression of all Catholic schooling and, in 1641, proscribed Catholicism in Ireland. These injunctions led to radical changes in the relationship between Ireland and England even given the raft of anti-Catholic legislation that had been enacted in the previous four decades, including a prohibition on serving in the army, holding public office and the handing over of Catholic churches to the Church of Ireland. In reality, Catholic practice continued without significant interruption, but the Cromwellian parliament pursued a strident and forceful programme of suppression and developed a chilling new conceptualisation of the nature and purpose of schooling for Catholics. In March 1657, Cromwell wrote to the Council in Dublin that:

> … the poorer sort of Irish in Ireland doe, as well as the rich, abound in children, and have for the most part noe other means to support them … but by begging or stealeing or both, by which means they not onely prove very burthensome but alsoe unnecessary members of the Comonwealth …

However, such children might prove:

> … of excellent use … if there were some course layd downe whereby they might att the age of tenn yeares and upwards be taken from their Parents and bound Apprentices to religious and honest people in England or Ireland …

Later, these children would leave these foster families to 'gett their liveings by their owne industry'. Hence, the 'great want of labourers and servants of all sorts' in England and the plantations could also be catered for. This vision is, obviously, utterly at odds with schooling as we understand it. The Cromwellian understanding of education as a preparation in utility, a way of making poor children useful to 'religious and honest people' is abhorrent but, at its root, is an understanding of schooling as having a utilitarian purpose and consequence, as being directly related to the wider good of the state and its mission. The schools founded under the Cromwellian regime were placed under a centralised board, in much the same way as the Board of National Education oversaw the founding and administration of the national system in 1831. However, as successive administrations found, the teachers' lack of Irish frustrated attempts at proselytism.

A restricted monarchy was restored in 1660 when Charles II (1660–85) acceded to the throne. He was faced with the difficult task of establishing his authority in the post-Cromwellian period and so needed Catholic support while placating an anti-Catholic parliament. Therefore, while Catholic schooling was tolerated, teachers were required to swear the Oath of Supremacy and the Oath of Allegiance, which they could not do in conscience. Hence, an effective prohibition remained although Catholic children were increasingly schooled in unofficial hedge schools operated by itinerant schoolmasters. In effect, Catholics subverted official restrictions by simply sending their children to learn the rudiments of writing, reading and arithmetic at these ramshackle but increasingly popular schools.

The reign of James II (1685–8), who was the first Catholic monarch since Mary I a century earlier, did little to improve the lot of Irish Catholics. After only three years on the throne, he was defeated at the Battle of the Boyne by William III (of Orange), who, in 1689, became joint monarch with his wife Mary, a daughter of Charles II. James fled to France and with him went a large number of Jacobites whom the new regime feared, would return as an organised invading force. So, in 1695, the Act to Restrain Foreign Education declared that: no 'child' could be sent abroad for education of any sort or stay with a Catholic family abroad. It prohibited the sending of money or any means of support to a child abroad and insisted upon the enforcement of all educational edicts since Tudor times, admitting that they had failed in large part because of Catholic 'connivance' in sending their children to hedge schools. Following William's death in 1702, an act to dissuade Irish Catholics further from sending their sons abroad stated that if a child could not be produced within two months then he should 'incur all the penalties of the 1685 Act', hence criminalising the child.

THE 18TH CENTURY

In 1703, a group of Protestant clergymen proposed the establishment in Ireland of a network of charity schools. They claimed that, past attempts having failed, the conversion of the Irish was more desirable than ever and by it 'the English interest would be better served'. They proposed, therefore, to establish schools in 'every parish' to provide free instruction in the 'English Tongue, Catechism and Religion of the Church of Ireland' and thereby 'establish the protestant religion more universally in this kingdom'. In 1727, by which time George II had become king, 130 charity schools had been established with an enrolment of approximately 3,000 children. However, this was only a fraction of the school-going population. Catholics shunned the schools, at which children were apprenticed to families and obliged to attend Protestant Sunday service, and continued to send their children to local hedge schools. A report of 1731 recorded the existence of at least 549 Roman Catholic schools in Ireland. Following this, in 1733, Hugh Boulter, Protestant Primate of Armagh, called on parliament to sanction the establishment of the Incorporated Society for Promoting English Protestant Schools in Ireland. The charter schools that this society established relied on private donations but between 1738 and 1831, also benefited from a government grant. The schools taught practical skills deemed to be useful to poor children and to sections of the wider community. The society declared, in its report of 1744, for example, that the schools represented a 'means of increasing industry and trade ... which must improve every Gentleman's Estate'.

Before long, however, the schools became the subject of bitter complaint and, between 1782 and 1788, John Howard, who had previously undertaken extensive investigations into the state of prisons in England, carried out a painstaking investigation of the society's *modus operandi*. He found that children lived in cramped, squalid conditions, were underfed, poorly clothed, and overworked on land adjoining schools, and were almost all illiterate. His report, which provided a catalogue of misery and neglect, caused much embarrassment both to the society and government and, in 1791, a Parliamentary Inquiry recommended that Catholics be appointed to management boards and children receive religious instruction from their own clergy. This represents the first attempt at democratising schooling for Catholics in Ireland and should, at least in part, be understood against the background of momentous social and political change triggered by the French Revolution, and the loss of the American colonies and agitation for male suffrage in England. The recommendations, in other words, appeared at a time when questions of social hierarchy and the rights of the disenfranchised were coming to the foreground of public political discourse. The changing dynamic is further evidenced by Gardiner's Third Relief Act (1782) which allowed Catholics to teach with impunity and Hobart's Catholic Relief Act (1783) which removed the obligation on Catholics to secure a licence to teach from a Protestant bishop.

The charter schools had, however, fallen into disrepute and little could be done to win Catholic sympathy. In 1799, the Parliamentary Report on Education of the Poor in Ireland made further recommendations including several which later became part of the machinery of the national school system. Turning its attention to teachers as a body of practitioners, it recommended that they be examined and licensed, that their salary be tied to performance and that a system of inspection be established to oversee schools in receipt of state monies. The United Irishmen revolt of 1798, however, hardened public opinion in England and the Act of Union (1800) meant that the 1799 recommendations were never acted on.

THE 19TH CENTURY

However, the absence of a formal system of schooling in Ireland could not simply be ignored. The Catholic population had persisted in subverting Protestant, state-sponsored attempts to provide schooling; a position encouraged and supported by their clergy. National non-compliance was insupportable and, between 1806 and 1812, a Statutory Commission on Education in Ireland surveyed education provision and produced 14 reports. It described the position of schooling as 'wholly unsatisfactory' and recommended the establishment of a body to oversee education. The commission insisted that no system would succeed in Ireland if it was not devoid of proselytism and suggested, as a means of achieving this, that religious and secular instruction be separate. These were radical proposals; in effect they conceded the right of Catholic children to receive religious instruction within schools funded by the state. The recommendations met with little sympathy in parliament, yet Catholic resistance to the culture of proselytism meant that schooling remained a key public battleground between government and the Irish Catholic hierarchy who rightly pointed out that various charitable groups received state funding, despite being avowedly set upon proselytism. The Lord Lieutenant's Fund, for example, which had been established in 1819 to aid the Catholic poor and oversaw the distribution of monies to such groups, had, in the six years since its inception, made 481 grants but only 12 of these were to Catholic undertakings. Continued Catholic pressure to provide an alternative had secured little sympathy.

However, in 1811, one year before the publication of the report of the statutory commission, the Society for Promoting the Education of the Poor in Ireland – known as the Kildare Place Society (KPS) – had been established to provide for the education of the poor regardless of creed and, according to a society report of 1820, to 'correct their turbulence' and 'turn their minds to industry and respect for the laws'. The KPS was, again, a philanthropic venture. It aimed to establish a network of schools in which scripture was read without note or comment. It received considerable government funding and, by 1831, had established 1,621 schools catering for 137,639 children. The KPS published its own schoolbooks, established model schools in which to train teachers and appointed inspectors. In many respects, the KPS represented the first formal, systematic, attempt to provide education in a religiously neutral setting. In this, it was radically different from the charitable bodies that had preceded it and, initially, won considerable Catholic support. However, by the mid-1820s the society was found to be contributing monies to three proselytising bodies overseeing 427 schools and to have employed teachers who commented on scriptures. Daniel O'Connell withdrew from board of the KPS in protest and, in 1824, the Bishop of Kildare placed a prohibition on Catholics assisting or utilising KPS schools, swiftly followed by official condemnation of the society from Rome.

The controversy led to increased agitation from the Catholic community, hierarchy and MPs for a solution to the problem of educating Ireland's poor. This resulted in yet another appraisal of provision, this time lasting three years (1824–7). The Parliamentary Review of Irish Education produced nine reports and, in what must have seemed rather familiar territory for all concerned, recommended the establishment of a board to oversee the distribution of monies for schooling, the appointment of schoolteachers and the selection of textbooks. It was critical of many proselytising bodies and recommended the withdrawal of funding from some. Like previous reports, it supported combined literary instruction. The Catholic hierarchy responded by stating that it wished to see the establishment of teacher training colleges in each province, to reserve the right to select texts chosen for religious instruction, and suggested that where one denomination was in the majority, a master of that denomination should be appointed. Progress, if there was to be any, foundered when the Catholic bishops would not accept the King James Bible for use without note or comment; while the Protestant bishops rejected texts approved by the Catholic hierarchy. Therefore, in 1827, a commission was appointed to review all previous reports into education in Ireland. At this point, while Catholics may have felt aggrieved that so little progress had been made, it should be kept in mind that, in principle, and in the face of a hostile Established Church in Ireland, a significantly progressive and forward-looking understanding of the position of Catholicism in Ireland had developed over the previous two decades. The Established Church had, for centuries, operated in Ireland as the spiritual arm of Westminster; its mission had been the conversion of Irish Catholics and, until the beginning of the 19th century, its position has remained almost wholly unchallenged. The several reports at this time undermined its role and called for parity of treatment for Catholicism, indeed, that the teaching of its religious tenets should be facilitated within a state-supported system of schooling. Hence, it was unsurprising when, in 1827, the commissioners of the Irish education inquiry recommended the creation of a non-sectarian system controlled by a multi-denominational government body with sole responsibility for education. This body was to establish procedures for founding schools and publish secular texts while religious texts were to be chosen by the respective denominations. The recommendations were informed by the principle of religious tolerance. The need to create some form of provision that would be embraced by the Catholic community was now imperative and it is not surprising that the recommendations informed the system proposed by Edward Stanley in 1831.

The Stanley Letter

Edward Stanley, a minister in the new Whig administration, presented to parliament a plan that incorporated the main provisions of the 1827 report. While rightly acknowledged as the founding document of the Irish national school system, Stanley's plan, while containing over 120 recommendations, contained little that was original in terms of broad informing principles. He proposed the establishment of a multi-denominational board to oversee a nationwide school system that would have authority over new schools and those wishing to join. The board should publish an annual report and so be accountable and transparent in its operations and have 'entire control' over the books used in its schools. While receiving state funding, local communities must contribute towards the cost of school building and maintenance. Teachers should keep attendance records, be employed by the school management and have first attended training in the Dublin Model School.

The informing principle of the system was that secular and religious instruction should be taught separately on days nominated for that purpose, each denomination receiving instruction from a clergyman of that faith. Stanley's proposals represented the culmination of two decades in which official thinking had gradually come to acknowledge that any system of schooling in Ireland must be utterly devoid of any hint of proselytism. For the Established Church, this represented the state's acceptance of the legitimacy of the Catholic voice; the state would now finance schools in which Catholic clergy could instruct children in the tenets of a faith which Protestantism had attempted to supplant for 300 years. It was a defining moment in the history of both churches in Ireland and in the relationship between this country and Westminster.

It should not be forgotten, however, that Stanley's proposals took place against the background of increasingly liberal and secular tendencies in political thought in England. The voice of the disenfranchised was, very slowly, beginning to make itself heard. The French Revolution had provided a warning to the ruling classes and a template for the disaffected. In England, the early 1830s saw half a million people added to the electoral register, and the beginnings of organised opposition to long working hours and conditions in its industrial regions, whilst in Ireland there were food riots in counties Clare and Limerick. While we cannot directly attribute Stanley's recommendations to notions of pluralism as we understand them in the 21st century, it is important to recognise that they were forged at a time of social change, when the dynamic of class relations were, very slowly, coming under scrutiny, when the relationship between Church and state was being questioned, and when the Catholic hierarchy in Ireland was becoming increasingly strident and confident in presenting its demands to Westminster.

Responses to Stanley

Under Stanley's proposals, the use of the Bible was prohibited for combined instruction. Each denomination was free to employ its respective version on days set aside for separate religious instruction, although the Commissioners of National Education reserved the right of veto on all texts used in its schools.

The Presbyterian Church, then experiencing a significant internal debate between traditional conservatives and an emerging liberal faction, condemned what it considered the usurpation of education by the state; a role that for centuries had been the preserve of the Presbyterian and Protestant bodies in Ireland. It, mischievously, decried the 'banning' of the Bible, by which it meant the prohibition upon its use for combined instruction. The Presbyterian Church also pronounced against allowing Catholics to operate separate religious instruction and the commission's control over books. A campaign to win concessions from the commissioners resulted in a change regarding separate religious instruction whereby the rule was modified so that it could be taught during the day, rather than on a day set aside, so long as children not belonging to that denomination were withdrawn. It was a significant concession given the sensitivity of what was a founding principle of Stanley's proposals and, in 1840, the Presbyterian community joined the national system.

The Church of Ireland refused to join the system and, in 1839, established its own network of schools under the auspices of the Church Education Society (CES). Like the Presbyterian community, the Protestant Church in Ireland: objected to government control over educational provision; rejected the distinction between religious and literary instruction and the limitation upon the use of Bible; objected to separate religious instruction; and was unwilling to accept the right of Roman Catholic clergy to use schoolrooms for Catholic instruction. As with the Presbyterian community, there was internal debate regarding the new system but, for many years, the Church Education Society prospered and, by the mid-1840s, was catering for approximately 100,000 children. This, however, was achieved without funding from the commissioners who refused applications on the basis that the CES was denominational in practice. Financial strain coupled with a falling off of contributions meant that, by the mid-1860s most CES schools had applied to join the national system in accordance with its rules and regulations.

Initially, the Roman Catholic Church was enthusiastic about the new system. While the Christian Brothers withdrew from the system in 1836, on the basis that the regulations prohibited daily acts of piety, such as the recitation of the Angelus and the display of religious icons, the 1838 Conference of Irish Bishops declared approval for the system. While, in 1840, they called for bishops to be granted the power of veto on religious books used in the schools and despite increasing wrangling between those who supported and disapproved of the system, the bishops were largely in favour, seeing the system as a long awaited opportunity for the Irish poor to secure a formal, systematic education.

Yet, within less than a decade of its founding, the national system had been ignored by the Church of Ireland, the Presbyterian community had forced a significant change regarding religious instruction and the Catholic Church had begun to seek ways to refine the system to accommodate its vision for the future of schooling in Ireland. It should be remembered that the Catholic Church in Ireland did not exist in a vacuum. It belonged to the wider international Catholic community and, like it, was conscious of the growth of secular thought in Europe. It was not intellectually removed from the wider concerns of the Church, and both Rome and the Irish bishops viewed the development of the national system from the perspective of both global and domestic Catholicism. Ultimately, the hierarchy wished to remould the national system so that it reflected the fact that Ireland was an overwhelmingly Catholic country and, perhaps understandably, believed that its schools should reflect that.

The Stanley Letter stated that teachers should receive training. A model school for this purpose was established at Molesworth Street in Dublin in the early 1830s and a decade later the commissioners were anxious to develop a network of such institutions which would, of course, be non-denominational.

The Catholic bishops vehemently opposed the plan, insisting instead upon denominational education, while the government was unwilling to countenance any alternative. In an attempt to settle the issue of university education in Ireland, Prime Minister Robert Peel announced, in 1841, that the government intended to establish three non-denominational colleges. These were the Queen's Colleges: Queen's College Belfast, University College Galway and University College Cork. Catholic response to this was equally hostile. Several of the great universities in Europe were Catholic foundations. Why then, the bishops argued, should these 'Godless colleges' be imposed upon Ireland?

MOULDING THE SYSTEM: THE ROLE OF THE CATHOLIC CHURCH

By the end of the 1840s, a number of issues divided Westminster and the Irish bishops, and the new decade began amidst an atmosphere of mistrust and acrimony. Failing to make ground, the bishops assembled at the Synod of Thurles in 1850 where they denounced the proposed Queen's Colleges and insisted again that the hierarchy alone should judge what books were to be used for Catholic religious instruction – a direct challenge to the Commissioners of National Education's right of veto. The synod's declarations represented a new era in the life of the system and reflected the growing confidence of the hierarchy in attempting to mould educational policy in Ireland.

The bishops' position that, in fact, the national system was essentially hostile to Catholicism was lent credence from an unlikely source in 1852. In a letter, Archbishop Whately, a Protestant commissioner, remarked that the neutral scripture extracts, agreed upon by all denominations as they were uncontroversial and so employed in religious instruction, were not being used by Catholics. The extracts were, he wrote, the means by which 'the minds of a large portion of the Roman Catholic [population] have been prepared ... and are now prepared for the reception of protestant doctrines'. Whately also stressed that if mixed (non-denominational) education was abandoned 'we give up the only hope of weaning the Irish from the abuses of popery' adding that he could not '... venture openly to profess this opinion. I cannot openly support the education board as an instrument of conversion.' The revelation caused considerable controversy. Catholics believed their suspicions were vindicated and the bishops immediately brought pressure to bear upon the commission, resulting in the scripture extracts being relegated to use before or after school hours for combined literary instruction (i.e. voluntary attendance) or for literary instruction in school if no parent objected; in effect, no child was obliged to use the extracts. This was a significant victory for the bishops, who always considered the extracts as inherently 'protestant'; it strengthened the influence of the churches in shaping the system and reinforced its increasingly denominational nature, encouraged the Catholic hierarchy to become more strident in its demands, and weakened the authority of the commissioners.

In 1854, the Lord Lieutenant, the Earl of Saint Germans, asked the commissioners to revisit the rules of the system as they had undergone much modification since their inception. In doing so, the commissioners re-emphasised the prohibition on religious iconography and acts of piety. This reassertion antagonised the Catholic community, particularly as so many schools were attended only by children of that denomination, and was duly condemned by the bishops.

In 1856, in a direct challenge to the government, the bishops announced that only a denominational system would be acceptable to them. It was inconceivable that the government would concede to such a demand, and the declaration was intended to bring as much pressure as possible to bear upon Westminster. Finding staunch resistance to their demands, the hierarchy decided, in 1859, to continue to bring pressure on the system rather than actually withdraw children from the schools. They complained to Lord Cardwell, the Chief Secretary, that the system represented a refusal to acknowledge their 'legitimate authority' in matters pertaining to education and demanded funding for the 'separate instruction of catholic children'. A pastoral letter of the same year attacked the commissioners' right to veto books, argued that the appointment and dismissal of teachers should be at the bishops' discretion, and objected both to the training of teachers in model schools, and the prohibition on acts of piety and the display of icons. The bishops were supported by 11 Catholic MPs and, in response, Cardwell reconstituted the Board of National Education to allow equal representation for each denomination.

The Royal Commission on Primary Education in Ireland 1870 (Powis Report)

During this period the issue of the non-denominational model schools caused a further deterioration in the relationship between the National Board and the hierarchy who, in 1860, again condemned the schools as unacceptable. Three years later, the bishops pronounced against Catholic children attending any schools attached to these training institutions, representing about 33 per cent of enrolments. While these provided the only state-funded teacher training available in Ireland, the government was not prepared to make further investments given the opposition of the hierarchy. In a pastoral letter of 1867, Cardinal Cullen condemned the model schools and the national system, announcing that no concession other than its abolition would be acceptable. In the face of such strident opposition, the government announced a royal commission to review education provision in Ireland.

The vast report of the Royal Commission on Primary Education in Ireland (Powis Report) was published in 1870. It provided an overview of the national school system between 1831 and 1870 and provides an invaluable insight into the workings of the system during that period. School books were found be of good quality, though rather unimaginative, and the commission recorded that many complained of their 'un-Irish character', a complaint later echoed by cultural nationalists. Enrolment figures as of 31 December 1870 stood at 998,999 representing over 90 per cent enrolment. However, attendance was very low. In the late 1840s and early 1850s, attendance was between 16 per cent and 58 per cent. Inspectors pointed to the correlation between attendance and poor performance but cited the terrible levels of poverty as the principle cause of children staying away from school. Figures for enrolment are more certain, showing that it had increased from 107,042 in 1831 to 998,999. The number of schools had risen from 789 in 1833 to 6,806 in 1870. While literacy and numeracy had improved, the Powis Report recorded that the system had failed to attract the numbers of pupils 'or meet the levels of proficiency that might reasonably have been expected of it'; an unwelcome verdict for Westminster and the board.

A striking feature of the Powis Report – and indeed the annual reports of the inspectorate, which had been returned, for schools connected to the national board, from the establishment of the system in 1831 – is the praise accorded to the teaching body. In reviewing the reports since 1831, Powis notes that the inspectorate repeatedly drew attention to poor remuneration. Initially, salaries were to be met by the local community, but parents were poor and Catholics were, understandably, opposed to paying for a system their clergy increasingly denounced. In 1847, a system of ranking teachers had been introduced (first, second and third 'class') to encourage 'increased zeal and diligence' but this only applied to those who had received training at a model school. A small increase was allocated in 1849 because of the suffering imposed by famine, but remuneration remained a bone of contention for the teaching body and even when referred to the House of Commons in the 1860s, the Treasury refused to commit to greater spending. It is hardly surprising that between 1863 and 1867 some 2,594 teachers left teaching, emigrated or were dismissed, representing approximately 35–40 per cent of the teaching body, or that an inspector reporting to the Powis Commission described them as 'watched, punished, starved…'.

Teaching conditions varied, depending largely upon income, and the inspectors recorded numerous instances where teachers used their private salary to effect improvements to their schoolhouses. Powis found that only 65 per cent of schools had 'good' roofs, floors and windows, and fewer than 50 per cent had playgrounds with walls. Over 33 per cent of schools lacked toilets, while approximately 25 per cent were deficient in desks, lighting, ventilation and heating. Although it should be noted that things were little different in England where, in 1860, one official described early 19th century schoolhouses as containing a 'teacher's desk, a rod, a cane, and a fools cap'! However, the Treasury would only provide greater funding in line with local contributions; a disingenuous position given the appalling poverty of post-famine Ireland. That little changed, in terms of the conditions in which teachers operated, may be gleaned from the observations of Inspector Dale in 1903 when he recorded that 'it is difficult to give in words any adequate conception of the building, which are classified by the Irish inspectors as bad'. Powis recorded that only 289 teachers, (34 per cent) had received formal training, yet inspectors found that, as a body, they were eager and the Powis Report presented a sympathetic view of teachers who, it suggested, were performing well in difficult circumstances. Yet in spite of this, proficiency was generally poor. Indeed, between 1862 and 1870 only three district inspectors reported any significant improvement in standards and the commission finally recorded that the progress of the children in the national schools of Ireland was 'very much less than it ought to be'.

The Powis Report made 129 recommendations. The most important was that a system of payment by results be introduced whereby schools and teachers could earn additional funding depending on the results obtained by their students; a system that had been introduced in England in 1862. It also recommended that:

- all state-aided schools should have management committees;
- where two small denominational schools existed in the same district, they could be adopted by the board;
- all teachers should have a period of 12 months pre-service training;
- teachers should be given written contracts of employment;
- state aid could be extended to religious institutions;
- model schools should be discontinued; and
- the National Board should cease publishing school texts (but retain its veto).

The recommendations immediately acted on were payment by results and written contracts of employment for teachers. Prophetically, one witness giving evidence to the inquiry argued that payment by results would 'formalize the work of the schools' and 'render it inelastic and mechanical', resulting in the teachers concentrating upon the 'paying subjects'. But the government believed that unsatisfactory proficiency demanded urgent remediation and the mechanism was introduced without delay. Reading, writing, spelling and arithmetic became obligatory for all grades, girls studied needlework and boys agriculture. Irish, it should be noted, only became an extra subject for which fees could be paid from 1879. Because subjects were accorded a result fee, teachers tended to concentrate on those that 'paid'. While illiteracy declined significantly and attendance rose from 37 per cent in 1871 to 65 per cent in 1899, when payment by results was finally abolished in national schools, the mechanism had the effect of concentrating teachers' minds on the paying subjects, thereby leading to unimaginative teaching, rote learning and an absence of innovation in methodology. Even the popular spread of child-centred understandings of education made little impact upon schooling in Ireland until late in the 20th century.

Towards the end of the 19th century, educational thinkers urged the introduction of science and practical, vocational subjects. Europe witnessed the rise of the kindergarten and associated movements and there was a general reassessment of the educative endeavour and, in particular, a desire to revisit the curriculum with a view to creating a balance between academic and practical subjects.

To this end, the Commission on Practical and Manual Instruction (Belmore Commission) began studying possible changes to the curriculum in 1897. Unsurprisingly, they concluded that the system was archaic, narrow, unchallenging, and restrictive, and made three recommendations: the abolition of payment by results; the establishment of kindergarten; and the introduction of practical subjects. The Belmore Commission resulted in the Revised Programme for National Schools (1900) which introduced new subjects, including manual instruction, elementary science, PE, cookery, singing, drawing and laundry. Problem solving and nature studies were also encouraged. However, the new programme was underfunded and, by 1904, manual instruction was dropped from the curriculum although most schools continued to provide PE, singing and drawing. Generally, the educational experience of children improved.

In 1900, the Roman Catholic hierarchy had declared that the national system was generally 'as denominational almost as we could desire'. In 1904, the attempt by the government to introduce a local rate aid for education and establish boards of management was successfully opposed by the hierarchy and Catholic MPs, who argued, in particular, that schooling should be supported by central funding rather than through local taxation. The period between this and independence witnessed a stand-off between Church and government over funding and control. The state remained unwilling to fund denominational schools in the absence of local contributions. The effect of this was that when the system came under the auspices of the Irish government, it inherited a network of poorly resourced schools that were almost wholly denominational in character. However, almost immediately, the old arguments of the 19th century gave way to the new crusade of the nascent state – the restoration of the Irish language.

INTERMEDIATE (SECONDARY) EDUCATION

Having outlined the development and informing ideologies that shaped the growth of the national school system, we now turn to the development of the intermediate system. It is important to realise that the intermediate, or post-primary sector, catered for a very small minority when it was founded in 1878. Intermediate schooling was not considered necessary or even appropriate for the majority of children – an understanding that informed official opinion in Ireland well into the 20th century – and those schools that did exist prior to 1878 were almost exclusively founded by religious congregations and received no support of any kind from the state, which was, of course, opposed to denominational schooling.

Catholic bodies had been quick to establish schools in the post-Penal period, and the following is illustrative of orders and foundations established in Ireland between the 18th and 19th centuries: Ursuline Order (1771), Presentation Sisters (1783), Christian Brothers (1802), the founding of Clongowes Wood College (Jesuit, 1814), Loreto Order (1822), Sisters of Mercy (1827) and the founding of Blackrock College (Holy Ghost Fathers, 1860). Each of these orders had established privately owned and managed schools prior to 1878 and this growing network of denominational intermediate schools posed the same problem for Westminster as the creation of the national system had in 1831. The solution, outlined in the Intermediate Education (Ireland) Act 1878, was to fund the schools using the payment by results mechanism, though the Intermediate Education Act did not initially envisage the inclusion of girls or the Irish language (Celtic).

An Intermediate Board of Commissioners was established to oversee the system, operate terminal examinations and allocate results fees. The board received £1 millon per annum from which it employed the annual interest of £32,000. At terminal examination, subjects were awarded varying marks (Latin and English, for example, received more), causing schools to focus upon paying subjects just as the national schools had done after 1870. This emphasis resulted in a 19th century 'points' fever and created a popular perception of schooling as utterly utilitarian and competitive. An example of the competition between schools, and of how their function was popularly viewed, may be gleaned from the following advertisements that appeared in *The Irish Times* in September 1908:

> St. Andrews College, Dublin: 'Distinctions won during the past year include – Trinity College, Dublin 1907 – First Junior Exhibition, Senior Exhibition, First Mathematical Award, First Science Award, First Science Entrance Prize, 1908 – Three University Scholarships.'

> Belvedere College, Dublin: 'Classical School for those preparing for University ...'

> Ranelagh School, Athlone: 'Boys prepared for University, Civil Service, Banks, Railways etc.'

> Rockwell College, Cork: 'This long established school, has under its large and capable staff, well maintained its high record of distinctions gained at public examinations...'

> Royal School, Cavan: 'Pupils are carefully prepared for Entrance to the University ... Intermediate and Commercial Life. Latest Successes ...'

There are also several advertisements for schools in England with the same emphasis upon preparing boys for university or commercial life. In his autobiography, Joseph O'Connor recalled, that when teaching in Killarney, County Kerry, the students entered into the 'hunt for medals and prizes with the keenness of greyhounds ... those were the days of published results when the college watched their position on the fateful prize day lists as anxiously as soccer clubs watch the league tables'.

In the early years of the intermediate system, only about 5–10 per cent of pupils remained until senior grade or sat senior grade examinations. Certainly, there was little change in the first two decades of its existence: the curriculum remained predominantly academic in nature; the imbalance in fees for subjects meant that some received significantly more attention in schools than others; only grudging provision was made for the Irish language, while Irish history, geography and literature were given scant acknowledgement in the curriculum.

In 1899, the Commission on Intermediate Education (Palles Commission) published the results of its inquiry into the 20-year-old system. It recorded that numbers sitting examinations had risen from approximately 4,000 in 1879 to around 9,000 in 1898 but was critical of the overly academic curriculum, noting that the emphasis on testing had resulted in poor teaching methodology coupled with little provision for weak pupils. While the report did not result in any significant immediate changes, the 1902 Rules and Regulations announced that all core subjects were to be awarded equal marks and that results fees were to be replaced with capitation fees, meaning that funding was to based on the average of pupils *sitting* and passing the intermediate examinations rather than solely upon examination successes.

The next major review of the intermediate system was the Dale and Stephens report of 1905. The authors were particularly critical of four areas: the payment by results mechanism, the lack of trained teachers, the poor level of funding and the high attrition rates, with less than 10 per cent of pupils finishing intermediate school. The report recommended: the creation of a central body to co-ordinate national, intermediate and university education; the abolition of results fees, to be replaced by direct funding for all recognised schools; the creation of Junior and Senior Certificate Examinations; and a registration council for trained teachers.

The proposals were certainly forward looking yet schools, particularly those owned and operated by religious bodies, feared that direct state funding might undermine their autonomy.

The Dale and Stephens report did not, therefore, lead to change, but, like so many reports before it, it pointed to the shape the system might take, given time and goodwill. Educational change is usually incremental and the multitude of reports and recommendations during the 19th century, while not always resulting in changes on the ground, moulded and informed the discourse surrounding schooling. As with the national school system, the intermediate system changed little between 1905 and 1922, although the Gaelic League brought pressure to bear on the curriculum regarding the Irish language, bilingual teaching, and the position of Irish history, geography and literature in schools. Standards were unimpressive, however, although increasing numbers of pupils sat for examinations, rising from 8,117 in 1901 to 11,900 in 1910.

In 1919, the Vice-Regal Committee of Inquiry (Molony Inquiry) undertook a review of the intermediate system, particularly funding mechanisms. Denouncing the payment by results system, it noted that 'too much importance has ... been attached to examinations in this country as a controlling force in education ... due to the results system' and recommended it be replaced with junior, middle and senior examinations. The inquiry made a number of recommendations, concluding that 'whole system should be reconstructed'. Many of its recommendations appeared in the MacPherson Education Bill (1919–20) which also included the creation of local education authorities (LEAs) to oversee schools in given regions. There was strong opposition to the bill, particularly from the Catholic hierarchy who perceived it as threat to the autonomy of Catholic-owned and -operated schools. It was also opposed by nationalist politicians, who, in post-1916 Ireland, were unprepared to countenance the proposed Department of Education answerable to a British parliament. The bitterness of the ensuing debate resulted in the withdrawal of the bill in December 1920 with the government unwilling to pursue the matter further given Ireland's imminent independence. In February of the following year, Hamar Greenwood, the new Chief Secretary for Ireland, remarked in the House of Commons that future questions regarding education in Ireland would fall under 'the jurisdiction of the Irish Parliament, to which the final solution of these questions must now be left'. There was, therefore, no major revision of the post-primary system before 1922. If schooling retained any lasting legacy of the pre-independence era, it was undoubtedly the strong tradition of terminal written examinations; an inheritance that continues to influence Irish education today.

SCHOOLING IN INDEPENDENT IRELAND

In the period immediately preceding independence, the Irish-language organisation the Gaelic League, had brought significant pressure to bear on government concerning the place of Irish in schools. They had won a number of concessions, in particular the introduction of the Bilingual Programme in Gaeltacht areas. The league's 1918 Educational Programme had urged that public money should be withheld from schools where Irish was 'not properly taught' and that all questions in language exams should be set in Irish, while those in other subjects be set bilingually. In 1921, the Irish National Teachers Organisation's annual conference called for the new state to 'frame a programme ... in accordance with Irish ideals and conditions ...'and to raise the 'status of the Irish language'. Where possible, instruction should be through Irish, although not where the 'majority of parents object', but should be taught for one hour per day in schools where this is not possible. Irish history should be taught in order to 'inculcate national pride' while all work in infant grade should be carried out through Irish.

The Dáil Commission on Secondary Education 1921–2 sought to allot Irish its 'due place' while identifying schooling as a means of reviving the 'ancient life of Ireland, as a Gaelic state ...'. Modern readers might find such an assertion as troubling as it is fanciful, but the commission also made a number of sensible, forward-looking proposals, including: the introduction of compulsory mathematics and science; the use of discovery learning; the encouragement of oral as well as written competence in languages; and the ability of teachers to choose texts, content and methodology freely. The commission enhanced teachers' self-image and generated a sense of partnership that had not existed in the pre-independence era as its work was informed by the contributions of a wide body of interested parties.

On 1 February 1922, the Irish state assumed control of education and the Department of Education came into being in June 1924, the same year in which the Intermediate Education (Amendment) Act 1924 modified its predecessor of 1878. This act established the Intermediate and Leaving Certificate examinations and made science optional at both levels. It incorporated the forward-looking proposals of the Dáil Commission, such as the emphasis upon Irish history, the freedom to choose texts and problem-solving methodology.

The government was not concerned with issues of ownership and management and the large network of schools that had been established in pre-independent Ireland was to remain firmly in the hands of respective boards, trustees and patrons. The prevailing understanding was that ethos and daily operation of the schools would be left in the hands of those that managed and owned them; very often religious groups. The sympathetic relationship between Church and state was both genuine and mutually beneficial. Of course, this has helped shape our present system, where up to very recently, many schools were owned and operated by religious bodies and almost all primary schools fell under the patronage of the Church.

The introduction of the Intermediate and Leaving Certificate was a direct consequence of the culture of terminal testing that had informed schooling in Ireland since 1870, the legacy of which continues to place examinations at the very heart of the educative endeavour. In effect, the state was content to allow schools to go about their business in much the same way as they had always done. The position at the time is best described by the Report of the Department of Education (1924–5) which noted that 'the state ... exercises a certain amount of supervision, but it neither founds secondary schools, nor finances ... nor appoints teachers, or managers, nor exercises any power or veto over ... appointments or dismissal of ... teachers or the management of schools'.

Yet, under the Cumann na nGaedheal administration that came to power in 1926, some significant changes took place. The School Attendance Act (1926) made attendance compulsory between the ages of six and 14. Irish became obligatory for registration as a secondary-school teacher, as an obligatory subject for 'recognised' (funded) schools (1927) and as a subject for the Intermediate Certificate (1928).

The establishment of the Commission on Technical Education in 1926 reflected the growing consensus about the need to begin investigating the provision of vocational training. The findings of the commission resulted in the 1930 Vocational Education Act. The act represented a significant shift in official thinking. It reflected the serious need for technical/vocational provision but also paved the way for the establishment and management of schools in which Church bodies had no role. The Catholic hierarchy was anxious to avoid competition from the new schools and after official reassurances, vocational schools quickly became part of Ireland's educational landscape.

Fianna Fáil came to power in 1932 and remained in government for 16 years, during which time, with the exception of nine months, Tómas Derrig held the post of Minister for Education. Fianna Fáil was anxious to pursue the Irish-language policy of their predecessors and tried to extend its use at primary and secondary level and raise competency among teachers. When, in 1938, the first vocational schools were established, they were situated in Gaeltacht areas, hence tackling the language issue and rural rejuvenation together. It should be noted that at the period, economic circumstances largely prevented considered examination of the curriculum, or, indeed, of pedagogy generally. Reviving the Irish language and the need for vocational education were the twin policy priorities.

The first significant review of the period, the Council of Education, was initiated by the Fine Gael administration of 1948–51, which was the first of two inter-party governments under Fine Gael (the second being between 1954–7). Richard Mulcahy acted as Minister for Education in both administrations. In 1950, the council convened to examine the nature of the curriculum at primary and secondary level and, in what perhaps reflects the inertia affecting educational thinking at the time, called for no significant changes in the primary curriculum. Perhaps most interestingly, the council referred to calls for greater access to secondary education as utopian; an extraordinary position given Ireland's economic plight. However, the correlation between economic growth and the provision of secondary schooling was not yet appreciated. The position was reaffirmed by Seán Moylan, Minister for Education under the 1951–4 Fianna Fáil administration, who dismissed 'this idea of equal opportunities for all …', and, instead, increased the number of vocational schools believing that they, almost exclusively, would provide the future training needs of the Irish economy. At the time, ministers identified secondary schooling as catering for a small, perhaps elite, minority of Irish society. For most families, the opportunity for secondary education did not arise and was not considered economically feasible. In 1954, for example, only 6,098 pupils sat the Leaving Certificate examination.

When Jack Lynch became Fianna Fáil Minister for Education in 1957, he continued the pattern of low ministerial interference. While 10 new vocational were schools built, secondary schools witnessed a 10 per cent cut in capitation grants between 1957 and 1959, although this was restored in 1960. However, this should be understood against a backdrop of strong support for the vocational sector at the time. Commentators pointed to the necessity of strengthening the sector as a prerequisite to economic growth and calls for greater expansion of the vocational sector were part of a growing public and political consensus regarding provision generally.

Patrick Hillery became Minister for Education under the Fianna Fáil administration that came to power in June 1959 and remained in the post until

1965. Hillery took over the portfolio at a time when official government thinking on education was beginning to lag behind more radical and egalitarian understandings. In particular, the period witnessed calls for wider access to secondary education and increased levels of funding. International comparisons revealed the paucity of investment. In 1959, Ireland's investment per pupil was 25 per cent of the United Kingdom and Northern Ireland's and 10 per cent that of the United States. Even given the precarious state of Ireland's economy, it was difficult to condone an allocation of only 50 pence per pupil, particularly as the country began to experience an economic uplift in the early 1960s. While 1960 saw plans to develop a further 35 vocational schools, Hillery was sensitive to the growing demand for wider access. The 'poor but clever' child was, he said, disadvantaged by a system where the schools were predominately private and, in 1963, the minister introduced a new category of school which would provide both the vocational and standard academic programmes in a comprehensive curriculum.

The planned comprehensive schools would offer this curriculum to intermediate level, after which pupils could enrol in a secondary or vocational school, depending upon his/her disposition and talents. Hillery envisaged that all schools would soon offer a comprehensive curriculum but both vocational and secondary schools were reluctant to adopt any such scheme and eight months after his proposal (which coincided with a by-election), Hillery had still not provided further information on the plan, leaving him open to accusations of playing politics with education. The first three comprehensive schools were finally opened in 1966 but the model never gained the popularity enjoyed by the vocational and secondary sector.

Traditionally, children moved seamlessly from primary school into one of the two standing systems, but Hillery's proposal, though owing much to the model pertaining in the UK, was a considered attempt to bring together two seemingly disparate systems. It also demonstrated the changing nature of the role of the minister and government, now increasingly inclined to affect direct and fundamental change upon the system. In an interview in 1965, Hillery noted that the role of the minister had changed considerably since Mulcahy's time:

> I have to take the initiative all the time. More and more the State is coming out as the only body geared to take the initiative ... instead of just going around with the oilcan keeping the machinery in order.

This was a timely development as the following year witnessed the publication of a report which forced the government to engage with education in a manner not witnessed since the founding of the state.

THE INVESTMENT IN EDUCATION REPORT

In October 1961, an OECD Policy Conference on Economic Growth and Investment in Education contributed to the growing debate regarding the role of education, at all levels, in Ireland. The following year, the government commissioned an OECD report which was published in 1965. The Investment in Education Report marked a turning point in how the state understood provision, particularly at second and third level. The aim of the review was to study the system with a view to probable 'manpower' needs 'for the next 10–15 years'. It provided a systematic analysis of the education system at all levels and attempted to identify weaknesses and future trends.

The report highlighted many areas, including:

- an inequality of opportunity, particularly the low levels of access to secondary education;
- a high instance of early school leavers, noting 'we find indications that some 8,000 leave school every year without reaching primary certificate level' at a time when 70 per cent of national schools had less than 100 pupils;
- the very low rate of vocational students entering third-level courses;
- the low rate of participation in university of 'many social groups';
- an inadequate number of national school teachers;
- the need for a 'very heavy programme of building replacement' for schools;
- inequality in the participation in post-primary education 'of children at all levels, based on social group and geographical location';
- the need for forward planning, noting that 'educational planning must be regarded as a continuous process which in its implementation must be open to revision and regular re-adaptation';
- the need for 'wider participation in education and for longer retention of pupils in the educational system';
- the need to 'increase the flow of educated people' as a 'minimum need of the Irish economy'; and
- the necessity of improving the 'efficiency' of 'important parts of the educational sector'.

Investment in Education was a most significant document. It provided the first comprehensive statistical, quantitative research regarding education in independent Ireland, and stressed the relationship between educational policy and economic development, employment and standards of living. It highlighted serious inequalities in provision, particularly regarding the imbalance between middle- and working-class and urban and rural levels of access. Although much debated in the previous five years, the report did hasten the announcement of free post-primary education in 1966 which, supported by the introduction of a free transport system in rural areas, dramatically improved participation levels.

While the report drew attention to inequality of access, low levels of participation and the wider issues outlined above, it also initiated ways of understanding the nature and purpose of schooling that are, perhaps, troubling. Certainly, the now common perception that education and the economy are inextricably linked had its origins in the mid-1960s, when economic concerns, rather than advances in pedagogy, influenced provision. While no one would question the notions of justice underpinning calls for wider access, we might exercise caution when such calls are based upon the needs of the economy, rather than the individual child. While these are not necessarily mutually exclusive, in observing the development of the education system in Ireland, it is important to recognise that, when documents such as the Investment in Education Report impact significantly on future policy, then a particular philosophy of education is accepted over others. Society and the economy are not the same thing, and it is important that policy is considered in the light of what it reveals about government understandings of the nature and purpose of learning and teaching. It is unusual, for example, for those entering teaching to claim national economic progress as a source of motivation!

The introduction of free secondary schooling had an immediate impact on enrolment. Between 1966 and 1967, secondary school enrolment rose by 15,000, resulting in 26,745 children in secondary boarding schools and 79,000 in day schooling. Approximately 92 per cent of day-school pupils opted for the free-school scheme.

In 1968, Brian Lenihan became Minister for Education, following the sudden death of his predecessor Donagh O'Malley, and, in the early 1970s, a plan to develop a new model of provision began to take shape. The community schools were to be non-denominational institutions, offering education and facilities to an entire community, adults as well as children. Not unlike the comprehensive model, the schools were to combine the curriculum of the traditional secondary and vocational schools, eventually replacing many of these. The community model was never popular and both it and vocational schools tended to be less attractive to parents than traditional voluntary secondary schools.

This period also saw the introduction of the new primary curriculum in 1971 representing a long overdue revisiting of a rather tired curriculum. The new curriculum was informed by the tenets of child-centeredness and it was welcomed by teachers and parents alike.

Following the findings of the 'Investment in Education Report', the vocational and technical sectors continued to witness growth and education generally saw increased levels of participation, while new technical subjects were introduced to the post-primary curriculum. However, in other areas, change was slow. Government had not devised any national strategy to address the social imbalance in access. As late as 1979, for example, the four higher socio-economic groups in Dublin (representing 21 per cent of its population) accounted for 72 per cent of entrants to higher education in that year. Almost 15 years after Investment in Education, radical initiatives to challenge early school leaving, participation rates and access to university were still absent. There was also a reluctance to revisit the predominantly academic nature of the Leaving Certificate syllabus or to consider seriously the place of children with special needs.

THE PROGRAMME FOR ACTION IN EDUCATION 1984–1987

These, then, were among the challenges facing the various administrations of the 1980s and were addressed in the Programme for Action in Education 1984–1987, a policy document published under the Fine Gael Minister for Education, Gemma Hussey. In many respects, this was the first policy document of the modern era, in that it proposed to treat aspects of the system that have now become common currency in discussions about schooling in Ireland. The document's preamble emphasised the notion of 'access' for all and outlined the need to update the curriculum to make it 'relevant to the modern world … to developments in technology' and 'changing employment opportunities'. It introduced the notion of 'permanent and continuing education for all citizens' and 'equal opportunities for educational advancement', stressing that educational provision should 'discriminate positively in favour of the educationally disadvantaged'. It also stressed that attempts should be made to achieve 'a full partnership between all the interests involved', a foreshadowing of the rhetoric of partnership that became popular in the 1990s.

The admission that the programme did 'not propose to set out a philosophy of education' is as troubling as it was contradictory, one need only revisit the aims as set out in the preamble to see that the programme was informed by a very explicit philosophy of education that included notions of social justice, while further study of the document reveals that it was also informed by gender considerations and social mobility. If we understand 'philosophy of education' to mean a value or moral position upon which education is founded and informed, then the programme is evidently based upon strong philosophical grounds. On the other hand, if the statement is an admission that the compilers of the programme did not present it as an articulation of what they understood the nature and purpose of education to be, one would question the extent to which they were qualified to engage in the issues at any level.

The challenge to education, according to the programme, was 'the relevance of the educational process to the world of work' and its adaptation to 'employment patterns'. Teachers may have been surprised by this as it implied that the purpose of teaching chemistry, for example, was directly related to 'patterns' of employment, rather than, as one would expect, a significant intellectual engagement with chemistry. This is not to be purposely obtuse, rather to question official understandings of the nature and purpose of schooling as articulated by outside parties; an essential engagement for professional educators.

The programme also drew attention to the 'participation of women' noting that 'all aspects of education must be available equally to both sexes', a long overdue statement of the place of women in school management and the imbalance in subject offerings in single-sex and co-educational schools. The document also noted that discussions would be initiated with publishers 'concerning the question of sexism [and] stereotyping in texts'. Regarding the teaching profession the programme undertook to initiate a review of the effectiveness of posts of responsibility and to secure the 'better distribution of employment opportunities' including 'job-sharing and early retirement'.

Concerning post-primary schooling in particular, the document stressed the need for 'reform of curricula' and a renewed emphasis upon the 'needs of lower achievers'. It also wished to initiate discussions concerning the role of continuous assessment, the needs of those not proceeding to further or higher education, and the need to introduce 'new technologies'. It also intended to initiate a reappraisal of vocational training in order to make it more co-ordinated and cost effective; the education system, it stated, must 'respond to ... increased mobility in the labour force generally'.

The Programme for Action had a significant impact on policy discourse. It set the tone and agenda for discussions in the early 1990s and was lauded for introducing issues that reflected contemporaneous concerns. It reflected shifts in thinking and couched them in a new vocabulary pointing to new directions for schooling. The success or otherwise of the programme, and others like it, should not simply be measured by the practical changes made at ground level. Often, these changes take time, particularly when the plans are radical, controversial or costly. While actual change at ground level is the most obvious criteria, we should also be mindful that, documents such as the Programme for Action have the effect of introducing concepts into the wider discourse and only later are these acted upon. An obvious example of this occurred in the mid-1990s when the notion of unsatisfactory teaching and its remediation entered the discourse. Sometimes, what is said is as important as what is done because it generates debate, which after modification, reflection and analysis can lead to genuine change. The Programme for Action did just this and impacted greatly upon the thinking that informed the two principal documents of the 1990s, the green and white papers. What change did occur was gradual, but, for many parties, the period witnessed progress in official thinking about education and improvements in the day-to-day experience of pupils in schools.

In 1990, Mary O'Rourke, Fianna Fáil Minister for Education, initiated a debate regarding the necessity of an Education Act. She outlined a number of concerns, many reflecting those advanced by the Programme for Action six years previously. In particular, the minister wished to examine: the possibility of devolving more power to schools, an approach popular in the UK at the period; the role of Church bodies in the provision of schooling; the development of models for life-long learning; and a consideration of the role of the disadvantaged, women, parents and multi-denominational schools.

In October 1991, therefore, a draft green paper outlined a number of key principles upon which education might be developed: education as holistic and as a partnership with all interested parties; the devolution of decision-making; quality and equity as the 'guiding principles' of provision and the balance between 'rights' and 'responsibilities'. The paper also sought to initiate a discussion around 'unsatisfactory' teaching and the vexed issue of the length of the school year.

O'Rourke was replaced as minister by Noel Davern in 1991, who was, in turn, replaced by Séamus Brennan in 1992. Building on the previous paper, Minister Brennan redrafted the green paper emphasising: greater equity with regard to access; the relationship between education and 'enterprise' culture; cost-efficiency; the need to prepare teachers for a constantly changing environment; the notion of quality assurance or accountability; and the need for greater transparency in provision. The minister's proposals were much influenced by business models and couched in the language of commerce. He suggested, for example, that school boards of management (BOM) include one person familiar with business models; that principals be redesignated as chief executive officers; that schools issue annual reports and, controversially, mooted testing for seven and 11 year olds. Minister Brennan's proposals reflect the political and economic vernacular of the period, poised as Ireland was on the edge of the 'boom' of the 1990s. Whether or not they reflected an engaged understanding of the nature and purpose of education was much debated by academics and commentators at the period and, ultimately, his proposals reappeared in a much diluted form in the green paper of 1992.

THE GREEN PAPER EDUCATION FOR A CHANGING WORLD

The green paper Education For a Changing World, was published in June 1992 and emphasised the need for education to be positioned: to react to change; to embrace enterprise culture; and to prepare pupils for the world of work. It also revisited the issues of the rights of parents and gender equality and paid lip service to notion of ongoing teacher training. The paper listed obstacles to change as including: disadvantage; the unsuitability of the senior cycle; assessment emphasis upon 'factual knowledge'; and a lack of 'openness' in the education system generally. It was intended as 'a discussion document' and Séamus Brennan, the Minister for Education, anticipated a 'reasonable consensus' concerning the issues raised.

Evidently, the vernacular of education had changed radically since the 1970s. The green paper was imbued with issues that had surfaced in the Programme for Action (1984) but presented a more detailed vision for provision. Without the benefit of data, it suggested that Irish teenagers tended to lack technical and communication skills, the language skills needed for European markets and tourism, as well as the initiative required by an 'enterprise culture'. In an effort to shape and further formalise the apparatus of school management, the paper suggested that there was a need to define the roles of management personnel in schools properly, in particular their exact roles and duties. In particular, it should be the responsibility of the BOM to 'ensure' that a 'high quality of teaching is maintained' and to take remedial action if necessary. Schools should formulate a plan detailing their aims and objectives and the means by which they would be achieved. The paper also advocated the inclusion of parents as having a 'critical role in the management of schools', having access to 'full information ... on all aspects of their [child's] progress'. Schools should become more proactive at identifying pupils with learning difficulties.

With regard to teaching as a career, the paper noted that teachers should have 'reasonable expectations' of promotion and that the future appointment of principals 'should not be for a fixed term', while appointments to posts should be open to competition. The quality of teaching was a 'matter for the Principal' and while the reality of unsatisfactory teaching must be accepted, teachers 'should be given every possible support' in overcoming difficulties.

The paper also touched on the establishment of a Teaching Council and outlined plans for whole school evaluation, to which we will return below. Interestingly, the paper suggested that every school should have a 'coherent and consistent policy' on assessment. Teachers and parents, it was felt, needed 'accurate information' and regular assessment provided 'valuable insights into the effectiveness of the work of the school'. While the paper accepted that assessment takes many forms (e.g. teacher observation, end of term/year examinations) wider issues regarding the type, validity and suitability of examinations were ignored. Certainly, the position of the terminal examinations for Junior and Leaving Certificate were left unexamined, although the Commission on the Points System was established in October 1997 to examine the system of student selection to third-level education. While a more flexible format for the Junior Certificate was envisaged, terminal testing has remained, with the notable exception of art.

Responses to the draft green paper reflected concern about the relevance and suitability of: the rhetoric of enterprise; the lack of emphasis upon the arts in education; and fears that the paper did not envisage any significant increased levels of funding to underpin the proposed changes. Concerns were also voiced about the lingering definition of school principals as CEOs, and the Association of Management of Catholic Secondary Schools pointedly suggested that the government might consider the provision of: an effective middle-management structure; in-service training in administration; pastoral-care requirements; plant maintenance; and enhanced salary and allowances.

THE NATIONAL EDUCATION CONVENTION

As noted, the 1992 green paper had been intended to initiate and inform a national discussion concerning education and, in October 1993, at the invitation of Niamh Bhreathnach, the Labour Minister for Education, a wide range of interested parties gathered in Dublin to draw up a response to the document under the auspices of the National Education Convention.

The convention was an important milestone in the development of education in Ireland as its response represented a consensus view, achieved by often disparate groups and it played a crucial role in informing the discussion that led to the white paper Charting our Education Future in 1995. The convention was concerned that the rhetoric of economic progress should be 'balanced by the other dimensions which should be integral to educational policy-making' and insisted that the state needed to formulate a philosophy of education that would provide a firm, intellectually robust basis on which the future of education might be structured. It found much to praise in the draft green paper including the need for new structures in management and the clarification of the role of patrons, trustees and owners. The declining numbers entering religious life led religious bodies to note that, while they did not oppose managerial change, they were anxious to safeguard the religious ethos and character of their schools. The convention supported the position of the green paper that the principal had a key role in school leadership and accepted the reality of underperforming teachers; indeed school principals felt that procedures for dealing with this were 'inadequate'.

Regarding the quality of education within schools, the convention commended the proposal regarding school planning but pointed out that staff would benefit from training in development planning. While the principle of school inspection, or evaluation, was accepted, the convention called for clear procedures to be agreed before any model could be implemented. There was broad support for a 'balanced holistic curriculum' at all levels although concerns were expressed regarding the resourcing of practical subjects and provision for teacher in-service and special needs education.

There was also broad support for combining formal testing with school-based assessment for Junior Certificate examinations. However, the convention expressed concerns regarding the neglect of the arts in education and many participants held that the green paper had not paid sufficient attention to 'religion and its role within Irish education'.

In addressing the issues of teaching and teacher education, the convention accepted the 'desirability of a Teaching Council' and the need to attract 'high quality applicants'. It stressed the 'imperative' of in-service training and suggested the establishment of an agency to co-ordinate this. Too much time was taken up with 'routine and organisational issues' and the convention stressed the need for support for teachers facing 'daunting difficulties'. It suggested that under-performance might be prevented by career breaks, in-service education and early intervention mechanisms, and stressed the importance of identifying the 'underlying causes' of underperformance and the need for a policy when it became persistent.

THE WHITE PAPER CHARTING OUR EDUCATION FUTURE

The National Education Convention represented the views of all interested parties in education in Ireland and provided direction, shape and content for the 1995 white paper, Charting our Education Future. Unlike its policy ancestor, the 1984 Programme for Action, the white paper recognised the need to provide a 'philosophical rationale' that 'systematically informs policy formulation and educational practise'. Consequently, the paper set out five key principles upon which future policy and provision should be based:

- Pluralism – 'Policy should value and promote all dimensions of human development and seek to prepare people for full participation in cultural, social and economic life.'
- Equality – Participation should not be impeded by 'physical, mental, economic or social factors … the education system … should … embrace all'.
- Partnership – 'The learner is at the centre of the educational process. The other principal participants are collectively referred to as the partners in education – parents, patrons/trustees/owners/governors, management bodies, teachers, the local community and the State. Other participants, including the social partners, businesses and the professions, should also be recognised as having legitimate interests in the system.'
- Quality – Students deserve the 'highest possible standard', the state should develop 'rigorous procedures for the evaluation of educational effectiveness and outcomes'.
- Accountability – What was publicly funded must be publically accountable.

The white paper ran to 231 pages and outlined government policy in all aspects of provision. It did not envisage significant changes at Junior Certificate level, despite previous discussions regarding continuous assessment. However, it stated that the 'traditional Leaving Certificate [did] not cater adequately for … the needs and abilities of students' and that there was a need to make the programme provide for the 'holistic development of all students', empowering them to 'actively shape the social and economic future of society'. The curriculum should continue to be based upon the provision of a broad, 'general education'. Two significant changes were envisaged. The Leaving Certificate Applied (LCA), under development at the time, was envisaged as preparing 'students for the transition from school to adult and working life, including further education' and was to be introduced on a phased basis from 1995. The Leaving Certificate Vocational Programme (LCVP) which would seek 'to foster skills … which assist young people to be successful as employees [and] entrepreneurs and employers' was to be fully implemented by September 1996.

The teaching profession was to benefit from a 'strategic framework of in-career development'; induction would be introduced while schools would develop 'staff development initiatives'. As a body, teachers needed to adapt to a climate of 'accelerating change' and it was envisaged that the provision of wide-scale in-service training would assist them in meeting the paper's targets of increased partnership with parents, accountability and quality assurance. Schools should promote partnership with interested parties and should ensure, where feasible, that a representative BOM is established, the task of which was: the identification and

ation of management, staff and student needs; the implementation of the plan; and the establishment of procedures that would give parents access to information pertaining to their child. The paper also outlined objectives regarding school planning and the role of whole school evaluation.

The white paper represented a wide and detailed exposition of the government's vision for the future of education in Ireland and an overview such as this can only hope to highlight its key points. Those seeking to understand the developments of the 1990s should become familiar with the original document.

As noted earlier, in the early 1990s, Minister for Education Mary O'Rourke had considered the desirability of an Education Act. The period between 1993 and 1995 witnessed perhaps the most significant review of education in Ireland since the founding of the state. Perhaps, most importantly, it was guided by the principle of partnership and so reflected, as far as possible, the concerns and hopes of all interested parties. Policy documents, however, are aspirational, and while they reflect and generate wider debate, they, or their parts, can remain little more than the good intentions of short-lived governments if not translated into action. The danger in reading the history of education in Ireland, or any other country, is that the aspirations of policy documents replace real, effective changes in provision. Governments and ministers come and go and the only true litmus test of policy is whether or not provision changes, for the better, for all concerned parties.

The white paper, however, was followed by the Education Act (1998), which was informed by what had preceded it and reflects many of the tenets of the green and white papers and the report of the National Education Convention. In defining the role of schools, the Education Act states that a recognised school, i.e. one operating under the auspices of the Department of Education and Science, must provide education which is 'appropriate' to the 'ability and needs' of its pupils; it must ensure that needs, including disability or other limitation, are identified and provided for; and that pupils have access to career guidance. Schools must promote the moral, spiritual, social and personal development of pupils; equality of opportunity for both genders (pupils and staff); and the development of the Irish language and heritage. Schools must ensure that parents have access to records pertaining to their child, and that the needs of management and staff development are provided for. They must establish means of assessing effectiveness in teaching and learning, as well as admissions policies that provide for maximum accessibility.

The inspectorate was defined as designated to support and advise schools, and evaluate their organisation, operation, quality and effectiveness, including 'the quality of teaching and effectiveness of individual teachers'. It should: assess the effectiveness of programmes for pupils with special needs; report to the minister or board, patrons, parents and teachers as 'appropriate and prescribed', as well as on 'successful educational initiatives', and observe and advise teachers and the BOM regarding the performance of their duties.

The management of schools had been a key issue in the green and white papers, and the Education Act provided definitions of all management bodies and personnel. Patrons should, 'where practicable', appoint a board of management the responsibility of which is to ensure the implementation of the act. The duty of a BOM was defined as follows: to manage the school on behalf of its patron; be accountable for the upholding of the school ethos; consult with and inform the patron regarding operational decisions and proposals; publish an admissions policy, including regulations governing expulsion and suspension; respect and promote diversity in the operation of the school; have regard to the efficient use of resources; use resources to make 'reasonable provision' for special educational needs and disability; and oversee the employment, suspension or dismissal of teachers. The board should also establish procedures for informing parents about the operation and performance of the school as outlined in the school plan and arrange for the circulation of the plan to all concerned parties.

The role of the school principal underwent considerable scrutiny during the mid-1990s and, while reflecting the move away from Minister Brennan's conceptualisation of the role as somehow akin to that of a CEO, the act was unambiguous regarding the leadership responsibilities of the position. The principal should: encourage and foster learning; ensure that students were 'regularly' evaluated and that parents were informed of progress; 'provide leadership to teachers'; be 'responsible' for creating an environment that was supportive of learning; and encourage the involvement of parents.

Importantly, paragraph 53 of the act stated that the minister may 'refuse access to any information which would enable the compilation of information (not otherwise available) in relation to the comparative performance of schools', in other words the compilation of so called 'league tables'.

The Education Act affected significant changes in definitions and obliged schools to become more accountable, introduce systems whereby pupils' needs were identified and provided for and ensure access to formal career guidance. It reflected the principles of accountability and transparency. In order to become more effective, schools must prepare plans which should be placed at the disposal of parents and the inspectorate. Leaving aside critical questions – and one would not expect a piece of legislation to be concerned with questions regarding, for example, the nature of effectiveness of schooling, such as might a child be said to be educated when s/he has failed examinations? What does it mean to be educated? To what extent are parents a transitory party in the educative process? How and when are teachers trained in the identification of pupil needs? Does regular testing result in better learning? – the act, at least, defined the key roles and duties of those involved in schooling. In this, it identified what each party might expect from the other; an important aspect of any publically funded system, particularly one as important as education.

THE TEACHING COUNCIL

The final development, having its roots in the discussions of the 1990s, took place in 2001. The 1992 green paper had touched on the establishment of a Teaching

Council of Ireland and the National Education Convention had supported the proposal. Discussions concerning the creation of such a body had been ongoing for about 15 years and all interested parties agreed upon its desirability. The Teaching Council Act (2001) set out the duties and role of the body with which all qualified teachers employed by the Department of Education and Science must register.

The act defines the Teaching Council as the regulatory mechanism for the teaching profession and 'professional conduct'. Its role is to promote the maintenance and improvement of standards of programmes for teacher education, including auditing and accrediting degrees and diplomas for initial teacher education offered by colleges and universities. The council's duties also include the promotion of teaching as a profession; the publication and review of codes of conduct and standards of competence; the establishment of a register of teachers; and procedures for the induction of new teachers and probation. It is also tasked with establishing criteria and sanctions regarding fitness to teach.

The council has, in the past four years, published an array of information pertaining to its purpose and is gradually taking shape as a professional body within the Irish educational and political landscape. The creation of the council is important in that, like other professional disciplines, such as law or medicine, it represents and regulates its practitioners, teachers register with the council and pay an annual stipend. A committee of 37 members, 22 of whom are elected by the teaching body, oversee its workings and it is to be hoped that its founding will further enhance and protect the very high quality of teaching that has traditionally been associated with the Irish education system.

RECOMMENDED READING

Commissioned, official and institutional reports, pre-1922

Reports of the Irish Education Inquiry, 1825–7.

Reports of the Commissioners of National Education (Ireland) 1835–1920.

Report of the Intermediate Education Board, 1898–1921.

Royal Commission of Inquiry on Primary Education (Ireland) 1870, vol. I., part I–X.

Conclusions and Recommendations in the General Report [C 6] H.C. 1870.

Royal Commission of Inquiry into Primary Education (Ireland) 1870, vol. I., part II, part III-Primary Schools [C 6a] H.C. 1870.

Royal Commission of Inquiry into Primary Education (Ireland) 1870 vol. II. Synopsis of Reports of Assistant Commissioners [C6-I] H.C. 1870.

Royal Commission of Inquiry into Primary Education (Ireland) 1870, vol. III. [C6-2] H.C. 1870.

Royal Commission of Inquiry into Primary Education (Ireland) 1870, vol. VIII. [C6-VII] H.C. 1870. Containing Miscellaneous Papers and Returns furnished to the Commission.

Commission on Manual and Practical Instruction in Primary Schools under the Board of National Education, Final Report by the Commissioners 1897, [C. 8923] H.C. 1898.

Revised Programme of Instruction in National Schools published in Appendix to the Annual Report by the Commissioners of National Education, 1902, [Cd 1890] H.C. 1903.

Report by Mr F. H. Dale, His Majesty's Inspector of Schools, Board of Education on Primary Education in Ireland, 1904, [Cd 1981] H.C. 1904.

Reports on Elementary Schools, 1852–82 (1908). London: HMSO.

Vice-Regal Committee of Enquiry into Primary Education Ireland (1918). Dublin: HMSO.

Policy documents and reports, 1922–95 (Ireland)

Coolahan, J. (ed.) (1994). 'Report on the National Education Convention'. Dublin: The National Education Convention Secretariat.

'Green Paper on Education, Education for a Changing World' (1992). Dublin: The Stationery Office.

'National Programme of Primary Instruction, Issued by The National Programme Conference' (1922). Dublin: Educational Company of Ireland.

'Programme for Action in Education 1984–1987: laid by the Government before each House of the Oireachtas, January 1984' (1984). Dublin: The Stationery Office.

'White Paper on Education: Charting our Education Future' (1995). Dublin: The Stationery Office.

Published primary source material

Bryce, R. J., Principal of the Belfast Academy (1828). *Sketch for a plan for a system of National Education for Ireland including hints for the Improvement of Education in Scotland*. London: George Cowie et al.

Buxton, Charles (1835). *A Survey of the System of National Education in Ireland*. London: John Murray.

Doyle, Rev. Dr. William, Archbishop of Dublin (1825). *Letters on the State of Education in Ireland: and on Bible Societies, Addressed to a Friend in England by J.K.L.* Dublin: (n.p.).

Frazer, Rev. William (1858). *The State of our Educational Enterprises, A Report of and examination into the Workings, Results and Tendencies of the Chief Public Experiments in Great Britain and Ireland*. Glasgow: Blackie and Son.

Frazer, Rev. William (1861). *National Education: Reasons for the Rejection in Britain of the Irish System; A Brief Exposition for Christian Educationists* (2nd edition). London: James Nesbit and Company.

Giffard, John (ed.) (n.d.). 'Mr Orde's Plan of an Improved System of Education in Ireland: submitted to the House of Commons, April 12, 1787', Caldwell and Orde's Speeches 1785, 1787, Absentees 1783, 1798, The Crisis. Union Pamphlets 8, Dublin.

Keane, Marcus (1874). *National Education and the Principles of Civil Government As Applicable Thereto.* Dublin: George Herbert.

Maguire, John Francis (1861). 'The Irish Education Question. The National System, Its Modifications and its Failure. Separate Education, Vindicated by its Necessity and its Advantages. The Case of the National Teachers'. Two speeches delivered in the House of Commons in 1860 and 1861 by John Francis Maguire, M. P. Dublin.

Nulty, Rev. T., Bishop of Meath (1884). *The Relations Existing Between Convent Schools and the System of Intermediate and Primary National Education.* Dublin: Browne & Nolan.

O'Donoghue, J. (1860). 'Letter to the Right Hon. Edward Cardwell, M.P., on the demand for a denominational system of Education in Ireland'. Dublin.

Orde, Thomas (1777). *Plan of an Improved System of Education in Ireland.* Dublin. Printed by W. Porter.

O'Sullivan, Mortimer D. D. (1841). *Reasons for Declining To Be Connected with the System of National Education.* Dublin: William Curry and Company.

Starkie, W. J. M. (1911). *The History of Irish Primary and Secondary Education During the Last Decade.* Dublin: A. Thom & Co.

Wyse, Thomas (1836). Educational Reform or the Necessity of a National System of Education. London: Longman, Rees, Orme, Browne, Green & Longman.

Secondary source material: journals

Coleman, Michael (1999). 'The Responses of American Indian Children and Irish Children to the School, 1850s–1920s: A Comparative Study in Cross-Cultural Education'. *American Indian Quarterly*, vol. 23, nos. 3 and 4, summer and fall.

Corcoran, Rev. Timothy (1931). 'The Dublin Education Bill of 1787'. *Irish Monthly*, August.

Corcoran, Rev. Timothy (1932). 'Financing the Kildare Place Schools'. *Irish Monthly*, June.

Elliot-Bonel, Imelda (1994). 'Lessons from the sixties: reviewing Dr. Hillery's educational reform'. *Irish Education Studies*, vol. 13, issue 1.

Garvan, Tom (1987). 'The Politics of Language and Literature in Pre-Independence Ireland'. *Irish Political Studies*, vol. 2.

Griffin, Sean (1994). 'Desegregating the national schools: Archbishop Murray 1832–1852 as a pioneer of church–state cooperation'. *Irish Educational Studies*, issue 1.

Hyland, Áine (1983). 'The Treasury and Irish Education: 1850–1922: The Myth and the Reality'. *Irish Educational Studies*, vol. 3, no. 2.

McElroy, Colm (1996). 'Thomas Orde and educational innovation 1786/87'. *Irish Educational Studies*, vol. 15, issue 1.

O'Buachalla, Séamus (1984). 'Educational Policy and the Role of the Irish Language from 1831–1981'. *European Journal of Education*, vol. 19, no. 1.

Quane, Michael (1961). 'The diocesan schools 1570–1870'. *Journal of the Cork Historical and Archaeological Society*, 2 ser., lxvi, Jan–June.

Raftery, Deirdre (2001). 'The academic formation of the fin-de-siècle schooling of girls in late nineteenth century Ireland'. *Irish Educational Studies*, vol. 20.

Raftery, D., Harford, J. and Parkes, S. (2010). 'Mapping the terrain of female education in Ireland, 1830–1910'. *Gender and Education*.

Redmond, J. and Harford, J. (2010). 'One man, one job: the marriage ban and the employment of women teachers in Irish primary schools'. *Paedagogica Historica*.

Walsh, Brendan (2006). 'The Challenge of Change: Secondary Schooling in Ireland 1922–1998'. *History of Education Researcher*, 78.

Walsh, Thomas (2007). 'The Revised Programme of Instruction 1900–1922'. *Irish Educational Studies*, vol. 26., issue 2.

Withers, Charles (1982). 'Education and Anglicisation: the Policy of the SSPCK toward the Education of the Highlander, 1709–1825'. *Scottish Studies*, No. 26.

Books

Akenson, Donald H. (1970). *The Irish Education Experiment, The National System of Education in the Nineteenth Century*. London: Routledge and Keegan Paul.

Akenson, Donald H. (1975). *A Mirror to Kathleen's Face*. Montreal and London: McGill-Queen's University Press.

Akenson, Donald H. (1991). *Small Differences, Irish Catholics and Irish Protestants 1815–1922*. Montreal and Dublin: Gill & Macmillan/McGill-Queen's University Press.

Akenson, N. (1970). *Irish Education, A History of Educational Institutions*. London: Routledge and Keegan Paul.

Balfour, Graham (1898). *The Educational Systems of Great Britain and Ireland*. Oxford: Clarendon Press.

Barnes, J. (1989). *Irish Industrial Schools, 1868–1908*. Dublin: IAP.

Beckett, J. C. (1981). *The Making of Modern Ireland*. London: Faber & Faber Ltd.

Boyd, William and King, Edmund J. (1968). *The History of Western Education*. London: Adam and Charles Black.

Bradshaw, B. (1974). *The Dissolution of the Religious Orders in Ireland under Henry VIII*. Cambridge: Cambridge University Press.

Clifford, Angela (ed.) (1922). *'Godless Colleges' and Mixed Education in Ireland*. Belfast: Athol Books.

Coolahan, John (1980). *Irish Education: History and Structure*. Dublin: Institute of Public Administration.

Coolahan, John (1984). *The ASTI and Post-Primary Education in Ireland, 1909–1984*. Dublin: Cumann na Meánmhúinteoirí.

Corcoran, Timothy (1916). *State Policy in Irish Education, AD 1539–1816*. Dublin: Fallon Brothers Ltd.

Corcoran, Timothy (1928). *Education Systems in Ireland from the Close of the Middle Ages*. Dublin: Department of Education, University College.

Corish, Patrick J. (ed.) (1968). *A History of Irish Catholicism*, vol. 5. Dublin and Sidney: Gill & Son.

Crowley, Tony (1999). *The Politics of Language in Ireland 1366–1922*. London: Routledge.

Dowling, Rev. P. J. (1968). *The Hedge Schools of Ireland*. Cork: The Mercier Press.

Dowling, Rev. P. J. (1971). *A History of Irish Education: A Study in Conflicting Loyalties*. Cork: The Mercier Press.

Durcan, T. J. (1972). *History of Irish Education from 1800*. Wales: Dragon Books.

Durkaz, V. E. (1983). *The Decline of the Celtic Languages, A Study of Linguistic and Cultural Conflict in Scotland, Wales and Ireland from Reformation to the Twentieth Century*. Edinburgh: John Donald Publishers, Ltd.

Foster, R. F. (1988). *Modern Ireland, 1600–1972*. England: The Penguin Press.

Foster, R. F. (1992). *The Oxford History of Ireland*. Oxford: Oxford University Press.

Harford, J. (2008). *The Opening of University Education to Women in Ireland*. Dublin: IAP.

Hannigan, K. (ed.) (1984). *The National School System, 1831–1924*. Dublin: Institutions of Science and Art.

Holmes, Brian (1967). *Educational Policy and the Mission Schools*. London: Routledge.

Hyland, A. and Milne, K. (1987). *Irish Education Documents*, vol. I. Dublin: Church of Ireland College of Education.

Kelly, Adrian (2002). *Compulsory Irish, Language and Education in Ireland 1870s–1970s*. Dublin: Irish Academic Press.

Lee Joseph (1973). *The Modernisation of Irish Society, 1848–1918*. Dublin: Gill & Macmillan.

MacManus, Antonia (2002). *The Irish Hedge School and its Books*. Dublin: Four Courts Press.

Macnamara, John (1966). *Bilingualism and Primary Education: A Study of Irish Experience*. Edinburgh: Edinburgh University Press.

McElligott, T. J. (1981). *Secondary Education in Ireland, 1870–1921*. Dublin: IAP.

McMillan, N. (ed.) (2000). *Prometheus's fire – a history of scientific and technological education in Ireland*. Carlow: History of Education Society and Cork University Press.

Milne, Kenneth (1997). *The Irish Charter Schools 1730–1830*. Dublin: Four Courts Press.

Mulcahy, D. G. (ed.) (1989). *Irish Educational Policy: Process and Substance*. Dublin: Institute of Public Administration.

O'Buachalla, Séamus (1988). *Educational Policy in Twentieth Century Ireland.* Dublin: Wolfhound Press.

Ó'Catháin, Seán (1951). *Secondary Education in Ireland.* Dublin: The Talbot Press.

O'Connell, Maurice (ed.) (1992). *O'Connell, Education, Church and State.* Dublin: IPA.

O'Donoghue, Thomas A. (2000). *Bilingual Education in Ireland, 1904–1922: The Case of the Bilingual Programme of Instruction.* Perth, Australia: Centre for Irish Studies Monograph Series, Number 1, 2000, Murdoch University Press.

Ó'Riagáin, Pádraig (1997). *Language Policy and Social Reproduction, Ireland 1893–1993.* Oxford: Clarendon Press.

Parkes, S. M. (1978). *Irish education in the British parliamentary papers in the nineteenth century and after, 1801–1920.* Cork.

Parkes, S. M. (2010). *A Guide to Sources for the History of Irish Education, 1780–1922.* Dublin: Four Courts Press.

Raftery, D. (2004). 'Female education in late nineteenth century Ireland'. In Susan Parkes (ed.), *A History of Women at Trinity College, Dublin.* Dublin, Lilliput Press.

Raftery, D. and Parks, S. M. (2007). *Female Education in Ireland: Minerva or Madonna, 1700–1900.* Dublin: IAP.

Randles, E. (1975). *Post-Primary Education in Ireland, 1957–1970.* Dublin: Veritas.

Sugrue, Ciaran (ed.) (2004). *Curriculum and Ideology, Irish Experiences International Perspectives.* Dublin: The Liffey Press.

Titley, E. B. (1980). *Church, State and the Control of Schooling in Ireland, 1900–44.* Dublin: McGill-Queen's University Press.

Walsh, B. (2005). *The Pedagogy of Protest: The Educational Work and Thought of Patrick. H. Pearse.* Oxford: Peter Lang.

Walsh, B. and Dolan, R. (2008). *A Guide to Teaching Practice in Ireland.* Dublin: Gill & MacMillan.

Chapter Three
Curriculum Studies
Rose Malone, National University of Ireland, Maynooth

As a student or practising teacher, you are probably teaching two or three subjects as part of your practicum. These subjects contribute towards the overall curriculum, experienced by your students. This chapter explains the structure and origins of that curriculum. Studying curriculum is a practical undertaking which will enable you to place your classroom experience in context. It is also a theoretical undertaking: the study of philosophy, history, sociology and psychology can all be applied to curriculum. Curriculum studies can be thought of as a place where theories run together to enhance the study of practice. Throughout this chapter exercises are given to help you review the points discussed. Firstly, we will consider the question: What is curriculum?

WHAT IS CURRICULUM?

One of the most frustrating problems in thinking or talking about curriculum is the difficulty in defining exactly what it is. In everyday conversation, the word is used in a variety of ways:

> 'The core curriculum in Ireland includes Gaeilge, English and Mathematics.' NCCA

> 'In this school we have drama and woodwork on the curriculum.' School principal

> 'The biggest problem with the science curriculum is that it is overloaded with too much information on too many topics.' Science teacher

These three statements come from different levels in the education system and they are also at different levels of generality. The first refers to subjects in the context of a broader vision of the nature and purpose of education, while the second refers to subjects within the programme of a school. The third refers to content within a subject. The white paper Charting our Education Future (Department of Education and Science, 1995) provides a very broad definition of curriculum which draws on the three levels.

The term 'curriculum' encompasses the content, structure and processes of teaching and learning, which the school provides in accordance with its educational objectives and value. It includes specific and implicit elements. The specific elements are those concepts, skills, areas of knowledge and attitudes that children learn at school as part of their personal and social development. The implicit elements are those factors that make up the ethos and general environment of the school. The curriculum in schools is concerned, not only with the subjects taught, but also with how and why they are taught and with the outcomes of this activity for the learner.

The word 'curriculum' is used in a number of different ways. It is, on the one hand, broader than a syllabus. Since the curriculum in Ireland is set centrally; the curriculum in the classroom must relate to a prescribed syllabus. The syllabus is a list of content to be covered within a subject. Each syllabus is part of a programme (e.g. Junior Certificate or Leaving Certificate Applied). The syllabus document may also contain a list if specific aims for that subject, the learning outcomes that are intended to result from the students' encounters with the content and, very often, some information about the modes and techniques of the associated assessment. The syllabus for each subject can be found online at www.education.ie. The curriculum documents set out the intention that young people participate in certain kinds of learning encounters and gain certain kinds of benefit as a result.

However, the curriculum does not become real until it is enacted in the interactions (Crooks and McKernan, 1984) that take place between teachers and students in the classroom. You plan those interactions when you write a lesson plan. The plan must relate to the overall curriculum intentions and to the reality of your classroom situation.

It then becomes part of the experience (Connelly and Clandinnin, 1986) of students and teachers. This experience is mediated through pedagogy: the way in which the subject content is taught. The experience is also mediated through the prior learning that each student brings to the learning situation and by the tacit assumptions about the subject, about learning and about society that teachers and students bring to the classroom learning situation.

Kelly (2004) suggests a number of different dimensions of curriculum. No matter how well you plan the curriculum, some students will interpret it and experience it differently from the way you expected. Thus, we distinguish between the intended curriculum and the received curriculum. Assessment, and especially formative assessment (Walsh and Dolan, 2009), helps us to identify and bridge the gap between the intended and the received curriculum. The students' experience in your classroom is, however, a part of their total school experience so you will need to develop an awareness of the way subjects and teaching styles fit together and, ideally, complement each other. All the individual subjects on the curriculum are intended to contribute to the overall aims of education and to the programme aims for junior or senior cycle.

Formal learning in the classroom is a key part of the curricular experience of students. This is complemented by the informal (or para-) curriculum. Different writers take different positions on the meaning of the 'informal' curriculum. For some, it encompasses the kinds of activities sometimes described as 'extracurricular', such as games, choir, drama productions and other enrichment activities. For others, it includes pastoral and disciplinary regulations, external to classroom teaching. In any event, these features of the curriculum may be central to the lives of the students and may have a major influence on their attitudes to school as an organisation. The planned curriculum of a school – formal and informal – does not tell the full story, especially when we think of curriculum as experience. As well as the overt messages conveyed by the curriculum, there are a variety of hidden messages implicit in the way schools are organised and the values and beliefs (Trant, 2007) that are espoused. Eisner and Vallance (1974, p. 74) refers to this as the 'hidden curriculum' which they describe as 'those non-academic but educationally significant consequences of schooling that occur systematically but are not made explicit at any level to the public rationales for education'.

The final dimension of curriculum to be considered here is a strange one – we could call it the curriculum that does not happen – and this is referred to by Eisner (1979) as the 'null curriculum'. This term refers to the subjects, pedagogies and experiences from which all students or certain groups of students are systematically excluded.

Curriculum is, above all, a human undertaking. You, as a teacher, do not just 'deliver' the curriculum. In a very real sense, you *are* the curriculum (or at least a very important part of it) for the students in your classes. If you think back on your own school experience, you will probably find that your memories of encounters with subjects, either as ways of thinking or as content, are coloured by memories, good and bad, of the people who taught them to you.

CURRICULUM IN IRELAND: THE JUNIOR CERTIFICATE

Ireland, like many developed countries, has a centrally defined national curriculum. Secondary education in Ireland is divided into two 'cycles', junior (commencing at age 12 to 13) and senior (commencing after the Junior Certificate) each lasting three years. Each cycle terminates in a formal, externally administered state examination. Junior cycle students follow the Junior Certificate programme which has been in operation since 1989. We will consider each cycle using the framework developed in the last section, that is: as intention, as interaction and as experience.

The Junior Certificate: curriculum as intention

The Junior Certificate is part of the compulsory educational experience of every young person in Ireland, so it must further or contribute to the general aims of education, included in every syllabus document:

The general aim of education is to contribute towards the development of all aspects of the individual, including aesthetic, creative, critical, cultural, emotional, intellectual, moral, physical, political, social and spiritual development, for personal and family life, for working life, for living in the community and for leisure.

These aims are listed on the inside cover of every syllabus document, and are intended to apply to every subject; at least to some extent.

- Select the three aims to which your principal teaching subject makes the most significant contribution. How does it do this?
- Select the three aims to which your subject makes the least significant contribution. How could it contribute more effectively?

The Junior Certificate, constructed as a list of subjects, was developed as a coherent programme and replaced two earlier programmes – the Intermediate Certificate and the Day Vocational (Group) Certificate – and represents an attempt to integrate the more academic programme of voluntary secondary schools with the more practically based and vocationally focused programme of vocational, community and comprehensive schools, in order to create a comprehensive curriculum. You can find the syllabus for your teaching subject(s) at www.education.ie.

The curriculum is more than a list of subjects. It is intended to contribute to the *areas of experience* that people have in their daily lives. These were identified as:

- language, literature and communication;
- mathematical studies and applications;
- science and technology;
- social, political and environmental education;
- arts education;
- physical education;
- religious and moral education; and
- guidance, counselling and pastoral care (CEB, 1984).

Some subjects clearly make most of their contribution in one defined area, but each subject is expected to make contributions to a number of areas, at least to some extent.

- To which area of experience does your subject make its principal contribution?
- To which other areas does it also contribute?
- To which areas does it make no contribution?

The Junior Certificate programme aims to:

- reinforce and further develop in the young person the knowledge, understanding, skills and competencies acquired at primary level;
- extend and deepen the range and quality of the young person's personal and social confidence, initiative and competence through a broad, well-balanced general education;
- prepare the young person for the requirements of further programmes of study, of employment or of life outside full-time education;
- contribute to the moral and spiritual development of the young person and to develop a tolerance and respect for the values and beliefs of others; and
- prepare the young person for the responsibilities of citizenship in the national context and in the context of the wider European Community (www.ncca.ie).

The general principles on which Junior Certificate is based are enunciated as follows:

- Breadth and balance – In the final phase of compulsory schooling, every young person should have a wide range of educational experiences. Particular attention must be given to reinforcing and developing the skills of numeracy, literacy and oracy. Particular emphasis should be given to social and environmental education, science and technology, and modern languages.
- Relevance – Curriculum provision should address the immediate and prospective needs of the young person, in the context of cultural, economic and social environment.
- Quality – Every young person should be challenged to achieve the highest possible standards of excellence, with due regard to different aptitudes and abilities and to international comparisons.

The syllabus also states that:

> The curriculum should provide a wide range of educational experiences within a supportive and formative environment. It should draw on the aesthetic and creative, the ethical, the linguistic, the mathematical, the physical, the scientific and technological, the social, environmental and political and the spiritual domain.

As well as listing the content to be covered in each subject, each subject syllabus must contain 'elements of learning'. These are knowledge, concepts, skills and attitudes (CEB, 1986). These elements are encountered by the students in engaging with each subject, in the context of an area of experience. Each subject introduces the student to content knowledge (for example, they will be able to describe the stages in the development of a river), in which over-arching ideas or concepts (for example, the concepts of deposition and erosion) are embedded. The students will develop specific skills (they will be able to interpret maps and draw sketch maps of rivers) and attitudes (they will understand the social and historical importance of rivers and understand the implications of planning decisions), relevant to each subject area.

> • Take any area of a subject that you teach and analyse the knowledge, concepts, skills and attitudes related to it. The syllabus document may be helpful here.

Syllabi are provided at different levels. Most subjects can be studied at either Ordinary or Higher level, but Gaeilge, mathematics and English can be studied at Higher, Ordinary or Foundation level. Civic, social and political education (CSPE) is available as a common level subject.

Curriculum and assessment: the 'backwash effect'

One of the factors that has the most profound effect on the reality of the curriculum in practice is the timing and nature of the assessment which accompanies it. Assessment is intended to establish whether, and to what extent, the curriculum intention has been achieved. However, the two processes, curriculum and assessment, are not independent: those features which are assessed are those on which most emphasis is placed in the classroom. Assessment, which is intended to follow after curriculum, tends to take precedence so that Hargreaves et al. (1996) refer to assessment as the 'tail that wags the curriculum dog'. Broadfoot (1979) refers to the 'backwash effect' of assessment on curriculum – those areas of the curriculum which are difficult or expensive to assess tend to be given less time and attention.

In this book, 'assessment' refers to any systematic way of estimating how well students have learned material or how well they can accomplish particular tasks. Assessment can be carried by a wide variety of methods, including written examination (see Walsh and Dolan, 2009). In Ireland, formal, terminal, written examination is the dominant mode of assessment, with little use of school-based assessment, such as assignment and project work. There is also a strong belief (Williams, 1992) that assessment for certification purposes must be carried out by someone external to the school. This means that even where project and practical work are used for assessment, the work is sent away to be marked anonymously.

This has the effect of influencing the teaching methods used, so that certain parts of the curriculum intention are carried out but others (those that cannot be assessed in this way) are under-represented. When the Junior Certificate was first introduced in 1989, it was expected that reform of assessment would quickly follow and syllabi and guidelines were written with this in mind. While changes to the format of the examinations were introduced, and while practical tests were introduced in certain subjects, the written examination remained dominant. In order to find out whether the curriculum intention was carried out, it was necessary to study curriculum interactions. This aspect is considered below.

Approaches to Junior Certificate: JCSP

The Junior Certificate is part of the compulsory phase of education in Ireland and is a programme for young people in the 12 to 15 age group. Within the programme, there is some choice of subjects but only one programme is available. While this programme is intended to be suitable for all, it is clear that some young people do not benefit from the programme to the extent that was intended. These include:

- students who show clear signs of not coping with the volume and complexity of the current mainstream curriculum;
- students who are underachieving significantly in literacy and numeracy;
- students whose attendance and/or behaviour and attitudinal patterns indicate a marked degree of alienation from school;
- students who have specific disabilities which preclude them from participating in regular courses; and
- students whose social and cultural environment does not equip them for the requirements of the normal Junior Certificate programme.

For these young people, a distinctive approach to the Junior Certificate has been developed and this is called the Junior Certificate School Programme. The programme is described on the NCCA website (www.curriculumonline.ie) as follows:

> The Junior Certificate School Programme is a national programme sponsored by the Department of Education and Science and the National Council for Curriculum and Assessment. It originated in the early school leavers' programmes initiated by the Curriculum Development Unit. Currently the programme is operating in over 240 schools throughout the country.

The aims of the programme are:

- to provide a curriculum framework that assists schools and teachers in making the Junior Certificate more accessible to those young people who may leave school without formal qualifications;
- to help young people experience success and develop a positive self-image by providing a curriculum and assessment framework suitable to their needs; and

- to provide a fresh approach to the Junior Certificate Programme for potential early school leavers who are struggling to cope with secondary school.

The Junior Certificate School Programme had its origin in a curricular project, the Early School Leavers' Programme developed by the City of Dublin Vocational Education Committee Curriculum Development Unit from 1980 onwards. The programme was subsequently developed under a number of names (Junior Certificate, Junior Certificate Elementary Programme, Junior Cycle Schools Programme) and has been in operation under its current name since 1998.

JCSP is an approach to Junior Certificate rather than a separate programme. Students following the JCSP take foundation-level mathematics and English and 'a suitable course' in Irish language and culture. The inclusion of 'school' in the programme title implies that local input at school level will be an important feature of the programme. An evaluation of the programme carried out by the Department of Education and Science (Department of Education and Science, 2005) found that cross-curricular work adds an important dimension to the experience of participants on the programme.

Literacy forms an important dimension of the programme and the approach taken is that 'every teacher is a teacher of literacy'. Since literacy is a dimension of every subject, students taking JCSP are explicitly taught the specific vocabulary for each subject. Posters are available that list the key words that students must learn to make the subject accessible. Materials such as *Who Wants to be a Word Millionaire?* Have been developed and evaluated. Literacy and arts activities are integrated in the annual 'Make-a-Book' competition and exhibition for schools involved in the programme and illustrated and three-dimensional 'books' are displayed to the public. An important dimension of the programme is the JCSP Library Initiative (Haslett, 2005).

A school-wide approach to literacy characterises the programme and numeracy is also emphasised. The numeracy dimension of the programme relates mathematical skills to real-life experience. Students' school experience is enriched by participation in sport and outdoor education and by involvement with arts activities such as music programmes and programmes provided by a community arts groups. JCSP runs parallel to initiatives such as the School Completion Programme and Home/School/Community Liaison Scheme, and shares their philosophy of positive engagement with parents. JCSP has developed an innovative approach to communicating 'good news' to parents via postcards designed by JCSP students. 'Celebration' forms a central part of the JCSP ethos and there is continuing emphasis on finding positive aspects to student activities.

JCSP is supported by a co-ordinator in each school who has slightly reduced teaching hours. There is also a programme support service based in the Second Level Support Service and in the CDVEC Curriculum Development Unit. The Department of Education and Science (DES) makes a time allowance available to schools for JCSP team meetings and there is a small financial allowance for resources. Schools are allowed by the DES to join the programme on the basis of DEIS (Delivering Equality of opportunity In Schools) status. Evaluations of JCSP and of the library programme have been carried out by the DES and by the NCCA.

JCSP: assessment and progression

The emphasis on affirmation is reflected in the assessment modes developed for JCSP, complementary to certification via whichever examinations individual students present for. Each JCSP student constructs a learning profile over the final two years of the course, based on the attainment of 'statements' which set out skill, abilities and tasks that the student has completed. Statements to be attempted are agreed jointly between the teacher and the student in question so that negotiated learning permeates the course. On completion of the programme, students receive a profile which is an official record of their achievements from the Department of Education and Science. Students can progress from the JCSP to the Leaving Certificate Applied Programme (see below).

The Junior Certificate: curriculum as interaction

The curriculum comes to life in the interactions that take place in the classroom: between teachers and students, between students and students, and, at school level, between teacher and teacher. These interactions are, to a large extent, hidden from outside scrutiny so, until recently, we have had little research evidence about the actual practices involved in the implementation of the curriculum intention described above. This gap in our knowledge has been addressed by the large-scale longitudinal study carried out by the ESRI between 2004 and 2007 and at international level, by the TALIS (Teaching and Learning in Schools) report for Ireland (Gilleece et al., 2009).

What does the research tell us?

First year: Moving Up
The ESRI study, carried out on behalf of the NCCA, used both quantitative and qualitative methods to explore the curriculum realities of Junior Certificate implementation across a comprehensive range of second-level school types, locations, student composition and school size. The study provided a general picture of approaches taken by the majority of schools and teachers and also provided some detail on the experience of individual students and teachers. This latter is described further in the next section.

The ESRI study is reported in three books: *Moving Up* (Smyth et al., 2004b), on the experiences of first years; *Pathways through the Junior Cycle* (Smyth et al., 2006) on the experiences of second years and *Gearing Up for the Exam* (Smyth et al.,

2007). The first phase of the study looked at how schools and students dealt with transition from primary to post-primary. It also explored the number of subjects taken, the issue of subject choice, the provision of taster subjects, ability grouping, literacy and numeracy of students, use of homework, use of class tests, and changes in student attitudes during the course of first year.

The curriculum intention, as discussed above, was that all of compulsory education in Ireland (ages six to 16) would be experienced as a continuum. Moving from primary to post-primary school represents a major challenge to this continuity. Smyth, McCoy and Darmody (2004b) found that a minority of students take a long time (over a month) to settle in and a majority of students still miss aspects of their primary school at the end of first year. Curriculum continuity is difficult to achieve because of the very different structure of curriculum that students begin to experience when they move into second level. They have been accustomed to having one teacher for all subjects and now must adjust to a new teacher at each change of class.

Students are typically exposed to a very wide range of subjects in first year. However, the number provided varies widely from school to school. The minimum number of subjects on offer in the schools surveyed was 11 but the average number provided was 18. A small number of schools offered as many as 23. This very large number of subjects generally implied that students were offered an opportunity to try out new subjects by doing short 'taster' courses. As you might expect, the biggest numbers of subjects are offered in co-educational community/comprehensive schools. In almost three-quarters of schools surveyed, students are offered some exposure to a variety of subjects before they make their final choice of subjects for Junior Certificate. In 20 per cent of schools, students choose their subjects before they begin secondary schooling or immediately on entry. Some very small schools offer no choice at all. Almost a third of students (29 per cent) reported that they felt they were taking too many subjects in first year. Students who felt this way were more likely to say that they were not enjoying first year and that they did not feel prepared for secondary-school work by their primary-school experience.

Ability grouping also has a profound effect on curriculum interactions. There is a considerable body of evidence to suggest that mixed-ability grouping has a positive effect on student performance, compared with strict streaming on the basis of ability. In particular, postponing choice of levels (that is, keeping students at the highest possible level for as long as possible) seems to have a positive effect. This finding has major implications for school organisation and for you, as a teacher (see Walsh and Dolan, 2009). Students in higher and lower streams may interact quite differently with the curriculum. Somewhat surprisingly, students in lower streams reported that teachers went too slowly and that they were bored in class. Students in higher streams were more likely to report that teachers went too quickly and some felt insecure and under threat of being moved to a lower stream if their grades were not good enough.

The TALIS report for Ireland (Gilleece et al., 2009) is based on a questionnaire to 2,227 teachers in 142 schools. The Irish survey is part of a larger study carried out on behalf of the OECD, which compares teaching and learning practices in Ireland with those in five other countries (Austria, Belgium, Denmark, Norway and Poland). In comparison with those countries, Irish teachers report the strongest belief in direct transmission method of teaching (teacher as instructor) and the lowest level of constructivist beliefs (teacher as facilitator of student learning). The study also identified three categories of instructional practices in the classroom, namely: structuring practices (checking homework, testing understanding by questioning); student-oriented practices (small group work, differentiated activities for different student abilities, student input into planning); and enhanced activities (projects, practical activities, debates). Irish teachers reported the highest rate of use of structuring activities and the lowest rate of use of enhanced and student-oriented activities of all the comparison countries.

A number of action research projects have attempted to enhance the capacity of teachers to engage in active learning methodologies and, as Hogan (2005) states, 'to become authors of their own work'. Reports of such projects are given by, for example, Trant (2007), Hogan (2005), Hogan et al. (2007) and Callan (2000, 2006). They all demonstrate that teachers can, given support and encouragement, engage in creative and collaborative practices within the framework of the Junior Certificate.

How do these findings relate to:
- Your memories of your own experience of secondary school?
- Your perception of the teaching strategies used and school management decisions taken in your teaching practice school?

Second year: Pathways through the Junior Cycle
The ESRI study also shows that, for many students, second year is a less positive experience than first year. The percentage of students who find schoolwork interesting falls from a high of 80 per cent at the beginning of first year to just 55 per cent by the end of second year. Attitudes to school are strongly influenced by gender and social class. Girls from professional backgrounds have the most positive attitudes and boys from working-class backgrounds have, on a percentage basis, the most negative attitudes. You will not be surprised to learn that teachers report a decline in student behaviour in second year and that some students report an increase in negative interactions with teachers. While some of this increase in challenging behaviour can be ascribed to adolescent development, the ESRI study highlights the role that curriculum organisation and teaching strategies play in maximising positive learning experiences for students. Students who choose subjects that they like are more positive about school in general. Students who

have little or no choice of subjects, or who choose the 'wrong' subjects, are generally more negative. Students show a preference for subjects that are perceived as practical or active, so subjects such as home economics tend to be popular. It is not, however, the subject itself that determines student attitudes. Students report more favourable attitudes towards any subject that is taught in a practical or active way, involving projects, games or group activity. By second year, students have developed a clear concept of what makes a good teacher. They put particular emphasis on the ability to explain things clearly and on approachability; they like to be able to talk to a teacher and they value a sense of humour. They also like and respect teachers who can keep order. Students particularly dislike teachers who just read the textbook or require them to copy large amounts of material from the board without explanation.

Streaming continues to impact on students' experiences and attitudes. Students are keenly aware of the level they are assigned to and students in lower streams tend to work down to expectations. They do less homework than their peers in higher streams and are less engaged in the classroom. Students in Ordinary and Foundation level classes may have a lower self-image and may not be challenged by the work expected of them. From second year onwards, students are increasingly aware of the impending examinations and of the need to study. Student attitudes to study are, however, quite complex. The need to study and do well is counter-balanced by a need to appear 'cool'. They also admit that they pretend not to study. This has the effect of making it appear that they 'don't care' if they do badly and they are 'naturally clever' if they do well.

> If you are teaching second years, note:
> - Strategies that you use that result in positive engagement with your subject.
> - Strategies used by your student colleagues and by experienced teachers.

The experience of third-year students: Gearing Up for the Exam
The third year of junior cycle tends to be dominated by the Junior Certificate examination and students note a trend of 'teaching to the test', and report that they experience less variety in teaching methods and less 'fun stuff'. A quarter of all students interviewed were taking 'grinds', and two-thirds of these were taking them in mathematics. The pattern was again related to social class: the majority of those taking grinds are from middle-class families. Significantly, a high proportion of students said that they would like extra tuition and cited maths and languages as the subjects they found most difficult. The study also found that patterns of behaviour and engagement with the curriculum, established in second year, continue into third year. Students who become disengaged in second year are likely to drift and students who are negative in second year become more negative. This is an important finding since it suggests that challenging behaviour in second year

cannot be ascribed simply and exclusively to a stage of adolescent development.

Curriculum organisation and interaction appear to play a significant role. A worrying finding is that those students who found first year easier than sixth class primary school achieve lower grades in the Junior Certificate examination. This would seem to indicate that lower teacher expectations result in students underperforming. This is related to streaming and the labelling of students in the lower streams who take subjects at Ordinary or Foundation level. The negative effects associated with streaming are confirmed by the ESRI study of third years. The study has some surprising findings regarding streaming. Students in lower streams report that the pace of instruction is too slow and that they have less access to practically oriented subjects. Students in mixed-ability classes actually outperform those in higher streams when they come to the Junior Certificate examination.

On the positive side, most third-year students are relatively positive about school and about learning. They have further developed their idea of the characteristics of a 'good teacher': explains things well, allows questions, asks for feedback to ensure that students have understood, uses a variety of methods, expects and demands hard work but does not 'give out'. This gives us a clear idea of the kinds of interactions which constitute a good curriculum experience.

- Talk to your co-operating teacher(s) and other experienced teachers in your teaching practice school about the effect the Junior Certificate examination has on their approaches to teaching third years.

The Junior Certificate: curriculum as experience

In this section we will imagine how the curriculum might be experienced by individual teachers and pupils. The case studies here are fictional, but their content is based on the findings from the research described above.

Junior Certificate case study 1: Marita

Marita started secondary school in Mount Armstrong Post-Primary (all-girls', voluntary secondary) school three years ago. She lives in a local-authority house about three streets away from the school with her parents, her younger sister and two younger brothers. Her father works in a factory and her mother works on the checkout of a supermarket three evenings a week and all day Saturday. Her mother chose the school on the advice of a woman up the street who said it was the best school around as her daughter had gone to college from it. It is also the nearest school and Marita had gone to the attached primary school. Both her parents left school after the 'Inter'. Her father started an apprenticeship as a carpenter but never finished it. He is good at making and fixing things and sometimes does jobs for people for extra money. Mount Armstrong, originally a convent school, is an all-girls' and now has a lay principal, Mrs Burke. It is small with just three class groups in first year and only one Leaving Cert group.

Marita loved secondary school in first year. Her primary-school experience had not been very good. Her class had 32 pupils and the building was old and decrepit. The secondary school building is a bit better and there were 26 girls in her class in first year. The school is designated 'disadvantaged' [DEIS Band 2] – there is a nearby co-educational vocational school to which some of her primary school class went. She knew most of the girls in her first year class, except for three 'posh' girls who came to school on the bus because their mothers had been to school there, and two new girls from other countries: one from Poland and one from Africa. The first year was mixed ability in two classes but there was another class with just 15 girls in it who were doing a special programme.

Marita had to pick her subjects at the start of first year and did not get to try any of the new ones before she picked them. She did Irish, English, maths, history, geography, CSPE, SPHE, PE, home economics, RE, art and business. She had a choice to pick two from science, music, home economics, art and business. She loved art, maths and history because she liked the teachers. She quite liked Irish, English, CSPE and home economics but really hated geography, business and SPHE. She had the same teacher for geography and SPHE and thought that the teacher was really 'mean'. She was disappointed in home economics because there wasn't much cooking in it and her mother didn't always get all the ingredients she wanted. Her partner never brought in her share either. She wished she had picked science because they had a man teacher for science – a young guy who was really cool. She asked her mother to go to the school to see if she could change but her mother wouldn't.

She settled in to secondary school quickly because she knew her classmates and the sixth class in primary school had prepared her well. She found that she was doing quite a lot of stuff that she had already done in primary but that meant that she was often ahead of her class, especially in maths. They didn't get too much homework and often did projects and other fun things. She found she was good at art but didn't get to do much of it at home because her mother said it was too messy and she never cleaned up afterwards. She was still friendly with the same three girls that were friends from primary school and also made friends with the Polish girl, Kamila, although Kamila didn't have much English and it was sometimes hard to talk to her. Kamila goes out for extra English lessons during Irish.

In second year, everything got harder. Marita grew a lot in the summer of first year and her uniform wasn't comfortable any more. She got into the Honours class in Irish and maths and the teachers seemed to be going much faster. They had a new teacher for Irish who would only talk Irish to them and half the time they didn't know what she was saying. The teachers all started to tell them to work harder or they wouldn't be ready for the Junior Cert. They got a lot more homework.

When Marita turned 14 she got a part-time job in the local hairdresser's and she loved it. She was just sweeping up and washing but everyone treated her like she was grown up and she sometimes got tips. She worked Thursday and Friday nights and all day Saturday. They were starting to get more and more homework in school and sometimes Marita didn't get it all done. She would just do the written work and hope she could learn the other stuff in between classes. She got five notes in her journal in the first term for homework not done or incomplete and her parents sat her down and asked her if she wanted to leave school. She was shocked because she knew she needed qualifications to get a good job and she promised to work harder. Some of the other girls in her class had started messing and giving back cheek and the teachers seemed to be cross most of the time.

Her Christmas tests gave her a shock – instead of As and Bs she was getting Cs and Ds. The Irish teacher's comment suggested that she might like to go back to Ordinary level. She decided to do this and found to her surprise that she liked Irish. She wanted to go to the Gaeltacht at the end of second year, but her parents couldn't afford it. At the end of second year, her report was fairly good and she stayed in the Honours class for maths and English in third year.

In third year, it seems to Marita that the teachers never stop talking about the Junior Cert. They have class tests very often and the 'mocks' will come shortly after Christmas. Marita has cut back a bit on her work hours but she still works all day Saturday. She has given up the Friday night work and goes baby-sitting instead so she can bring her books and do some studying. She hopes to do well in the Junior Cert and maybe go to college.

> - In your own reflective journal describe how Marita's curriculum experience compares with your own experience at that age.
> - Compare Marita's experience of the curriculum with what you know of that of the students you teach.
> - Identify the resources that Marita brings to her schooling experience and the obstacles she must overcome.
> - Consider the hidden curriculum of Mount Armstrong School as it is portrayed here. What expectations do you think the school conveys to its students? How do these compare with her parents' expectations? With her own expectations?

Junior Certificate case study 2: Simon

Simon goes to Tiermoghan Community School, a large community school in a big rural town with a socially mixed intake. He lives about three miles from school with his mother who is separated from his father, who is a vet. His mother is a teacher in a primary school in a village about a mile on the other side of the town. His mother drives him to school in the mornings. His parents chose Tiermoghan Community School because they thought he would get the help he needs as Simon is dyslexic and dyspraxic.

Simon does not cope well with change and his father works unsocial hours so Simon seldom goes to stay with him during school term time. In school, he has a special needs assistant who writes down the homework for him and helps him to organise himself. Simon was in a mixed-ability class in first year, a class of 14 girls and 10 boys. He had not done entrance tests prior to entering the school because of his dyslexia but his mother had given the school comprehensive information about his progress and his needs. He found first year very difficult. He doesn't like noise and had attended a small rural primary school. He found the transition to a big, noisy, bright school very difficult at first. The school has a policy of postponing subject choice until second year and offers a wide taster programme in first year. Simon started out in this programme but his dyspraxia made practical subjects difficult and hazardous and the school requested that he drop woodwork and metalwork. His mother reluctantly agreed. She is a tireless advocate for Simon and spends hours helping him with homework, reading books to him and listening to audiobooks with him.

Simon loved science and tolerated maths in first year. He has a vivid imagination and likes to compose and dictate stories. He can do aspects of art that do not involve fine work. He can sing well and has a good sense of rhythm. Somewhat to his parents' dismay, he is fascinated by religion and with his parents' approval, he likes to be involved in social justice issues. He is greatly interested in history and got on very well with his geography teacher in first year. Simon is exempt from Irish but his mother encourages him to listen to Irish language programmes on television. His biggest problem in first year was bullying. He is tall and thin and very conspicuous in the corridors. Other students imitate his unco-ordinated walk and intense adult-focused mode of speech. Because he is exempt from traditional 'male' practical subjects and does art and home economics, a rumour has spread that he is gay. He also hates PE, particularly team games and the PE class is a weekly ordeal for him. He has a short temper and twice in first year was in trouble for fighting, each time hitting a much smaller boy. His mother is not aware of the homophobic bullying and he has taken to finding excuses for missing PE.

Simon spent some time in the summer of first year with his father and discovered some skill with animals. Simon had a somewhat better time in second year. He was allowed to drop some of his most hated subjects and began to make some tentative friendships with boys and girls. He continued with English, maths, CSPE, SPHE, RE, art, science, music, technical graphics, history and geography. He found science practicals and technical graphics difficult but he dropped home economics even though he liked cooking to give himself some 'street cred'. His mother continued to support his education and got him some extra tuition to help him stay with higher level maths. Some other students continued to call him 'gay' but he became more discreet in dealing with the taunts. He also did music and ceramics outside school and went to a computer club. He works tirelessly when motivated by interest. He has begun to spend more time with his father and has begun to think he might like to be a farrier. His lack of metalwork might pose a problem but the school refused to consider allowing him to take up the subject again. He did not find the work more intense in second year but found himself bored when the rest of the class spent so much time writing.

Simon went to the Gaeltacht at the end of second year but came home after a week because he was bullied and miserable. He spent time working with horses and begged to be allowed to leave school and become a groom. His parents refused to consider this and he is now in third year, preparing for the Junior Cert.

* In your own reflective journal describe how Simon's curriculum experience compares with your own experience at that age.
* Compare Simon's experience of the curriculum with that of Marita.
* Compare Simon's experience with that of any student you teach who has special needs.
* Identify the resources that Simon brings to his schooling experience and the obstacles he must overcome.
* Consider the hidden curriculum of Tiermoghan Community School as it is portrayed here. What expectations do you think the school conveys to its students? How do these compare with Simon's parents' expectations? With his own expectations?
* Reflect on the null curriculum as experienced by Simon. How does this limit his opportunities?

Junior Certificate case study 3: the student teacher

Karen is a student teacher doing her teaching practice in Ticknevin Community College, in a large new working-class suburb in southwest Dublin. Ticknevin Community College is a co-educational school of 620 students with 60 teachers, three guidance counsellors, two learning support teachers, a chaplain and a resource teacher. There are seven classes in each of first, second and third year; two Transition Year classes, four fifth-year and four sixth-year classes. Karen holds a BSc with first class honours in physics, with mathetatics as her minor subject. She has also taken mathematical physics and chemistry, the latter just in first year. She has always been a high achiever and got 480 points from her Leaving Certificate results. She did a very focused Leaving Certificate: Higher level maths, maths physics and physics, chemistry, English and Irish with Ordinary level business and geography. She has now been asked to teach Junior Certificate science and maths to first and second year classes, and one class per week of SPHE to first years. She was delighted when the principal showed her the facilities in the school: four laboratories, all well-equipped and well-kept. There were interactive whiteboards in two of the general classrooms and she was told that she would have the use of these for teaching maths. Karen was delighted to see a poster about Rosalind Franklin in a science lab: she is passionate about encouraging girls to do science and especially to think about taking physical sciences rather than biology.

Karen's co-operating teacher is Anne who has been qualified for a few years. Karen is delighted to be working with someone young and they have been getting on very well and sharing a few laughs and moans. Just recently, though, things got a little tense when Karen told one of the second years (a really 'bright' student) that she would be wasting her time doing biology for Leaving Cert and going into nursing; Karen thinks she should concentrate on physics and maths. Anne feels really hurt about this and they have been avoiding each other in the staff room. This means that Karen doesn't get to discuss SPHE with Anne and she feels really lost in this subject which she believes is too 'touchy-feely'. She is living in dread of a visit from her college supervisor when she is teaching this subject.

Karen is surprised that so many of her students seem to find maths so difficult. She feels that even though she breaks down each problem really clearly, writing each step on the interactive whiteboard, students sometimes come in without any homework done and say that they couldn't understand it. She does it again patiently, step-by-step, exactly as she did the previous day, and the students say 'yes' when she asks them if they understand. Anne tells her not to worry as they will be covering the material again when they revise for the Junior Cert.

- Note in your reflective journal the ways in which you interact with your co-operating teacher about curriculum issues. Do you agree with the sequencing of material that s/he proposes? Do the sections that you teach draw on your strengths or challenge you in areas where you are less confident?
- Do you agree with her/his pedagogical approach? How do you deal with disagreements?
- How can you use formative assessment to address any difficulties students might have with curriculum content?

THE JUNIOR CERTIFICATE IN THE FUTURE

Evaluations of Junior Certificate have indicated that the programme has not fulfilled all the expectations that were held for it in 1989 when it was introduced. As was mentioned above, the curriculum content was designed separately from the in-service programme and the assessment modes and techniques. It had been anticipated that curriculum reform would be quickly followed by assessment reform but the terminal examination remained the dominant mode of assessment for almost all subjects. In 1999, the NCCA carried out a large-scale evaluation of the Junior Certificate programme, based on a survey of school principals. They found that the curriculum was less suitable for students described as 'at risk' and for those referred to as 'educationally disadvantaged'. They also found that schools made little reference to 'areas of experience' but based their curriculum around separate subjects.

During the 1990s, the focus of curriculum reform was at senior secondary level (see below) and at primary level. The introduction of a new primary school curriculum in 1999 was accompanied by a comprehensive in-service programme which brought teachers together for six days in each school year. The ESRI study (discussed above) demonstrated the lack of cohesion between primary and secondary curricula and emphasised the need for more continuity of experience for students throughout the compulsory period.

The NCCA also found that, since each subject had been developed separately and individually, there was sometimes a lack of co-ordination. As a result some subjects were overloaded with content and there was sometimes overlap between subjects. Following consultation in 2008 (www.ncca.ie), they embarked on a process of 're-balancing' of syllabi which aimed to:

- reduce overload within and overlap between subjects; and
- provide more space and time to have the quality of learning engagement with students that teachers would like.

Five subjects have gone through the rebalancing process: English, history, music, home economics, and art, craft and design.

Rebalancing has involved:

- rewriting each syllabus to a common template;
- writing learning outcomes for each syllabus;
- updating each syllabus and removing unnecessary overlap;
- lining each syllabus up with changes in the primary school curriculum and with any changes at Leaving Certificate; and
- making minor changes to assessment.

The NCCA is currently engaged in a consultation about the shape of junior cycle in the future. The document 'Innovation and Identity: Ideas for a New Junior Cert' can be downloaded from www.ncca.ie. You can be part of the consultation process by completing the online questionnaire. You can also be involved in curriculum decision-making through your teachers' union (ASTI or TUI) and by joining your subject association.

THE CURRICULUM IN IRELAND AT SENIOR CYCLE

As a student teacher or educational practitioner, you are likely to have less experience of teaching at senior cycle than junior cycle. Nevertheless, it is important for you to understand the structure of and rationale for senior cycle curricula, as you will need to be familiar with these issues as a qualified teacher.

The senior cycle: curriculum as intention

Senior cycle in Ireland consists of either two or three years, depending on whether Transition Year is taken. Senior cycle begins after the Junior Certificate examinations and spans the end of the compulsory period (for students not yet 16 at Junior Certificate) and the beginning of the non-compulsory period of education. Because most of the programme is in the post-compulsory phase of education, the overall intention of senior cycle is not expressed in terms of entitlement as is the intention of junior cycle. The senior cycle must also serve a range of different, and sometimes conflicting, purposes (e.g. preparation for adult and working life, preparation for further study). Nevertheless, the general aims of education also apply to senior cycle. In 1993, the NCCA proposed a set of aims for senior cycle which stated that the senior cycle programmes aim:

- to reinforce and provide continuity and progression from the aims and content of the Junior Certificate programme and coherence across the curriculum;
- to prepare the young person in particular for the requirements of further education, for adult life and for working life; and
- to develop in the young person a capacity for self-directed learning and for independent thought.

In 2005, the NCCA expanded that list as follows:

- to ensure coherent and meaningful continuity from the junior cycle of post-primary education and to allow progression to further education, the world of work and higher education;
- to provide a curriculum characterised by breadth and balance, while allowing for some degree of specialisation;
- to ensure improved access to, and equality in, senior cycle education for all, within a context of lifelong learning;
- to contribute to the emergence of Ireland as a knowledge society;
- to educate for participative citizenship at local, national, European and global levels;
- to contribute to each individual's moral, social, cultural and economic life, and enhance their quality of life;
- to ensure that the highest standards of achievement are obtained by every person, appropriate to their ability; and
- to ensure that the educational experience at senior cycle is in line with good practice and developments internationally.

> - Do you notice any changes of emphasis between junior and senior cycle aims?
> - How do the aims for senior cycle relate to the overall aims of education, listed above?

Until 1994, the majority of students had access to just one senior cycle programme, called simply 'the Leaving Certificate'. During the 1990s, a number of programmes were developed and students now have the option of taking Transition Year (if the school provides it), followed by a choice between Leaving Certificate Applied, Leaving Certificate Established and Leaving Certificate Vocational Programme.

Extended senior cycle provision and increased uptake of programmes have, however, increased the necessity for more coherence in senior cycle planning and for more clearly defined rationales for any senior cycle and for each of the various options within it. The overall list of aims given above comes from a document which is still under discussion as part of an ongoing review of senior cycle which has involved committees, conferences, the production of discussion documents using scenario planning tools, and online questionnaires and comments. This process has run in parallel with the review of existing syllabi for the Leaving Certificate Established programme, evaluations of the Leaving Certificate Applied and Leaving Certificate Vocational programmes, and major research into the Transition Year programme. Each of these programmes will be considered in turn.

Transition Year

Transition Year (TY) was introduced for the first time in 1974 and, from 1994 onwards, all second-level schools have had the option of offering the programme. The programme remains optional for both schools and students: in 2009–10, more than 27,000 students in 540 schools took part in the programme. Some schools make TY compulsory for all students; the majority of those providing it offer the programme as an option and have a limited number of places. Usually, students seeking a place on the programme are interviewed. Patterns of provision were studied by ESRI (Smyth et al., 2004a). Girls' secondary schools are most likely to provide the programme and over 90 per cent of such schools do so. The lowest levels of provision are found in vocational schools and in designated disadvantaged schools. Jeffers (2002, p. 60) relates the low take up of Transition Year in designated disadvantaged schools to a perception that Transition Year is not an intervention targeted at disadvantage and that its capacity to make a difference is therefore underestimated. The patterns of provision are related to school size, opportunity, logistics, school traditions and 'assumptions about the suitability of the programme for certain groups of students' (Smyth et al., 2004a, p. 21).

Transition Year is unique in Ireland in the degree of freedom allowed to schools to design their own Transition Year curriculum within the overall programme mission statement given in the programme guidelines, namely:

> To promote the personal, social, educational and vocational development of pupils and to prepare them for their role as autonomous, participative and responsible members of society (Department of Education, 1993, p. 4).

The aims listed in the guidelines include 'education for maturity', 'personal development', 'social awareness and social competence', 'general, technical and academic skills', interdisciplinary and self-directed learning', and 'experience of adult and working life' (Department of Education, 1993, pp. 6–14). More than any other programme, Transition Year provides an opportunity for schools to get involved in designing their own curricula. The curriculum is described on the TY website in terms of layers:

- the *calendar* layer consists of once-off activities, such as work experience, trips out, visitors to the school, social outreach, a musical or drama;
- the *TY specific* layer consists of modules and subjects provided in Transition Year only, such as mini company, Young Social Innovators, photography;
- the *subject sampling* layer provides opportunities for students to try out subjects that they might consider taking for Leaving Certificate or for further study, such as physics, Spanish, music or business; and
- the *continuity subject* layer consists of Gaeilge, PE, ICT, mathematics, English and religious education.

In the final two years of senior cycle, students take one of three Leaving Certificate programmes: Leaving Certificate Applied, Leaving Certificate Established or Leaving Certificate Vocational. Each of these will be considered in turn.

Leaving Certificate Applied

The Leaving Certificate Applied (LCA) is currently provided in 368 centres and taken by about 8,000 students (about 8 per cent of the cohort). Most of these centres are second-level schools, but the list of providers also includes a welfare and probation service, youth service, senior education centres (for members of the Travelling Community) and 34 Youthreach centres. The programme is supported by a lower pupil–teacher ratio (PTR), by provision of some funding for resources and by in-career development of teachers carried out by the Second Level Support Service (SLSS). The most recent ESRI survey (Banks et al., 2009) notes that the programme is provided in about 40 per cent of schools. This compares with just 15 per cent of schools in 1997.

The Leaving Certificate Applied was introduced on a pilot developmental basis in 1995, following intensive work by the NCCA. The programme built on the curricular initiatives, namely the Senior Certificate (developed by the Shannon Curriculum Development Centre) and the Vocational Preparation and Training Programme (VPT1) developed by schools according to guidelines produced by the Department of Education and supported by the CDVEC Curriculum Development Unit. All of these programmes had their origins in concern regarding the suitability or appropriateness of the Leaving Certificate programme in existence (now known as LCE) for those who were taking all or most subjects at Ordinary level and were unlikely to proceed to study in higher education (Curriculum Awareness Action Group, 1990). A second and more significant factor was concern regarding the levels of youth unemployment throughout Europe in the late 1980s and early 1990s. Prior the Treaty of Maastricht (1991) the EC was precluded from involvement in the education systems of member states but was involved in supporting training initiatives, especially those designed to address youth unemployment. Accordingly, a number of initiatives, based wholly or partly in schools, and containing the term 'training' or 'vocational' in their titles, were developed in member states. All of these programmes, in receipt of EC funding, had a common structural framework of vocational education, vocational preparation and general education. The Leaving Certificate Applied (LCA) is a modular programme described by the NCCA as 'pre-vocational'. Key objectives for the programme are:

- preparing students for adult and working life; and
- meeting the needs of students who are not adequately catered for other Leaving Certificate programmes or who choose not to opt for such programmes (Department of Education and Science, 2000, p. 25).

LCA is a two-year programme which must be taken as a self-contained option and cannot be combined with elements of any other Leaving Certificate programme. Some schools offer LCA as a choice against Transition Year so that students cannot take both programmes while others appear to give LCA a relatively low profile within the school's activities. The DES survey which evaluated the programme (Department of Education and Science, 2000, p. 31) reported that some schools had concerns 'that the academic reputation of the school would be diluted by possibly attracting a greater number of students from more disadvantaged areas'.

The two years of the programme are each divided into two half-year sessions. Students take 40 modules, each generally of three to four classes per week throughout the course. The distribution of the modules is as follows: 14 in general education, 16 in vocational education and 12 in vocational preparation. General education incorporates social education (LCA is the only Leaving Certificate programme, at present, to include social education as a discrete, certificated category), courses in conversational Irish (Gaeilge chumarsaideach) and in a modern European language, and leisure and recreation and arts education. Vocational education includes vocational specialisms (students take two options (four modules in each) from a list of 11 options), mathematical applications and information and communication technology. Vocational preparation includes English and communications, preparation for work, work experience, and enterprise.

The structural innovation of the programme is mirrored in its assessment procedures which include seven cross-curricular 'tasks', key assignments associated with the vocational specialism modules and credit for 90 per cent attendance (the minimum acceptable) in the programme. There are a small number of terminal, written examinations in the language and mathematical areas. The seven tasks include a practical achievement task and a personal reflection task. Certification is only available to students who complete the entire programme and take terminal examinations. Progression to LCA is generally available to JCSP students so that LCA groups will usually contain students who have come from at least two different courses.

The Leaving Certificate Established

The Leaving Certificate Established is the paradigmatic Leaving Certificate programme and until 1995 was referred to simply as the 'Leaving Certificate'. It can fairly be described as a collection of subjects rather than a programme and is perhaps the area of secondary schooling which best exemplifies the tradition of 1878. The LCE is comprised of some 33 subjects, taken by most students over a two-year period, only one of which (Gaeilge) is compulsory. The tide of reform which resulted in the development of the Junior Certificate and a number of other senior-cycle programmes did not result in change in the Leaving Certificate at a programmatic level. Revision of LCE syllabi, however, was undertaken on an individual basis resulting in the introduction in 1995 of new courses in Gaeilge, French, German, Spanish, Italian, accounting, business, and music, and the introduction of Foundation level in mathematics. Further revision followed in most other subjects and the NCCA state that:

> In addition to updating the content and relevance of syllabuses (to the needs of students), the vocational orientation of each subject, where relevant, has also been increased.

The impetus for this revision appeared to come, not so much from the consultative reform process as from the economic imperatives reflected in documents such as the OECD review, the 'Industrial Review Group Report' (Culliton, 1992) and continued by the EU policy documents such as the Lisbon Strategy (2004).

The new and revised syllabuses introduced are characterised by:

- modernisation and increased relevance;
- an outcomes-based approach to expressing course and assessment objectives;
- increased attention to the vocational aspects of subjects – to the application of learning to real-life situations;
- greater attention to differentiation, often in the form of different learning outcomes for Ordinary and Higher levels;
- broadening of the basis for and the methods for the assessment of achievement; and

- greater consideration of gender issues and of special educational needs (www.ncca.ie).

The introduction of these syllabi has resulted in the provision of in-career development courses for teachers, on a subject basis, on a much larger scale than before. The Leaving Certificate Established plays a pivotal role, different from that of all other programmes, in the Irish education system. Because of its gatekeeper role in controlling access to further and higher education, the Leaving Certificate is a high-stakes examination and the 'points system' exerts an influence on all second-level programmes, and, arguably, even on primary education. Because of this, LCE has been much slower to change and tends to be thought of in terms of separate subjects, rather than as a coherent programme. To remedy this, the NCCA has embarked on a process of embedding key skills across all programmes, but especially in LCE. These key skills are based on the work of Bentley and are identified as: information processing, communicating, being personally effective, working with others, and critical and creative thinking.

> - From your experience of senior-cycle programmes, identify where one or more of the key skills can be developed in a subject or module.

The Leaving Certificate Vocational Programme

The Leaving Certificate Vocational Programme was introduced in 1994 with a very specific focus on the business and vocational environment into which young people would move. It can be described as a vocational orientation to the Leaving Certificate Established and is sometimes described as the 'Leaving Cert plus'. Students taking LCVP typically take seven subjects from the Leaving Cert Established programme together with two link modules (described below). The subjects taken must include two from either of the Vocational Subject Groupings (VSGs) listed below.

Specialist grouping
1. Construction studies; engineering; design and communication graphics; technology (any two).
2. Physics and construction studies or engineering or technology, or design and communication graphics.
3. Agricultural science and construction studies or engineering or technology or design and communication graphics.
4. Agricultural science and chemistry or physics or physics/chemistry.
5. Home economics; agricultural science; biology (any two).
6. Home economics and art – design option or craft option.
7. Accounting; business; economics (any two).
8. Physics and chemistry.

9.   Biology and chemistry or physics or physics/chemistry.
10.   Biology and agricultural science.
11.   Art – design option or craft option and design and communication graphics.

Services groupings
12.   Engineering or technology or construction studies or design and communication graphics and accounting or business or economics.
13.   Home economics and accounting or business or economics.
14.   Agricultural science and accounting or business or economics.
15.   Art design or craftwork option and accounting or business or economics.
16.   Music and accounting or business or economics.

Source: www.lcvp.slss.ie (2010)

An important dimension was added to the programme with the inclusion of two 'link modules' which link the vocational studies to the other aspects of the programme and to link the in-school and out-of-school aspects of student learning. The content of the link modules is described on the LCVP website as follows.

Link Module I – Preparation for the World of Work
Students will research and investigate local employment opportunities, develop job seeking skills such as letter writing, CV presentation, interview techniques; gain valuable practical experience of the world of work; interview and work shadow a person in a career area that interests them.

Link Module II – Enterprise Education
Students will be involved in organising visits to local business and community enterprises; meet and interview enterprising people on-site and in the classroom; plan and undertake interesting activities that will build self-confidence, creativity, initiative and develop teamwork, communication and computer skills.

The programme is currently provided in 522 schools. The curriculum intention underlying LCVP is that students are educated 'to cope and thrive in an environment of rapid change' (www.lcvp.slss.ie).

Students taking part in LCVP are expected to develop good ICT skills and schools taking part in the programme receive support towards computer facilities. The link modules are assessed by some innovative, school-based assessment techniques including role-play based on a video presentation. Students need to develop a range of information-processing and presentation skills to be able to do this. The link modules collectively constitute a 'subject for points' purposes and are recognised (although at a diminished level in comparison with other subjects, i.e.

80 points for a Distinction (80-100 per cent)) by universities and institutes of technology.

Senior cycle: curriculum as interaction

Transition year

Evidence about curriculum interaction in Transition Year comes from a number of sources. An evaluation of the programme was carried out by the Department of Education. Detailed studies were carried out by Smyth, Byrne and Hannan (2004b) and by Jeffers (2007). These studies note considerable variation between schools in the content, organisation and assessment of Transition Year programmes. Where Transition Year programmes are deemed to have been successful, very positive student outcomes have been observed. Parents and teachers remark on the increase in maturity and the enhanced capacity to engage with adults (Jeffers, 2007) displayed by students who have completed Transition Year, compared to their peers who went directly to fifth year. Strong bonds between students and improved classroom climate have also been noted. The longitudinal study found that students who took TY out-performed their peers who had gone straight to Leaving Certificate by one and a half grades on average. TY students were also more 'educationally adventurous' – they were more likely to take subjects for Leaving Certificate that they had not previously studied at Junior Cert. Students surveyed were very positive about the use of active learning methodologies in TY. Jeffers found, however, that these were not as widely used as was recommended by the DES.

Leaving Certificate Applied

LCA has been evaluated by the inspectorate of the Department of Education and Science (Department of Education and Science, 2000) who established that the key objectives of the programme were being met in most schools. They note (p. 73) that 'the reported retention of many of these students in schools until the completion of Senior Cycle education was an indicator of the success of the programme'. They also remark on the extension of the developmental ethos of the programme to other areas of the school's activities, such as professional development of teachers, personal and social development of students and the development of links with out-of-school agencies in the community and in business. Areas of concern identified include: the selection of students for the programme; the involvement of parents and community interests in the development of the programme; the monitoring of attendance to ensure that the 90 per cent requirement is met; and the provision for social education and for vocational preparation and guidance. More diverse provision of work experience and reduced reliance on part-time work of students to provide this experience was recommended.

The Department of Education and Science (2000, p. 78) survey also made reference to gender differentiation in the provision of vocational specialisms. The recommend that 'gender balance in the uptake of Vocational Specialisms should continue to be a focus for schools in programme planning and implementation'. Since the DES evaluation was based on questionnaires to school principals and teachers together with school visits and some interviews with teachers and principals, the student voice has not informed the findings to any extent. Hence there is no data on the satisfaction levels of male and female students with the courses on offer.

A significant percentage of students in LCA experiences literacy difficulties. The ESRI study found that students who had lower scores in reading and mathematics in first year were more likely to be offered LCA. The programme literature and the DES evaluation make no mention of literacy support. English and communications is an LCA module within the area of Vocational Preparation rather than general education, so its scope to address such difficulties may be limited.

Two aspects of the LCA programme have been particularly controversial and have impacted on the esteem in which the programme is held. The first is the discrete or 'ring-fenced' nature of the programme. Students cannot combine elements of the programme with elements of other Leaving Certificate programmes. This may be limiting for students with specific aptitudes or intelligences who are focused on a vocational option. Their possibilities for continued, lifelong learning in their area of expertise are very limited. The second is the limited range of progression options which follow on from the programme. The Leaving Certificate Applied does not generate 'points' for entry to third-level education. Limited access to further education is available via post-Leaving Certificate courses which link to certificate courses in institutes of technology. The LCA thus has a complex and difficult dual role as a programme which can cater for a diverse range of student abilities and aspirations. On the one hand it seeks to further the education of those students who would find the academic Leaving Certificate Established programme too challenging and who wish to proceed directly to the workplace; on the other, it seeks to provide a pathway of opportunity into further and higher education for those whose engagement with education is mediated through vocational activity. If it were part of the 'points system', the important benefits noted from the programme (e.g. increased self-confidence, motivation, maturity) might be the very features that would be at risk of being lost. The challenge for the LCA is to retain its identity while claiming parity of esteem with other Leaving Certificate programmes.

Leaving Certificate Established

The existence of three Leaving Certificate programme testifies to a level of dissatisfaction with the Leaving Certificate, especially for those who will take the majority of their subjects at Ordinary or Foundation level. The LCE as a programme, however, has received little systematic evaluation. At the time of writing, the ESRI longitudinal study is nearing completion of its work on LCE.

Leaving Certificate Vocational Programme

The LCVP has not been studied to the same extent as the programmes named above. Gleeson and Granville (1999) evaluated the in-service provided for teachers of LCVP and noted that while the LCVP is a programme, the term tended to be used in schools to refer to the link modules only. The DES has carried out a number of evaluations of LCVP programmes in schools as part of whole school evaluations, which can be found on the DES website (www.education.ie). Some concerns expressed referred to the way in which the vocational subject groupings are allocated, the need to strengthen the cross-curricular dimension of the programme and the timetabling of the ICT component against other curriculum areas, and the need for support and guidance in subject choice. In most reports, the inspectors noted the use of active learning methodologies and positive awareness of the programme on the part of students.

Senior cycle: curriculum as experience

The student teacher

Evan is a PGDE student doing his teaching practice in Aylmer College, a 600-student all-boys' voluntary secondary school in a large town. He teaches French and history and spent a year abroad teaching English after his degree. He attended a co-educational community school himself and finds himself surprised by some aspects of school life. Relations between staff and students are somewhat more formal than he remembers from his own schooldays and the school places a lot of emphasis on examination results and sporting prowess, especially in hurling. During teaching practice, he has had the opportunity to teach a Transition Year class and has been asked to develop a module on history. He did not do Transition Year himself and was a little apprehensive for a number of reasons. The school puts a lot of emphasis on examination success and he was not sure how best to contribute to this while at the same time giving the students a good experience of Transition Year. He spoke to a colleague in his PGDE class who suggested a module on the First World War. He decided to talk to one of the English teachers in the school and together they put together a module on the poetry of the First World War. The students responded well and contributed pictures and added poems of their own, making links with contemporary wars in Afghanistan and Iraq. Evan was delighted but felt very deflated when one of the senior teachers made critical and cynical comments like, 'I wonder how much that lot will remember, they probably think George Bush was in the trenches.' Together with his colleague who helped him to design the module, Evan decided to upload the module on to the Transition Year website and was delighted to receive feedback by email from a number of teachers.

- Reflect on your own experience in teaching Transition Year or any other area of the curriculum where you had the opportunity to design materials.
- Reflect on ways in which your PGDE colleagues and the teachers in your school have supported you or criticised your work. What have you learned from this?

The student of Leaving Certificate Applied

Amber is a fifth-year student in Ballinafagh Community College. She took JCSP at Junior Cycle and made a lot of progress. She had always struggled with reading but had good friends in primary school and the teachers liked her. She enjoyed the project work in JCSP and her group won a prize in the Make-a-Book exhibition. She went for extra help with reading and got a good mark in Foundation level mathematics. When she was in third year the Leaving Certificate Applied Co-ordinator suggested to her mother that she might do Leaving Cert Applied. Her parents were not very sure what the programme was about or about the implications of doing it. In the beginning, she did not like it much. Her two best friends left school after the Junior Cert and as she is quite shy, she did not find it easy to settle in. She didn't know most of the teachers and found the pace quite fast in some subjects. She no longer has any extra help with reading and finds some of the work difficult. Her vocational subjects are childcare and catering and she really looks forward to the days when she has them. She greatly prefers the LCA approach to the home economics she did for Junior Cert as it is more practical and she doesn't have to write so much. She has been involved in a cross-curricular task which included catering for foreign expert visitors to the school. Her group had to do the budgeting and shopping as well as writing menu cards on the computer. They wrote up a report afterwards. She found some of these tasks challenging but enjoyed working in a group and being treated like an adult. She has done some work experience in a crèche and found she has real aptitude with small children. She had thought of leaving as soon as she turned 16 but now thinks she will stay to the end of the programme and maybe do a Post-Leaving Certificate FETAC qualification in childcare.

- Which elements of the LCA curriculum, in your opinion, would be most challenging for Amber?
- If the LCA counted for 'points' do you think this would have a positive or a negative effect on Amber's experience?

The student of Leaving Cert Established

Joseph is in his second Leaving Certificate year in Colaiste Aonghusa, a 700-student all-boys', fee-paying secondary school. He did 11 subjects for Junior Cert and got eight As and three Bs. He did Transition Year and spent a term in a French school during that time. He was also involved in a mini-company which made and sold picture frames. He greatly enjoyed the experience and found that he had a flair for business.

When it came to choosing his Leaving Certificate subjects, he considered doing LCVP but found that his subject choice would be quite limited. In particular, he found that he would not get as many points for the 'link modules' as he would for a 'regular' subject, no matter how well he did. As he wants to study law, he chose subjects that he felt would give him the maximum points. These included mathematics and physics. He must take a European language, so he chose French. He is doing Higher level English but has decided to drop to Ordinary level Irish, although he got an A in the subject in Junior Cert.

He has chosen subjects where he feels he will get the most points so has opted for accounting and business. He liked art at Junior Cert level and studied piano outside of timetabled classes but no longer takes part in these activities as he wants to concentrate on maximum achievement. He continues to take part in debates as he feels that this will be an advantage in doing law and he plays rugby although he has cut back on training. He attends supervised study every day after school and does a further three to four hours after he goes home. He considers the constraints on his life to be worthwhile if they will enable him to achieve the college course and the career to which he aspires.

- Compare Joseph's school experience with that of Amber, described above.
- Would you enjoy teaching Joseph? Why or why not?
- If you were Joseph's Irish teacher, how would you feel?

RECOMMENDED READING

Websites

This chapter has dealt with the second-level curriculum in Ireland in a largely descriptive fashion, with the needs of pre-service education students in mind. Some of the key references mentioned above are websites.

www.education.ie (website of the DES. Syllabus listings for all subjects; evaluation reports for LCVP; links).

www.ncca.ie (website of the National Council for Curriculum and Assessment. Programme information for all major programmes; consultations on areas of development; research results).

www.slss.ie (website of the Second Level Support Service. Programme information on JCSP, LCA, LCVP, TY and subjects for which a support team is in place).

www.curriculumonline.ie (a section of the NCCA website with specific curriculum information).

www.sess.ie (website of the Special Education Support Service).

www.cdu.cdvec (website of the Curriculum Development Unit of City of Dublin VEC; variety of resources, especially for JCSP).

www.esri.ie (website of the Economic and Social Research Institute; research on a number of areas of the curriculum).

www.pisa.oecd.org (website for the OECD's PISA project of international comparisons.

www.oecd.org/country (website that gives OECD statistics for Ireland).

Reports

Banks, J., Byrne, D., McCoy, S. and Smyth, E. (2009). *Student Experiences of the Leaving Certificate Applied*. Dublin: ESRI.

Callan, J. (2000). *School and Curriculum Development Initiative, Context, Activities and Analysis, Interim Report*. Maynooth: NUI Maynooth Education Department.

Callan, J. (2006). *Developing Schools, Enriching Learning, The SCD Experience*. Maynooth: NUI Maynooth Education Department.

CEB (Curriculum and Examinations Board) (1984). *Issues and Structures in Education*. Dublin: Curriculum and Examinations Board.

CEB (Curriculum and Examinations Board) (1986). *In Our Schools*. Dublin: Curriculum and Examinations Board.

Commission of the European Communities (2005). *Progress Towards the Lisbon Objectives in Education and Training*. Commission Staff Working Paper. Brussels: Commission of the European Communities.

Commission on the Points System (1999). *Final Report and Recommendations*. Dublin: The Stationery Office.

Cosgrove, J., Shiels, G., Sofroniu, N., Zastrutzki, S. and Shortt, F. (2004). *Education for Life: the Achievements of 15-year olds in Ireland in the Second Cycle of PISA*. Dublin: Educational Research Centre.

Culliton, J. (1992). *A Time for Change: Industrial Policy for the 1990s*. Dublin: The Stationery Office.

Curriculum Awareness Action Group (1990). *Low Achievement in Senior Cycle: a Survey of Principals of Voluntary Secondary Schools*. Dublin: Marino Institute of Education.

Department of Education (1993). *Transition Year Guidelines*. Dublin: The Stationery Office.

Department of Education (1994). *Evaluation of the Transition Year Option*. Dublin: The Stationery Office.

Department of Education and Science (2000). *Report on the National Evaluation of the Leaving Certificate Applied*. Dublin: The Stationery Office.

Department of Education and Science (2005). *Building on Success: An Evaluation of the Junior Certificate School Programme*. Dublin: The Stationery Office.

Gilleece, L., Shiel, G., Perkins, R. and Proctor, M. (2009). *Teaching and Learning International Survey (2008): National Report for Ireland*. Dublin: Educational Research Centre.

Government of Ireland (1995). *Charting our Education Future*. White Paper. Dublin: The Stationery Office.

Granville, G. (1999). *In Support of Change: An Evaluation of the LCVP In-Career Development Programme*. Dublin: Leaving Certificate Vocational Programme.

Haslett, D. (2005). *Room for Reading: JCSP Demonstration Library Project Research Report*. Dublin: JCSP Support Service.

Jeffers, G. (2007). *Attitudes to Transition Year*, Maynooth: NUI Maynooth Education Department.

Smyth, E. (1999). *Do Schools Differ?: Academic and Personal Development among Pupils in the Second-Level Sector*. Dublin: ESRI.

Smyth, E., Byrne, D. and Hannan, C. (2004a). *The Transition Year Programme: an Assessment*. Dublin: Liffey Press/ESRI.

Smyth, E., McCoy, S. and Darmody, M. (2004b). *Moving Up: The Experiences of First Year Students in Post-Primary Education*. Dublin: Liffey Press/ESRI.

Smyth, E., Dunne, A., McCoy, S. and Darmody, M. (2006). *Pathways through the Junior Cycle: the Experiences of Second Year Students*. Dublin: Liffey Press and ESRI.

Smyth, E., Dunne, A., Darmody, M. and McCoy, S. (2007). *Gearing Up for the Exam: The Experience of Junior Certificate Students*. Dublin: Liffey Press and ESRI.

Some curriculum texts

Text that deal with curriculum in general

Apple, M. (2004). *Ideology and Curriculum* (3rd edition). New York: Routledge-Falmer.

Connelly M. and Clandinnin J. (1986). *Teachers as Curriculum Planners: Narratives of Experience*. Toronto: The Ontario Institute for Studies in Education/OISE Press.

Crooks, T. (ed.) (1989). *The Changing Curriculum: Perspectives on the Junior Certificate*. Dublin: O'Brien Press.

Flinders, D. J. and Thornton, S. J. (1997). *The Curriculum Studies Reader*. London: Routledge.

Goodson, I. (1995). *The Making of Curriculum: Collected Essays* (2nd edition). London: Falmer.

Hargreaves, A., Earl, L. and Ryan, J. (1996). *Schooling for Change: Reinventing Education for Early Adolescents*. London: Falmer Press.

Kelly, A. V. (2004). *The Curriculum: Theory and Practice* (5th edition). London: Sage.

Lawton, D. (1983). *Curriculum Studies and Educational Planning*. London: Edward Arnold.

Ross, A. (2000). *Curriculum: Construction and Critique*. London: Falmer.

Stenhouse L. (1976). *An Introduction to Curriculum Research and Development*. London: Heinemann.

Sugrue, C. (ed.) (2004). *Curriculum and Ideology: Irish Experiences, International Perspectives*. Dublin: Liffey Press.

Texts dealing with specific curriculum issues
The Hidden Curriculum

Apple, M. W. (2006). *Educating the 'Right' Way: Schools and the Conservative Alliance*. New York: Routledge.

Eisner, E. and Vallance, E. (1974). *Conflicting Conceptions of Curriculum*. Berkeley: McCutcheon.

Kelly, A. V. (1995). *Education and Democracy*. London: Paul Chapman.

Lynch, K. (1989). *The Hidden Curriculum: Reproduction in Education, A Reappraisal*. Lewes: Falmer Press.

Paechter, C. (2000). *Changing School Subjects: Power, Gender and Curriculum*. Buckingham: Open University Press.

White, J. (1990). *Education and the Good Life: Beyond the National Curriculum*. London: Kogan Page (in association with The Institute of Education, London).

Curriculum change and innovations

Crooks, T. and McKernan, J. (1984). *The Challenge of Change*. Dublin: Institute of Public Administration.

Gleeson, J and Granville, G. (1999). 'The Case for the Leaving Certificate Applied'. *Irish Educational Studies*, 15.

Jeffers, G. (2002). 'Transition Year Programme and Educational Disadvantage'. *Irish Educational Studies*. 21 (2), 47–64.

Trant, A. (1999). *The Future of the Curriculum: Papers to Celebrate the 25th Anniversary of the CDVEC Curriculum Development Unit*. Dublin: CDVEC Curriculum Development Unit.

Trant, A. (2007). *Curriculum Matters in Ireland*. Dublin: Blackhall Publishing.

The vocational dimension of curriculum

McCoy, S. and Smyth, E. (2004). *At Work in School*. Dublin: Oak Tree Press.

Pring, R. (1995). *Closing the Gap: Liberal Education and Vocational Preparation*. London: Hodder & Stoughton.

Young, M. F. D. (1998). *The Curriculum of the Future: From the 'New Sociology of Education' to a Critical Theory of Learning*. London: Routledge/Falmer.

Curriculum and assessment

Broadfoot, P. (1979). *Assessment, Schools and Society*. London: Methuen.

Eisner, Elliot W. (1979). *The educational imagination: on the design and evaluation of school programs*. New York: Macmillan.

Reay, D. and Wiliam, D. (1999). '"I'll be a nothing": structure, agency and the construction of identity through assessment'. *British Educational Research Journal*. 25 (3), 343–54.

Walsh, B. and Dolan, R. (2009). *A Guide to Teaching Practice in Ireland*. Dublin: Gill & Macmillan.

Williams, K. (1992). *Assessment: A Discussion Paper*. Dublin: ASTI.

Transition from primary to post-primary

O'Brien, M. (2004). *Making the Move: Students', Teachers' and Parents' Perspectives of Transfer from First to Second-level Schooling*. Dublin: Marino Institute of Education.

Active learning and curriculum

Hogan, P. (ed.) (2005). *Voices from School: Interim Report of the TL21 Project*. Maynooth: NUI Maynooth Education Department.

Hogan, P., Brosnan A., De Roiste, B., MacAlister, A., Malone, A., Quirke-Bolt, N. and Smith, G. (2007). *Learning Anew*. Maynooth: NUI Faculty of Philosophy.

Ability grouping

Ireson, J. and Hallam, S. (2001). *Ability Grouping in Education*. London: Paul Chapman.

Alternative approaches to curriculum: care and well-being

Noddings, N. (1992). *The Challenge to Care in Schools*. New York: Teachers' College Press.

Noddings, N. (2003). *Happiness and Education*. Cambridge: Cambridge University Press.

O'Brien, M. (2008). *Well-being and Post-primary Schooling: a Review of the Literature and Research*. Dublin: NCCA.

Chapter Four
Sociology of Education
James O'Higgins-Norman, Dublin City University

INTRODUCTION

Sociology is the scientific study of social life. It involves the description and analyses of social behaviour with a particular focus on how human society has come to be the way it is, revealing the social forces that shape people's lives. A fundamental assumption in sociology is that society has a major influence on what people do with their lives and on the way we understand what we do.

It has been argued that 'in the game of life we may decide how to play our cards, but it is society that deals us our hand' (Macionis and Plummer, 2005, p. 9). In other words, although we have a choice in how we may respond to our social environment, humans have little control over the societal context into which they are born and how it may initially affect them. This is a view that is not shared by some who emphasise the capacity of the individual over societal influences. A well-known quotation from former British Prime Minister Margaret Thatcher famously sums up what is sometimes described as the neo-conservative view 'there is no such thing [as society] there are individual men and women' (Thatcher, 1987). In arguing against social forces, neo-conservatives seek to highlight the role of individual ability and merit in achievement over societal circumstances. Such disagreements are not uncommon among sociologists. Arising out of the study of social behaviour, sociologists have developed a number theories and concepts to help reveal the structures of social life. Throughout the past two centuries sociologists have engaged in numerous forms of research to test and develop their theories. Of particular interest to sociologists is the way in which people construct knowledge, meaning and understanding. Another common concern for sociologists is the way that social behaviours and structures promote or inhibit relationships of power and equality.

Education is a major social structure that can effect what an individual knows and understands about society and its *modus operandi*. It has been argued that education, and in particular schools, play a major role in reproducing dominant social forces and inequalities. It is not surprising, therefore, that sociologists have examined the relationship between education and its effect on what people do with their lives. As such, the sociology of education has evolved into an important area of scholarship and is a core component of teacher education, as it is a discipline that helps us understand the context in which teaching and learning occurs.

In common parlance, the terms 'education' and 'schooling' are often used synonymously. However, for the purposes of this chapter, some precision in the use of these terms is required. 'Education' is understood here as more than just the acquisition of knowledge, understanding and skills. It is a process of teaching and learning that occurs within the context of a concerned relationship ordered towards the lifelong development and well-being of the student. I understand 'schooling' to be the formal processes, often state sponsored, whereby education is facilitated. This chapter will initially introduce some of the founders of the study of sociology and education and will then go on to examine some of the issues in schooling that are considered to be of importance in the sociology of education.

Earlier studies in sociology tended to conceptualise society in terms of one central apex around which human life was controlled. For example, the German scholar Ferdinand Tönnies (1855–1936) contended that there were just two distinct types of social groups: *Gemeinschaft* and *Gesellschaft*. On the one hand, he designated *Gemeinschaft*, or 'community', as an association of people based on feelings of togetherness and mutuality. In this type of society, the individual acts to achieve the goals of their group, seeing him/herself as an actor in the realisation of communitarian values. Examples of *Gemeinschaft* include traditional families and neighbourhoods in rural settings. Tönnies compared this traditional type of social grouping with *Gesellschaft*, or 'civil society', where individuals exist to achieve personal goals and material success, and so society exists to facilitate individuals and the economic connections between them. For Tönnies, the modern state and commercial corporations were increasingly perpetuating this type of social grouping (Tönnies, 1912). His approach to society as a single coherent unit reflects the works of other early sociologists such as Émile Durkheim (1858–1917) and Max Weber (1864–1920). However, it is now argued that these early theorists underestimated the complexity and diversity of modern societies (Vanderstraeten, 2004) and that society is differentiated according to subsystems such as law, education and politics, each concentrating on one function and thus requiring a specific focus within sociological research (Luhmann, 1995). This chapter takes the view that education is a subsystem within wider society.

EDUCATION AND SOCIAL COHESION

Sociology of education is the study of how education, as a social force or structure, impacts upon individual lives. It is the study of how schooling is organised and the implications of this for determining how individuals can access and participate in educational processes, leading to participation in wider society and well-being. As a field of study, the sociology of education was first considered in a systematic way by Émile Durkheim (1858–1917) who was appointed Professor of Science of Education and Sociology at the University of Paris (La Sorbonne) in 1902. The circumstances in which Durkheim lived and worked in France had a significant impact on the focus of his teaching and research. By 1871, France was in a political crisis which resulted in a decline in its national unity. In response to this, from 1880 onwards, the government began to pursue policies of political consolidation to rebuild France's national identity. Within this context of national consolidation, two important themes were linked to the rebuilding of France's national identity. The first of these themes was a focus on science and social progress which led to the elevation of the scientific method in solving social problems. The second theme centred on the increasing autonomy of the individual in relation to society. This theme of individualism could be traced back to the turmoil of the French Revolution (1789–99) which gave rise to the belief that the individual was separate from society and only engaged with society out of economic necessity and self-interest. This belief, that the individual was placed ahead of society, was perceived by Durkheim to threaten notions of national unity and social cohesion. Arising out of this political and social context, Durkheim was interested in education as a cohesive function of society.

Strongly influenced by the positivism of French philosopher Auguste Comte (1798–1857), Durkheim argued that values, cultural norms and social structures were social facts that could be studied and compared in an external and objective manner. This perspective became known as 'social realism' and was based on the belief that external social realities exist in the outer world and that these realities are independent of one's perception of them. Morrison explains that in this context 'the realist perspective takes the view that our awareness of and knowledge about the outside world is a straightforward encounter with the visual perception of reality' (Morrison, 2006, p. 152). This was not a view shared by some of Durkheim's contemporaries, particularly philosophers such as David Hume, who belonged to a group known as the 'empiricists' who held that all realities in the outside world were only products of human sense perception and would not exist if they were not perceived by humans (Hanratty, 1995). Furthermore, empiricists argued that as external reality did not exist on its own, it could not be confirmed by observation. Durkheim took an opposing view. He not only believed that all external realities could be observed but that these realities had causal powers that could affect individual acts. He argued that his method of study would, in turn, enable informed decisions to be made about the state of society and how to address problems therein (Durkheim, 1895).

Fundamental to Durkheim's work was the belief that collectives of people naturally exist and that these groupings contained a 'conscience collective', that is 'the totality of beliefs and sentiments common to the average citizen in that society' (Linde, 2003, p. 325). Durkheim (1893) argued that, in traditional groupings, clan, family or religion played an important part in uniting members through the creation of a common consciousness. Where religion, for example, was less prominent or emphasised individual conscience, then society would be more individualistic. Durkheim was interested in the way that education could also play a role in supporting social cohesion. In this, he was strongly influenced by his own political context. Durkheim argued that education plays an important role in reinforcing 'social solidarity'; a concept that relates to the degree to which individuals and society are integrated together. It has to do with the bonds that tie people together within a society. According to Durkheim (1893), two types of social solidarity exist based on two different types of society, primitive, or 'mechanical', and industrialised, or 'organic'. As Tönnies would also later write, Durkheim argued that the received collective conscience of the primitive society would result in a strong sense of connectedness, and therefore responsibility to the community. On the other hand, Durkheim understood modern industrialised societies to be more individualistic and therefore the state needed to impose rules and norms so that differences could be worked out in a peaceful manner. He argued (1897) that the transition from primitive to advanced society may result in a state of 'anomie', that is a position where the norms of society fail to allow for the needs of individuals to be met. In other words, having gone through a period of change, society fails to provide the means by which it is possible for individuals to achieve the ideological goals that are commonly held in society. An example of this can be seen where the state allows an economy to develop at such a fast rate that individuals are unable to find the means to live the lifestyle expected in that society. Such normlessness would lead to individuals experiencing alienation and purposelessness, as they are unable to achieve societal goals.

Durkheim believed that the common beliefs, or collective consciousness, of society could be differentiated from the beliefs of individuals and groups within society. He believed that society held certain beliefs about what a child should ideally become and that education played a central function in achieving this. Education reflects and perpetuates societal values and beliefs. Durkheim argued that because education was a system that arose out of society's collective values and beliefs, then it must possess and express those collective beliefs and values. In other words, society created formal education in order to perpetuate societal values and beliefs. On the other hand, if societal values and beliefs changed, for example if society became more secular, then education needed to reflect these changes, otherwise, a gap would occur between what society held to be important and what schools held to be important and, in this case, schools would eventually lose out to the power of the collective conscience which had created them in the first place (Giddens, 1972). In so far as schools are required to play a role in the regulation of society, they contribute to stability and well-being. This raises interesting questions for schools that have evolved, historically, in a confessional state which later becomes more secular or pluralist. Ireland provides a case in point, where over 93 per cent of primary schools and 60 per cent of second-level schools continue to be under the direct management and control of the Roman Catholic Church. Having achieved independence from the United Kingdom in 1922, Ireland has increasingly developed into a more pluralist and, some might say, secular state, raising questions about the appropriateness of Church domination in the provision of schooling. For the most part, it appears that the majority of the population are content with the status quo and it has yet to be seen if the recent changes in society will result in a new collective consciousness, where schooling is concerned, ultimately demanding a greater pluralism in the ownership and management of schools.

For Durkheim, society can only survive if there is sufficient homogeneity among its members. Education plays an important role in perpetuating and reinforcing this homogeneity by establishing in young people from an early age the similarities required to sustain social life. Such *socialisation* provides young people with the skills and knowledge that are necessary and required for successful participation in society. Socialisation then is the means by which social and cultural continuity are attained (Clausen, 1968, p. 5).

For Durkheim, then, schools are servants of society and as changes occur in society, schools need to change to reflect the common values and beliefs that sustain them. For example, during certain periods of history when society placed birthright at the centre of social status, the education system reflected this by only admitting those from higher levels of society into some educational institutions. This, in turn, caused these educational institutions to be associated with prestige and status. Society then moved to a more democratic and meritocratic value system and, consequently, the education system became more open and students were encouraged to achieve individually in an examinations system. From Durkheim's perspective, the education system is merely a function of society replicating itself and inducting new members into the normative experience of belonging to society. Changes in society, no matter how subtle, eventually leave their mark on schools and schools, in turn, pass on these changes to young people. This raises questions about the type of people required to make the education system work. If all we expect of schools is that they replicate societal values and beliefs and induct young people into societal customs, then we will not require a high degree of critical thinking or innovation from those who administer and teach in these schools. However, many scholars reject this idea of teachers as agents of society who merely inculcate the dominant ideals, values and beliefs of society in their students. For others, teachers play a central role in teaching young people to become independent thinkers, to critique society and play a role in changing their society. It is argued that the purpose of teaching in a democratic society is to be an advocate for social change and that this is achieved through promoting critical thinking among young people (Giroux, 1997; Freire, 2006; Cochran-Smith et al., 2009; Marshall and Klein, 2009).

EDUCATION AS MERITOCRACY

Ideas of equality in society are not necessarily a modern development. For example, Plato's description of the ideal government is essentially egalitarian (Plato, 1908) while Thomas Jefferson's commitment to equality in society can be seen in his attempts to abolish both slavery and the system of primogeniture inheritance in Virginia (Brown, 1954). For Karl Marx (1818–1883), education was strongly connected with social class and played a role in the struggle between the classes. Marx recognised the existence of two broad classes in society and related these to capitalist values. Firstly, he identified the *proletariat*, or lower classes, who possessed little wealth or access to infrastructure and natural resources or what Marx called the 'means of production'. The other group identified by Marx were the *bourgeois*, or upper classes, who owned the means of production and therefore possessed wealth, and therefore power.

According to Marx, each society created a ruling class and a subordinate class and the relationship between them, what he called the 'relations of production', was necessarily antagonistic. In this context, schooling was viewed as a system used to perpetuate bourgeois ideologies and to maintain economic dominance over the proletariat. For Marx, the education system was tied to the class nature of society and, through it, to the perpetuation of the economic system; as such, the education system served to reproduce relations of production. Marx would argue that ideas are not neutral and that each new ruling class creates its own version of the truth, or *ideology*, which becomes accepted as common sense. The dominant class creates ideas that reflect the existing relations of production. For Marx, these hegemonies are reproduced and set in the minds of the proletariat by the education system. This did not mean that there was a sinister plot to employ the education system to oppress the lower classes, rather, that the institutions of society, including education, reflect the human circumstances, ideas and material conditions that created them. Apparently, modern ideas – such as freedom, democracy and meritocracy – are not neutral ideas serving the common good, they are, in fact, ruling class ideas accepted by everyone as if they were for the common good. On the other hand, Marx also highlighted the possible role that the education system could play in transforming society, arguing all children should receive an equal education in public schools (Marx and Engels, 1848).

Western education systems are not always the most suitable environments for the teaching or modelling of this type of transformational process. Apart from a strong focus on scholastic achievement, modern schools often reflect what Bauman (1991) refers to as society's 'solid' form and attempt to remove all unknowns and uncertainties in the educational process. As such, schools are highly organised and hierarchical in nature, with learning managed in a structured manner by professionals (teachers) who impart knowledge to non-professionals (students). A school's instrumental goals, those that are concerned with the transmission of academic learning, are closely related to its organisational goals which have to do with the administration and structures that have been put in place to facilitate the teaching and learning envisioned by the instrumental goals. A modern concern with instrumental and organisational goals has resulted in other aspects of education receiving less attention in many schools. These somewhat intangible aspects of a school's outcomes include: cultural activities; the formation of character; the cultivation of attitudes; the transmission of values and freedom of thought. While these expressive goals are important as a source of cohesion and unity within a school, as well as providing the foundations of democracy and collaboration in wider society, they are too often displaced by instrumental and organisational goals (Bernstein, 1975). This can contribute to a society where citizens are competitive, individualistic and ill suited to participating in a democratic way of life. In response to this problem of goal displacement, some new syllabi now integrate 'real-world problems' so that students begin to understand and learn how to solve issues with a global perspective from a less individualistic perspective.

Related to the displacement of the expressive order of school life is the concern that the apparent rise in societal violence and conflict has been in some way fed by anti-social expressive behaviour, which began with the alienation of those for whom their school's instrumental and organisational methods did not work. Bauman (1991) argues that despite the tendency to manage and arrange society into categories, there are always individuals and groups who cannot be administered and controlled. If we fail to recognise and facilitate the nature of such *undecidables*, under repression they can become further alienated from mainstream society and are left to find expression of their alienation in violence and other forms of anti-social behaviour. Recent research confirms that although acts of high-level violence are rare, low-level violence and conflict in schools between students is increasingly a cause of stress to both teachers and students alike (Welsh et al., 1996; Welsh, 2000; Leach and Mitchell, 2006; Martin, 2006a; Meyer-Adams and Connor, 2008). It is argued that, to some degree, schools have become environments that are so extremely organised and controlled that young people experience themselves as strangers in an environment that does not appreciate the weneed to core characteristics of their generation, such as a sense of confidence and an expectation that one will make a positive contribution to society (Howe and Strauss, 2000). A further concern is the fear that the violence which has become widespread in society will find its way into schools, thus changing them from the safe havens they are meant to provide for students (Martin, 2006a). From a Marxist perspective, our modern schools can be said to reflect the class struggle that is found in wider society. The *alienation* which arises among students can be linked to powerlessness and self-estrangement (Krahn and Lowe, 1993) within society and schools. The challenge to our school systems is to find, as a priority, a way to need develop a participatory environment in which the instrumental and organisational goals give way to the intellectual development and well-being of young people.

The term meritocracy is believed to have been first coined by British sociologist Michael Young (1915–2002) in his somewhat depreciatory work *The Rise of Meritocracy* in which he ruminates about a dystopian future where one's place in society is determined by a combination of IQ and effort, i.e. meritocracy. Traditionally, estimations of merit have mostly been based upon birth (aristocracy), family connections (nepotism) or friendship (cronyism). However, Young asserted that advanced societies would be just as narrow in determining merit in that they would use success in schooling to determine social mobility. He argued that in such societies, any individual should be able to achieve advancement and promotion based on merit rather than on the authority of another (Young, 1961).

American sociologist Irving Louis Horowitz explains that Young's hypothesis of a shift to meritocracy in modern society does not necessarily result in more intelligence in the work place or in creative processes, but instead in a separation of those who are educated from those who possess physical skills (Horowitz, 2006, p. 283). In other words, by replacing aristocracy, nepotism and cronyism with a meritocracy, we have not opened up the processes of social mobility to everyone but instead have merely established new rules for achieving success or merit through education alone. Horowitz argues that the 'most serious problem with the concept of meritocracy is its failure to distinguish merit from education', which means that those who are deemed to have achieved or succeeded are often those who have received the most amount of formal education rather than those who actually possess the best talents for a particular task or role (2006, p. 284).

The concept of meritocracy is now firmly rooted in our *conscience collective*, however it is argued that the way we measure merit is merely the measurement of academic achievement, and, in doing so, we have created a new elite who control society and determine the mobility of others. Critics of meritocracy argue that while the concept has taken hold in modern democratic societies, it is flawed at its core. The flaw relates to how merit is determined and measured and who decides these processes. As soon as we begin to determine what merit is, we have begun to create a new structure to which individuals must adhere if they are to succeed in society. A fundamental flaw with the concept of merit is that, rather than creating an egalitarian society, it becomes a new mechanism in the struggle between the classes. In other words, if we designate academic performance as the form of merit that enables social mobility, then, to a large extent, schools will inevitably become involved in reproducing social and cultural inequalities.

EDUCATION AS CULTURAL CAPITAL

After the Second World War, most Western states revisited the economic, social and political role of education, resulting in compulsory secondary education being introduced in England and Wales in 1949 and in the Republic of Ireland in 1966. With the introduction of state-sponsored education, it was expected that all young people would do reasonably well and that social mobility and well-being would be achieved for all citizens. However, it was not long before governments and scholars alike realised that bourgeois young people, namely those from middle- to upper-class backgrounds, were more successful in schools than those from the proletariat, namely those from lower- to working-class backgrounds.

In trying to explain the phenomena of failure at school among young people in France in the 1960s, Pierre Bourdieu (1930–2002) developed the concept of 'cultural capital'. In economics, 'capital' is one of the factors of production used to create goods or services. In this sense, capital can be defined as that amount of wealth which is used in making profits (Sombart, 1953). Traditionally, we associate capital with ownership of natural resources, land and money. However, some scholars, such as Bourdieu, have identified other forms of capital that are not necessarily linked to money or land but are equally important, if not more so, in terms of social mobility. The term 'cultural capital' refers to non-financial assets, such as education, which might promote social mobility beyond economic means. Since it was first articulated by Bourdieu, this sociological concept of cultural capital has gained considerable popularity among scholars and is used to explain the hidden linkages between apparent academic ability and cultural heritage (Bourdieu, 1998). It is argued that, for the most part, the education system has been designed and maintained by individuals from bourgeois backgrounds and, as such, their language, values, symbols and general cultural heritage are deeply embodied within the ethos of most schools. Consequently, when the children of middle- to upper-class people come to school, they are advantaged because they share the same cultural heritage as that embedded within the education system, and therefore are predisposed to succeed within the school system which is bourgeois in nature.

Bourdieu distinguished between three types of cultural capital: 'embodied', 'objectified' and 'institutionalised'. The first, 'embodied cultural capital', refers to both the consciously acquired and the submissively inherited qualities of one's self. These are received over time through socialisation within one's family, culture and traditions. In this sense, cultural capital is not transmissible instantaneously like a bequest from one's parents, instead, it is acquired over time as it impresses itself upon one's character and way of thinking, which, in turn, becomes more attentive to, or primed to receive, similar influences. Bourdieu designated the second type of capital as 'objectified cultural capital', which relates to physical objects that one might own, such as a painting or a work of art. These types of cultural goods can be used for economic profit, when others are willing to buy them, and also for the purposes of symbolically conveying the cultural capital associated with the ownership of such items. However, there is a difference between owning and *consuming* the object. For example, in order to fully understand the cultural significance and meaning of a painting, one has to have acquired the cultural foundation which enables a full appreciation of a work of art, and this type of prior cultural capital does not necessarily accompany the purchase of the painting. If we see education in this way, there are those for whom the consumption of education is easier than for others who, although they have access to the same education, do not have the same shared cultural heritage to enable them to appreciate what they own.

Finally, Bourdieu designated a third form of capital with the term 'institutionalised cultural capital'. This type of cultural capital relates to institutional recognition of one's cultural capital, most often in the form of

③ academic and professional awards. This aspect of cultural capital is crucial for social mobility and is most evident within the labour market. The fact that an employer will seek a certain educational background or that an individual can present certain academic qualifications relates to more than a person's capability for a particular job. The possession of a university degree signifies that the graduate carries with him/her a certain cultural capital and presumes the presence in the individual of highly developed linguistic, social, symbolic and cultural skills. The process by which institutions recognise this type of capital enables individuals the possibility of easily converting their cultural capital into economic capital. Social institutions have formalised this process by creating gateway qualifications that are required for entry into particular professions, such as law and medicine. Many of these professions have traditionally been populated by individuals from the same families which attests to the importance of institutionalised cultural capital.

In so far as schools are involved with social reproduction, they are about the status quo and, as such, the importance of one's cultural heritage, as a form of wealth, is an extremely significant variable in predicting educational outcomes. It is argued by some scholars that the link between success in school and economic and social possibility is becoming more pronounced. In fact, rather than neo-liberal societies discovering new ways to provide pathways to success and well-being for young people, the narrowly defined experience of schooling, as we have come to know it in the West, has become an essential ingredient for social mobility in contemporary economies (Weis and Dimitriadis, 2008). Research regarding the type of individuals who succeed in schools reveals that, in Western societies, those from middle-class backgrounds tend to out-perform those from lower class and sometimes also ethnic backgrounds. In fact, the research indicates that socio-economic factors, rather than ethnicity, are more important as indicators of achievement in education, once again pointing to the importance of cultural capital (Rumberger and Palardy, 2005). Furthermore, the research suggests that schools serving mostly lower income students tend to be organised and operated differently than those serving more affluent students which, when taken with the lower levels of academic achievement, suggests that teachers and school administrators working in these lower socio-economic contexts may have different instrumental and organisational goals than their colleagues working in more bourgeois environments (Rumberger and Palardy, 2005; Leavy, 2005).

Teachers' beliefs about education and their students are heavily influenced by their cultural heritage and have been found to influence classroom practices. Furthermore, teachers' beliefs about their students are an important indicator of educational achievement. Consequently, teacher education programmes often seek to address immature and underdeveloped beliefs through engagement and reflection on teaching practice (Nespor, 1987; Pajares, 1992; Fenstermacher, 1979, 1994; Leavy, 2005).

The majority of pre-service teachers come from bourgeois backgrounds and have usually had little contact with people from minority populations and cultures tending to prefer to teach children and young people who come from backgrounds similar to their own (Zimpher, 1989; Law and Lane, 1987; Larke, 1990; Barry and Lechner, 1995; Valli, 1995; Wiggins and Follo, 1999; Delpit, 1988; Mahan and Boyle, 1981). In fact, research has shown that students entering teacher-education programmes tend to see *diversity* as a problem and often have negative attitudes towards children and young people who come from a different cultural or social background to their own, resulting in negative outcomes for those children and young people (Zeichner and Hoeft, 1996; Law and Lane, 1987; Terrill and Mark, 2000).

An indication of the extent to which pre-service teachers come from bourgeois culture and have limited contact with people from lower socio-economic and diverse backgrounds, is seen in the findings of recent research in Ireland which found that 59 per cent of pre-service teachers had practically no prior exposure to members of the Travelling Community. Furthermore, the same study found that 65 per cent of pre-service teachers had no prior contact with refugees or asylum seekers. The same study found that 52 per cent had almost no contact with non-Christians and almost half of the respondents report almost no contact with people who identify themselves as gay or lesbian. Finally, the same study found that 92 per cent of pre-service teachers had no ethnic, religious or cultural diversity in their own personal background (e.g. parent or grandparent), leading the researchers to conclude that Ireland still has a predominantly monocultural teaching population (Leavy, 2005).

The possibility for a clash of cultures between teachers and students is clear where teachers from bourgeois backgrounds are increasingly being asked to work with ethnic minorities and those from lower socio-economic backgrounds. Mills and Gale (2010) warn that, without access to the educative effects of the cultural capital of the dominant group (i.e. bourgeois), those from minority or marginalised populations will not succeed at school.

EDUCATION AND RELIGION

The relationship between society and religion and the implications for educational systems have always been important to sociologists. Modern concerns with the role of religion in society can be traced back to Durkheim's 1897 study of suicide in which he compared the rates of suicide among Catholic and Protestant populations. Durkheim's work was strongly influenced by his own preoccupation with social cohesion and some scholars today argue that his findings were strongly biased by his assumptions about modern industrialised societies (Kushner and Sterk, 2005). In his work on suicide, Durkheim identified a high level of social cohesion (Durkheim, 1888). Finding a lower rate of suicide among Catholic compared to Protestant populations, he attributed this to a stronger emphasis on social cohesion in the former group; in other words, he argued that the type of social relationships that existed in Catholic-based societies made a difference to individual well-being. From this basis, later sociologists argued that, among other social entities, religion can be a source of social capital by providing individuals with a community-based network, a form of civic engagement and identity, and promoting reciprocity and trust among people (Coleman, 1988; Putnam, 2000). However, Bourdieu (1983) linked social capital to his concept of cultural capital and recognised the possibility of its use in maintaining elite status and inhibiting social mobility.

More than one scholar has been concerned with the role of religion as a form of social capital in post-independence Ireland and the longer term effect on modern Irish schooling (Inglis, 1998, 2007; Mackey and McDonagh, 2004; Williams, 2005; Tovey and Share, 2007). We will now turn our attention the role of religion in Irish society and how this relationship has impacted on Irish schooling as a form of cultural capital.

As a consequence of the historical development of Irish education (see above Walsh, Chapter Two), the contemporary form of provision is unique, in that the Catholic Church, in one form or another, manages the majority of schools in Ireland. At primary level, according to the 2008 Irish government statistics, there are 3,175 ordinary primary schools in Ireland of which 67 are multi-denominational. The rest of the primary schools are denominational with 93 per cent under the patronage of the Catholic Church. At secondary-school level, there are 388 Catholic voluntary schools catering for approximately 200,000 students, which accounts for 60 per cent of the total school enrolment of this age group. Another 15 per cent of students attend 91 community/comprehensive schools, in which, for the most part, the Catholic diocese or Religious Orders act as co-trustees. The remaining 25 per cent of the post-primary student population attend the 253 vocational schools and community colleges which, while multi-denominational in theory, most commonly have a majority of Catholic students, parents, teachers and representation on their boards of management from the local Catholic diocese.

These statistics regarding the ownership and management of Irish primary and second-level schools, reveals a rather homogeneous picture of the control and management of Irish education; a picture that can be described as mainly denominational and, for the most part, Catholic. These statistics confirm the Irish Catholic Church's concept of ethos and its desire to influence the character of schools through its managerial role. At no stage from 1831 until quite recently has the official Church sought to promote or develop any other form of schooling except that over which it has complete or decisive influence. This has resulted in the Catholic Church achieving a lion's share of control in Irish schooling. Even in the vocational/community-college sector, which is the nearest thing in Ireland to a state-school system, the official Church will usually have representation on the boards of management and will be involved in the selection of teachers. Clearly then, apart from the 67 multi-denominational schools, every other type of school in Ireland will have some degree of influence in its management from the Catholic Church.

It could be argued that the present situation regarding the Catholic Church's control and management of Irish schools is reflective of the traditionally homogeneous nature of Irish society. However, whatever about the past, Irish society today is increasingly more diverse and, as with other Western societies, there have been many changes in how we perceive ourselves and the world in which we live. Many of these changes can be summed up in the expression 'postmodernism', which describes our time, a time when the traditional culture based on the value of ultimate meaning in life has been replaced by a culture of convenience and consumerism. Boundaries have been pushed back and for many Irish people, consumerism and self-need have replaced any abiding religious values. Large shopping malls have been described as the new cathedrals replacing the churches as the focus of communities. In this context, it is not surprising that some Irish people are now demanding a choice in every aspect of their lives including religion and education. On the other hand, outside of the occasional media flashpoint, the status quo regarding the Catholic Church's role in Irish education remains for the most part unchallenged. There are three reasons for this: firstly, the strength of the Church in the control and management of most Irish schools can be said to prevent others from entering this field of endeavour; secondly, the weakness of student and parental influence compared to the power of teachers and management bodies in the Irish education system; and finally, for the most part, the majority of the population seem to be satisfied with the standard of education provided under Church management.

Notwithstanding the broad satisfaction enjoyed by many, an implication of the homogeneous nature of Irish education is that children whose parents belong to an ethnic minority, or whose religious affiliations are non-Catholic, have found it particularly hard to realise educational choice despite the fact that such is a constitutional right (Article 42.3.1). Consequently, parents who are not Catholic, especially those in rural and in lower socio-economic areas, often find themselves with no choice but to opt for the local Catholic school due to various restraints, such as distance, inconvenience and finance. Furthermore, because of the largely homogeneous nature of the student population in Irish schools, it can be hard to assess if non-Catholic students in Catholic schools experience religious or racial intolerance. However, some research seems to suggest that there is a degree of religious prejudice in Irish Catholic schools (Lynch and Lodge, 1999; Connolly and Keenan, 2002; Devine et al., 2008). While many children of ethnic minorities have had a good experience in Irish Catholic schools to date, the high numbers of migrants, refugees and asylum seekers who have come to Ireland in recent years, as well as the broader changes in society, have forced the government and the Catholic Church to revisit the issue of pluralism in education. This was illustrated by a number of statements in recent years from Dr Diarmuid Martin, Catholic Archbishop of Dublin, in which he has called for new forms of school patronage and greater accountability in how schools are managed (Martin, 2004, 2006b). If parents in Ireland are to have a real choice in education, the government will have to revisit how schools are planned and funded, whether Catholic, Jewish, Muslim or multi-denominational. At the same time, the Catholic Church in Ireland will have to realise that such a development is not a challenge to its involvement in education, but rather a recognition of all people's freedom of conscience and belief as espoused in national and international legal instruments not least of which include the Universal Declaration of Human Rights (Article 26), the European Convention (Article 9), and the Charter on Fundamental Rights of the European Union (Articles 10 and 14).

So far, we have seen how the Catholic Church's role in Irish education, particularly in terms of the ownership and control of schools, is largely influenced by what can be described as a paternalistic concept of ethos. A closer look at the internal life of Catholic schools reveals that the actual influence of the Church is somewhat weaker than it is at the level of management (McDonnell, 1995; O'Keefe, 1998; Sullivan, 1998; Donnelly, 2000; Norman, 2003). This is a possible indication that, in its desire to influence the ethos of schools, the Church has failed to employ an effective method other than to be involved in school management, which by its very nature tends to be removed from the ongoing life of the school. At the level of curriculum, the Church now has to compete with the influence of commerce and industry as well as the media and popular fashion. The Irish Catholic Church's response to some curricular changes over the past decade or so reveals a particular vision of ethos that can be described as somewhat paternalistic.

In recent decades, the curriculum of schools has been expanded by state action to include issues of morality, such as family planning, Aids/HIV, drugs and sexuality, which have all, at least initially, brought the official Irish Church into dispute with the state. According to some sociologists such as Tom Inglis, young Irish people today 'appear as likely to be more informed and guided in what is right and wrong by what they hear discussed in the media, as by what they are told by priests and bishops' (Inglis, 1998, p. 241). However, it would be far too simplistic to interpret recent changes to the curriculum as a sign of the Church losing its influence in Irish schools. As with the rest of Irish culture, the Irish Church, particularly at grass-roots level, has changed and is changing in its outlook. Many of the changes in the school curriculum reflect the desire of many in the Church to provide an education that will help young people to interpret their experiences of the modern world in a meaningful way. Consequently, it is expected that Irish Catholics in the future will be far better equipped than they were in the past to make personal decisions in terms of morality and ethics and constant recourse to the bishops will no longer be desirable or necessary.

However, at the level of the Irish Catholic hierarchy, there was a considerable resistance to the state's attempt to increase its influence in the area of relationships and sexuality education (RSE). Initially, the Catholic bishops welcomed the announcement in 1995 by the then Minster for Education, Niamh Breathnach, that a new RSE programme would be introduced into the national curriculum for schools. By the time RSE came into being in 1997, it had been reduced to a set of guidelines rather than the full programme that had been originally expected. Although the minister had guaranteed from the beginning that the programme would be taught within the context of each school's ethos, the bishops wanted a further guarantee that RSE would only be taught in religious education classes (Irish Bishops' Conference, 1995a). A compromise was eventually reached with the state agreeing that there would be no specific syllabus, but rather a set of guidelines and resource materials that would be made available to schools. Each school was to work out its own RSE policy and programme with the co-operation of parents, teachers and boards of management in the context of the school's own character or ethos.

While the bishops had no objection to the teaching of RSE (for the most part it already formed a considerable part of the religious education programme) they were anxious that they could control the context in which it was taught. They stressed in their statement that they trusted their teachers to teach RSE to children in accordance with the Christian ethos of the schools. Once again, the bishops' words and actions reflect their perception of their role as guarantors of the good with a duty to protect the young people in their care.

> In the formation of its policy [the Catholic school] should reflect the Catholic moral teaching on sexual matters. Even more fundamentally, it needs to be specific in excluding approaches which are inconsistent with the very foundations of Catholic moral thought (Irish Bishops' Conference, 1997).

This statement implies that Catholic moral teaching on sexuality is static and it does not allow in any way for the amount of interpretation and debate that actually occurs, even within the realm of official Church teaching. It is without question that young people should seriously engage with the Catholic Church's teaching on moral issues, such as relationships, sexuality and marriage, however, the bishops approach to the RSE programme is somewhat narrow and may result in young people rejecting the values and standards put to them in schools. Effectively, the original programme intended by the Minister for Education has been subsumed into existing RSE programmes in many Irish Catholic schools. The state has minimal control over the content of RSE and the Catholic Church, as patron of most Irish schools, continues to exert its influence over the content and the manner in which RSE is taught. On the one hand, this means that RSE is taught as part of an integrated curriculum, in which the young person is helped to consider the values of the Christian tradition in terms of relationships and sexuality. However, on the other hand because of the Church's paternalistic approach to RSE and to school ethos in general, one wonders to what extent students and teachers will be free to dialogue with this tradition in their classrooms. Research indicates that between 30 and 40 per cent of schools have yet to develop an RSE policy which is a government requirement (Mayock et al., 2007; O'Higgins-Norman, 2008). If schools themselves have not been able to begin the process of dialogue required to develop an RSE policy, then it is hardly to be expected that young people will be able to engage in such critical enquiry as part of the delivery of the RSE programme.

Having considered the role of religion in Irish education and in particular, the Irish Catholic Church's contribution to the education debate of the last decade of the 20th century, it seems that for the most part the official Church has taken a strongly paternalistic approach to many of the important issues now affecting society and schools. When we take into account the restrictive way in which the Church had to operate before the foundations of the Irish state, it is not surprising that it developed such a paternalistic concept of ethos, seeing itself as the protector of the moral character of Irish people and their education. However, as we continue into the new millennium, Ireland has become a very different place. The significant number of people who voted in favour of legalisation for divorce in November 1995 is a clear sign that, today, many Irish Catholics openly differ in their views from official Church doctrine while remaining generally committed to their religion. Others have left the Church as is seen by the decreased numbers attending mass, while others again are members of other denominations or hold no religious faith in particular. All of this reveals a picture of Irish society that is increasingly pluralist, and, consequently, people's expectations and demands on schools are changing. In the face of this, the education system will be forced to change and adapt to meet the needs of society. From a sociological perspective, we have already asserted, in the earlier parts of this chapter, that society created formal education in order to perpetuate societal values and beliefs. If societal values and beliefs continue to change and become more secular and pluralist in tone, then regardless of how hard school patrons try to resist, the ethos of the school system will change or otherwise face becoming irrelevant to the society that has created it in the first place (Giddens, 1972).

EDUCATION, GENDER AND SEXUALITY

The past 50 years have seen the emergence of a new discourse on the roles of men and women in society. For quite some time, the discourse centred on perceptions of binary differences between men and women resulting in 'an unwitting regulation and reification of gender relations' (Butler, 1990; Gray, 1992; Belenky et al., 1997; Kazemek, 1989). Earlier feminist scholars had tended to talk about men and women as if they were two separate species with their own characteristics, motivations and behaviours. This is illustrated in the popular book by John Gray entitled *Men are from Mars Women are from Venus* (1992) where he compares male and female as if they were from different planets unable to communicate through a common language. However, in more recent times, the discourse has developed to focus on the possibility of gender being a more individual construction, and the presence of masculinity in women and femininity in men (Butler, 1990; Cameron,

2007). For example, both Connell (1995) and later Cameron (2007) note that masculinity does not exist solely in contrast with femininity. They argue that the terms not only highlight the way men and women differ between themselves but they also point to the ways men and women differ among themselves in matters of gender. Connell claims that 'gender is social practice that constantly refers to bodies and what bodies do, it is not social practice reduced to body' (1995, p. 7). Gender then, is a complex and fluid concept that refers to 'specific social and cultural patterns of behaviour and the social characteristics of being a man or a woman in particular and social circumstances' (Measor and Sikes, 1992, p. 5). However, Butler (1990) argues that certain constructions of gender have taken hold in our society and are hegemonic in that they permeate every aspect of life, resulting in stereotyping of certain lifestyles. For example, research has identified gender stereotyping in Irish schools regarding the different type of vocational choices made by boys and girls in relation to future careers. It seems that the type of guidance provided to students reinforces concepts of what was a *real* girl and what was a *real* boy in that girls were more likely than boys to be given guidance on traditionally feminine careers, such as nursing, and boys were more likely to receive guidance on careers that were traditionally considered to be more masculine, such as a trade or engineering (Sheridan, 1995; Darmody and Smith, 2005). Furthermore, Renehan (2006) in her research into teaching and learning in Irish second-level schools found evidence of gender-stereotyped attitudes among student teachers resulting in different pedagogical interaction with male and female pupils. It seems that, rather than challenge gender stereotyping, schools are sites where these stereotypes can be exaggerated and validated. The implications for young people's construction of their social and personal identities can be significant and even restraining.

While *sexuality* is distinct from gender, it is intimately linked to it. It involves a social construction of a biological drive. An individual's sexuality is defined by who they have sex with, in what ways, why, under what circumstances and with what outcomes. It is also more than sexual behaviour; it is a multidimensional and dynamic concept (Gupta, 2000). There are many influences on an individual's sexuality, including explicit and implicit rules imposed by society (Zeidenstein and Moore, 1996). It has been argued that human sexuality can be understood in terms of a continuum with heterosexuality at one end and homosexuality at the other and varying realities between them (Kinsey et al., 1948). Not only might there be a continuum of sexuality, but it might also have the element of being fluid, that is, depending on our education, development, emotions, needs for intimacy, and so forth, our sexual preference may move along the continuum as the years go on.

Foucault (1987) highlights the complexities of how humanity has come to understand homosexuality and same-sex behaviour through the centuries. He argues that the modern concept of a fixed sexual orientation would not have been recognised in pre-1800 societies. Foucault argued that same-sex behaviours were regarded as 'abominable acts', viewed as being 'contrary to nature' and punishable as such but that the entirety of the person was not determined by these acts

(Foucault, 1987, p. 38). The modern concept of a fixed homosexual orientation as something that is fixed was 'forced into being by the development of a rigid medical discourse in the late nineteenth century that insisted on categorizing sexual behaviour in order to regulate it' (Duberman et al., 1989, p. 519; Foucault, 1987, p. 43). Epstein and Johnson deconstruct this concept of homosexuality as a fixed and discreet identity, arguing instead that 'there is no homosexuality' but rather 'homosexualities' (1998, p. 146). In other words, homosexual identity is as individual as each person who calls himself/herself gay or lesbian or whatever s/he chooses.

While acknowledging that schools are not the only places where sexual relations are established, Epstein and Johnson (1998) argue that schools are important sites for both the production and regulation of sexual identities for both heterosexuals and homosexuals alike. They give the example of the paradoxical situation where, on the one hand, many schools go to great lengths to control expressions of sexuality by students and teachers alike through rules, while on the other hand expressions of sexuality provide a 'major currency and resource in the everyday exchanges of school life' (ibid., p. 108). So, for instance, schools impose on all students the requirement to wear a uniform, which has the effect of undermining their individuality, which includes, among other things, sexuality. However, despite this, in the areas of dress or accessories and the way that students relate to each other, sexuality can remain quite evident. Epstein and Johnson observed how students would adorn their school bags, which were not covered by the uniform rule, with sexualised images of their favourite pop star, and how boys and girls would segregate themselves along gender lines when sitting in groups in classes. Consequently, we can reaffirm that schools are significant places where young people create meaning about themselves, their gender identities and their sexualities.

The role of the teacher in the production of sexual identity is also very important. Epstein and Johnson argue that the formation of teacher identities is part of the informal curriculum both in initial teacher education and in schools. They go on to make the point that teachers 'bear the primary responsibility for the desexualisation of schooling required by government and the dominant sexual culture' (ibid., p. 122). Consequently, if schools generally are places where students and teachers are to be desexualised, then any possibility of addressing the issue of sexual orientation is really beyond the bounds of possibility. However, while the majority of the population who consider themselves to be heterosexual have the support of the dominant sexual culture outside school and in resisting desexualisation within school, those who experience themselves as homosexual or bisexual are at risk of experiencing social isolation and oppression of their sexual expression in both spheres. Their heterosexual peers, meanwhile, are at risk of creating meaning around homosexuality that is based on stereotypes and prejudice.

In recent times, Foucault (1967) has dominated the discourse on sexuality while attempting to deconstruct the societal structures that enable heterosexual relations to dominate. Foucault has identified the use and distribution of *power* and *knowledge* within sexuality as cultivated and continuously shaped sociological roles and society's interpretation and understanding of human sexuality. He argued that power relations are not fixed; in fact they are fluid. Each person can have and exercise power, and can resist power. Foucault poses the question: has a repression of silence been the central link between power and knowledge in regard to thinking about human sexuality? He goes on to say that if this repression of silence has existed, then it will be an almost impossible task for anyone to change the dominant perception of sexuality and homosexuality:

> It stands to reason that we will not be able to free ourselves from it except at a considerable cost: nothing less than a transgression of laws, a lifting of prohibitions … a reinstating of pleasure within reality and a whole new economy in the mechanisms of power will be required (Foucault, 1987, p. 5).

Until very recently, there has often been a refusal by Western societies, such as Ireland and Greece (Tovey and Share, 2003; Phellas, 2005), to listen to gay and lesbian people and their experiences of sexualities. For a long time, both civil and religious society have treated any attempt to even question the predominant assumptions about sexuality (and homosexuality) with a prohibiting silence, which inhibits any further questioning. Specifically from a Church perspective, a prominent professor of Catholic moral theology has commented that where sexuality is concerned 'a great silence is now the norm' (Gallagher, 2003). There seems to be little room for discourse about sexuality, lest the Roman Church put the beleaguered speaker or writer 'under a cloud of official suspicion' (ibid., p.131). However, it is not only the Churches that have appeared to maintain this reign of silence prohibiting and condemning affirming opinions about homosexuality. This conditioning of silence has been maintained and carefully controlled historically through a variety of processes in our wider society. A primary function of schools, like other social institutions, is the reproduction of the dominant social ideology. Schools legitimate and sustain cultural practices. Studies have shown that the daily worlds of our schools 'teach' scripts for what is considered to be appropriate gender and sexual behaviour during adolescence and later on in adulthood (Mac an Ghaill, 1994; Epstein and Johnson, 1998; O'Higgins-Norman, 2008).

RECOMMENDED READING

Books and chapters

Bauman, Z. (1991). *Modernity and Ambivalence*. Ithaca, NY: Cornell University Press.

Belenky, M. F., Goldberger, N. and Tarule, J. (1997). *Women's Ways of Knowing*. New York: Basic Books.

Bernstein, B. (1975). *Class, Codes and Control*, vol. 2. London: Routledge.

Bourdieu, P. (1983). 'Forms of capital'. In J. C. Richards (ed.), *Handbook of Theory and Research for the Sociology of Education*. New York: Greenwood Press.

Bourdieu, P. (1998). *Practical Reason*. Cambridge: Polity Press.

Brown, S. G. (1954). *The First Republicans: Political Philosophy and Public Policy in the Party of Jefferson and Madison*. Syracuse, NY: Syracuse University Press.

Butler, J. (1990) *Gender Trouble*. New York: Routledge.

Cameron, D. (2007). *The Myth of Mars and Venus: Do Men and Women Really Speak Different Languages?* Oxford: Oxford University Press.

Clausen, J. (1968). *Socialisation and Society*. Boston: Little Brown and Company.

Connell, R. W. (1995). *Masculinities*. Cambridge: Polity Press.

Devitt, P. (1992). *That You May Believe*. Dublin: Dominican Publications.

Devitt, P. (2000). *Willingly to School*. Dublin: Veritas.

Dewey, J. (2001). 'Education and social change'. In F. Schultz (ed.), *SOURCES: Notable selections in education* (3rd edition), 333–341. New York: McGraw.

Duberman, M. B., Vicinus, M. and Chauncey, G. (eds) (1989). *Hidden from History, Reclaiming the Gay Past*. New York: New American Library.

Durkheim, É. (1893). *The Division of Labour in Society*. Glencoe, IL: The Free Press.

Durkheim, E. (1895). *Les Règles de la méthode sociologique*. (trans W. D. Halls (1982). *The Rules of Sociological Method*. New York: The Free Press).

Durkheim, É. (1897). *Suicide*. New York: Free Press Reprint.

Durkheim, É. (1922). *Éducation et Sociologie*. Paris: Alcan.

Durkheim, E. ([1897] 1951). *Suicide: A Study in Sociology*. (trans. J. A. Spaulding and G. Simpson (ed.) New York: The Free Press).

Epstein, D. and Johnson, R. (1998). *Schooling Sexualities*. Buckingham: Open University Press.

Fenstermacher, G. D. (1979). 'A philosophical consideration of recent research on teacher effectiveness'. In L. S. Shulman (ed.), *Review of Research in Education Volume 6* (pp. 157–85). Itaska, IL: F.E. Peacock.

Foucault, M. (1967). *Madness and Civilisation*. London: Tavistock.

Foucault, M. (1987). *The History of Sexuality: An Introduction*. London: Pelican.

Freire, P. ([1970] 2006). *Pedagogy of the Oppressed*. (trans. M. B. Ramos). New York: Continuum.

Giddens, A. (ed.) (1972). *Émile Durkheim Selected Writings*. Cambridge: Cambridge University Press.

Giroux, H. (1997). *Pedagogy and the Politics of Hope: Theory, Culture and Schooling*. Boulder, CO: Westview.

Gray, J. (1992). *Men are from Mars Women are from Venus*. New York: Harper.

Gupta, G. R. (2000). *Gender, Sexuality, and HIV/AIDS: The What, the Why and the How*. Washington, DC: International Centre for Research on Women.

Hanratty, G. (1995). *Philosophers of the Enlightenment: Locke, Hume and Berkeley Revisited*. Dublin: Four Courts Press.

Howe, N. and Strauss, W. (2000). *Millennials Rising: The Next Great Generation*. New York: Vintage.

Inglis, T. (1998). *Moral Monopoly, The Rise and Fall of the Catholic Church in Modern Ireland*. Dublin: Gill & MacMillan.

Inglis, T. (2007) 'Individualisation and Secularisation in Catholic Ireland'. In: *Contemporary Ireland: A Sociological Map*. Dublin: University College Dublin Press.

Kinsey, A. C., Pomeroy, W. B. and Martin, C. E. (1948). *Sexual Behaviour in the Human Male*. Philadelphia: W.B. Saunders.

Krahn, H. J. and Lowe. G. S. (1993). *Work, Industry, and Canadian Society* (2nd edition). Scarborough, Nelson, Canada: University of Alberta.

Leach, F. and Mitchell, C. (2006). *Combating gender violence in and around schools*. New York: Trentham.

Luhmann, N. (1995). *Social Systems*, Stanford: Stanford University Press.

Lynch, K. and Lodge, A. (1999). *Equality in Education*. Dublin: Gill & MacMillan.

Mac an Ghaill, M. (1994). *The Making of Men, Masculinities, Sexualities and Schooling*. Buckingham: Open University Press.

Mackey, J. and McDonagh, E. (2004). *Religion and Politics in Ireland: at the Turn of the Millennium*. Dublin: Columba Press.

Macionis, J. and Plummer, K. (2005). *Sociology: A Global Introduction*. New Jersey: Prentice Hall.

Marx, K. ([1844] 1932). *Economic and Political Manuscripts of 1844*. (trans. M. Mulligan. Moscow: Progress Publishers).

Marx K. and Engels, F. ([1848] 1998). *The Communist Manifesto*, introduction by Martin Malia. New York: Penguin group.

Measor, L. and Sikes, P. (1992) *Gender and Schools*. London: Cassell.

Mills, C. and Gale, T. (2010). *Schooling in Disadvantaged Communities*. Dordrecht: Springer.

Morrison, K. (2006). *Marx Durkheim and Webber, Formations of Modern Social Thought*. London: Sage.

Norman, J. (2003). *Ethos and Education in Ireland*. New York: Peter Lang.

O'Higgins-Norman, J. (2008). *Homophobic Bulling in Irish Secondary Education*. Palo Alto, CA: Academica Press.

O'Keefe, T. (1998). 'Values in a Christian School'. In M. Feheney (ed.), *From Ideal to Action, The Inner Nature of a Catholic School Today*. Dublin: Veritas.

Plato, (1908). *Republic*, Book IV, Section 434a–c. (trans. B. Jowett (ed.)). Oxford: Clarendon Press.

Putnam, R. (2000). *Bowling Alone: The Collapse and Revival of American Community*. New York: Simon and Schuster.

Renehan, C. (2006). *Different Planets: Gender Attitudes and Classroom Practice in Post Primary Teaching*. Dublin: Liffey Press.

Robinson, R. and Garnier, M. (1986). 'Class Reproduction among Men and Women in France: reproduction theory on its home ground'. In D. Robbins (ed.) (2000), *Pierre Bourdieu Volume I* (pp. 144–53). London: Sage.

Sombart, W. (1953). 'Medieval and Modern Commerical Enterprise'. In F. C. Lane and J. Riemersma, *Enterprise and Secular Change*. Homewood, IL: Irwin.

Tönnies, F. ([1912] 2002). *Community and Society*. (trans. C. P. Loomis. Mineola, NY: Dover Publications).

Tovey, H. and Share, P. (2007). *A Sociology of Ireland* (2nd edition). Dublin: Gill & MacMillan.

Williams, K. (2005). *Faith and the Nation: Religion, Culture and Schooling in Ireland*. Dublin: Dominican Publications.

Young, M. (1961). *The Rise of Meritocracy*. London: Thames and Hudson.

Zeichner, K. M. and Hoeft, K. (1996). 'Teacher socialization for cultural diversity'. In W. R. Houston (ed.), *Handbook of Research on Teacher Education* (2nd edition). London: Macmillan.

Zeidenstein, S. and Moore, K. (eds) (1996). *Learning About Sexuality: A Practical Beginning*. New York: Population Council.

Journals

Barry, N. H. and Lechner, J. V. (1995). 'Preservice teachers' attitudes about and awareness of multicultural teaching and learning'. *Teaching and Teacher Education*, 11:2, 149–61.

Cochran-Smith, M., Shakman, K., Jong, C., Terrell, D. G., Barnatt, J. and McQuillan, P. (2009). 'Good and Just Teaching: The Case of Social Justice in Teacher Education'. *American Journal of Education*, 115:3, 347–77.

Coleman, J. C. (1988). 'Social capital in the creation of human capital'. *American Journal of Sociology*, 94, S95–120.

Connolly, P. and Keenan, M. (2002). 'Racist Harassment in the White Hinterlands: minority ethnic children and parents' experiences of schooling in Northern Ireland'. *British Journal of Sociology of Education*, 23:3, 341–55.

Delpit, L. D. (1988). 'The silenced dialogue: power and pedagogy in educating other people's children'. *Harvard Educational Review*, 58:3, 280–98.

Devine, D., Kenny, M. and MacNeela, E. (2008). 'Naming the 'other': children's construction and experience of racisms in Irish primary schools'. *Race, Ethnicity and Education*, 11:4, 369–85.

Donnelly, C. (2000). 'In Pursuit of School Ethos'. *British Journal of Education*, June, 143–4.

Durkheim E. (1888). Suicide et natalite: etude de statistique morale. *Rev philosophique France L'étranger*, 26, 446–63.

Gallagher, R. (2003). 'The Great Silence'. *The Furrow*, 55:3, 131–4.

Horowitz, I. L. (2006). 'The Moral Economy of Meritocracy'. *Modern Age*, 48:3, 281–6.

Kazemek, F. D. (1989). 'Feminine Voice and Power in Moral Education'. *Educational Horizons*, 67:3, 76–81.

Kushner, H. I. and Sterk, C. E. (2005). 'The limits of social capital: Durkheim, Suicide and Social Capital'. *American Journal of Public Health*, 95:7, 1139–43.

Larke, P.J. (1990). 'Cultural diversity awareness inventory: assessing the sensitivity of preservice teachers'. *Action in Teacher Education*, XII: 3, 23–30.

Law, S.G. and Lane, D.S. (1987). Multicultural acceptance by teacher education students. *Journal of Instructional Psychology*, 14:1, 3–9.

Leavy, A. (2005). '"When I meet them I talk to them": the challenges of diversity for preservice teacher education'. *Irish Educational Studies*, 24:2, 159–77.

Linde, G. (2003). 'A Journey with Durkheim through an Examination Driven School System'. *Education Studies*, 29:4, 323–35.

Mahan, J. and Boyle, V. (1981). 'Multicultural teacher preparation: an attitudinal survey'. *Educational Research Quarterly*, 6:3, 97–103.

Marshall, J. and Klein, A. M. (2009). 'Lessons in Social Action'. *Social Studies*, 100:5, 218–21.

Meyer-Adams, N. and Conner, T. B. (2008). 'School violence: bullying behaviours and the psychosocial school environment in middle schools'. *Children and Schools,* 30:4, 211–21.

Nespor, J. (1987). 'The role of beliefs in the practice of teaching'. *Journal of Curriculum Studies.* 19 (4), 317–28.

Pajares, M. (1992). 'Teachers' beliefs and educational research: Cleaning up a messy construct'. *Review of Educational Research.* 3, 307–32.

Phellas, C. N. (2005). 'Cypriot Gay Men's Accounts of Negotiating Cultural and Sexual Identity: A Qualitative Study'. *Qualitative Sociology Review*, 1:2, 65–82.

Rumberger, R. W. and Palardy, G. J. (2005). 'Does Segregation Still Matter? The Impact of Student Composition on Academic Achievement in High School'. *Teachers College Record*, 107:9, 1999–2045.

Sheridan, A. (1995). 'An Analysis of the Factors Influencing The Sex Stereotyping of Nursing as an Occupation'. *An Bórd Altranais News*.

Sullivan, J. (1998). 'Compliance or Complaint'. *Irish Educational Studies*, 17, 183.

Terrill, M. M. and Mark, D. L. (2000). 'Preservice teachers' expectations for schools with children of color and second-language learners'. *Journal of Teacher Education*, 51:2, 149–55.

Valli, L. (1995). 'The dilemma of race: learning to be colourblind and colour conscious'. *Journal of Teacher Education*, 46:2, 120–129.

Vanderstraeten, R. (2004). 'The Social Differentiation of the Educational System'. *Sociology*, 38: 255–72.

Weis, L. and Dimitriadis, G. (2008). 'Dueling Banjos: Shifting Economic and Cultural Contexts in the Lives of Youth'. *Teachers College Record*, 110:10, 2290–2316.

Welsh, W. N. (2000). 'The effects of school climate on school disorder'. *Annals*, 567, 88–107.

Wiggins, R. A. and Follo, E. J. (1999). 'Development of knowledge, attitudes, and commitment to teach diverse student populations'. *Journal of Teacher Education*, 50:2, 94–105.

Zimpher, N. (1989). 'The RATE project: a profile of teacher education students'. *Journal of Teacher Education*, 40:6, 27–30.

Reports and other sources

Council of Europe (1950). *European Declaration of Human Rights*. Rome.

Darmody, M. and Smith, E. (2005). *Gender and Subject Choice: Take-up of Technological Subjects in Second-Level Education*. Dublin: ESRI.

European Parliament (2000). *The Charter of Fundamental Rights of the European Union*. Bruxelles: Official Journal of the European Communities.

Government of Ireland (1938). *Constitution of Ireland*. Dublin: The Stationary Office.

Irish Bishops' Conference. (1995a). *Statement on Relationships and Sexuality Education*, 23 January.

Irish Bishops' Conference. (1995b). *Response to the Education Bill*, 12 March.

Irish Bishops' Conference. (1997). *Relationships and Sexuality Education Policy Document*, 1997, Article 3.

Martin, M. (2006a). *School Matters: Report of the Taskforce on Student Behaviour*. Dublin: Department of Education and Science.

Mayock, P., Kitching, K. and Morgan, M. (2007). *RSE in the Context of SPHE: An Assessment of the Challenges to Full Implementation of the Programme in Post Primary Schools*. Dublin: Crisis Pregnancy Agency.

McDonnell, M. (1995). *Ethos and Catholic Voluntary Secondary Schools*, Phd. Thesis. Vol. II. University College Dublin.

Thatcher, M. (1987). *Interview for* Women's Own *magazine*, 23 September. Sourced from Thatcher Archive online [http://www.margaretthatcher.org/document/106689], 19 July 2010.

United Nations (1948). *Universal Declaration of Human Rights*. New York.

Welsh, W. N., Jenkins, P. H. and Greene, J. R. (1996). *Building a climate of safety in public schools in Philadelphia: School based management and violence reduction, final report*. Washington DC: National Institute of Justice.

Websites

Martin, D. (2004). Archbishop's *Commencement Speech for the Opening of the School Year 2004–2005* (Dublin: Archdiocese of Dublin) accessed online 22 July 2010, at http://www.dublindiocese.ie/index.php?option=com_content&task=view&id=3&Itemid=372.

Martin, D. (2006b). *Launch of Graduate Diploma in Education* at Dublin City University accessed online 22 July 2010, at http://www.dublindiocese.ie/index.php?option=com_content&task=view&id=441&Itemid=372.

Chapter Five

Psychology of Education

Geraldine Scanlon, Dublin City University

WHAT IS PSYCHOLOGY?

Psychology can be described as the scientific and systematic study of animal and human behaviour (Carlson et al., 2006; Child, 2007). The discipline of psychology is concerned with investigating, from a scientific perspective, the essence of human behaviour which is underpinned by physiological, cognitive, social and emotional processes. From a historical perspective, the mind was regarded as a primarily independent spirit and deemed unobservable; this later came to be defined and recognised as a 'functioning brain' which controlled behaviour (Carlson et al., 2006). The limitations of observing the brain that existed at the time facilitated a shift in interest to observing behaviour. However, because the brain both contains the mind and controls behaviour, it was inevitable that the study of psychology would incorporate both of these components. Consequently, one of the main goals of research in psychology is to understand, predict and change human behaviour, that is, to provide explanations about why people do what they do (Carlson et al., 2006).

From a scientific perspective, there are many different ways to explain behaviour. For example, two psychologists might be interested in depression in primary-school children but may approach the subject from different perspectives because they are specifically concerned with different explanations with regard to the phenomena of depression. Therefore, a clinical psychologist might look at the causes of the child's depression and how it impacts on the child's social functioning in school (relating events to behaviour); in contrast, a neuropsychologist might explore the brain using magnetic resonance imaging (MRI) to identify the relationship between the child's brain and spinal cord, known as the central nervous system, which is responsible for maintaining and producing behaviour (relating brain functioning to behaviour). As a result, the complexity that surrounds human behaviour has given rise to the development of several branches of psychology that compare, contrast and complement research methods to support professionals across several domains including medicine, business, human resources and education. For a full overview see Table 5.1.

Table 5.1 Branches of psychology

AREA DESCRIPTION	
Physiological psychology	Studies the biological basis of behaviour.
Psychophysiology	Measures people's physiological relations, e.g. heart rate, blood pressure.
Neuroscience	Examines the relationship between the central nervous system and behaviour.
Behaviour genetics	Examines the role of genetics in behaviour.
Cognitive psychology	Studies mental process and complex behaviours, such as perception, attention, learning and memory.
Developmental psychology	The study of physical, cognitive, emotional and social development in children, adolescents and adults.
Social psychology	Examines attitudes, opinions, interpersonal relationships and group dynamics.
Individual differences	Examines individual differences in temperament and patterns of behaviour.
Clinical psychology	Identifies and treats neurological and psychological disorders.
Educational psychology	Applies psychological theories and research to respond to individual differences.

However, at its core, psychology establishes the scientific foundations to enable professionals to understand human beings and their challenges, as well as the problems associated with them. It also promotes the cause of human welfare by providing interventions and supports to enable behaviour change and improve social functioning (MacKay, 2010).

RESEARCH IN PSYCHOLOGY AND ITS APPLICATION TO EDUCATION

The discipline of psychology is underpinned by rigorous research methods with researchers engaging in a wide variety of research questions to assist professionals across a broad range of disciplines to improve outcomes for both individuals and organisations. From an educational perspective, some comprehensive research topics include:

- The impact of diet on behaviour and intelligence (Benton, 2008).
- Understanding drugs and behaviour (Parrott et al., 2004).
- Temperament (Putnam and Stifter, 2008).
- Special educational needs (Scanlon and McGilloway, 2005).
- Peer attachment in adolescents (Wilkinson, 2009).
- Day-care and academic achievement (Cooper et al., 2010).
- Cyberbullying (McGuckin et al., 2010).
- Positive behaviour support in schools (Scanlon et al., 2010).
- Teacher efficacy (Tschanned-Moran and Woolfolk Hoy, 2001).
- Relationships between parental school involvement and academic outcomes for pupils (Tan and Goldberg, 2009).
- The adolescent brain (Weinberger, et al., 2005).

The findings from some of the research topics above have been instrumental in contributing to teacher knowledge in both school and education programmes, informing educational professionals about best practice, and creating suitable learning environments for all learners. From a psychological perspective, the topics extend across the four domains of developmental psychology, which describe the stages and sequences of physical, social, emotional and cognitive development. In practice, developmental theory describes changes within areas of behaviour (e.g. language and social skills), the relationships between these areas of behaviour and accounts for the transitions from one point of development to another. In short, it establishes a set of rules or principles that can explain change and also describe individual differences.

Consequently, the function of psychology in education is distinct from educational psychology. Specifically, the former is concerned with how psychological theories and research inform and support the work of educational professionals working across a wide variety of educational settings; whereas the latter applies psychological theories, research and techniques to assist teachers to appraise individual differences, create more efficient learning environments for all students and become reflective in their own teaching practice. The term 'educational psychology' is more generally associated with educational psychologists who are particularly concerned with children and young adults who may be experiencing difficulty in communication, cognition and learning, behaviour, social and emotional development, and sensory and/or physical needs, and how this might impact on their development in general in school settings (Child, 2007). Educational psychologists are trained specifically to assess children in the areas where they might be experiencing difficulty (e.g. reading, mathematics or remembering information).

The assessment tests used within the Irish context for cognitive ability include:

- The Wechsler Intelligences Scale for Children (2003) (WISC), which generates an overall intelligence quotient (IQ) score and four other indices scores, including verbal comprehension, perceptual reasoning, processing speed and working memory.

- The Wechsler Individual Achievement Test-111 (WIAT-111) measures reading and numerical attainment in written and oral language.

Behavioural assessments employed include:

- The CONNERS-3 (2008) which assess a broad range of psychopathology and behaviour problems.
- The Adaptive Behaviour Assessment System (ABAS, 2nd edition) helps to evaluate the level of adaptive skills and specify treatment goals.
- The Achenbach Child Behaviour Checklist assesses adaptive and maladaptive functioning in home and school settings.

The results of these assessments are then compared to what is construed as 'normative development' and interventions and supports are identified to help and develop the pupil's learning in school. Other interventions may also be included to develop social skills, increase levels of self-esteem and improve behaviour where required. These interventions may be articulated through the development of an Individual Education Plan (IEP), the allocation of resource teaching hours within the school and the assistance from outside agencies (e.g. speech and language therapy, and counselling). These interventions are usually implemented and monitored by the Learning Support Department or Special Educational Needs Team in conjunction with class teachers. The implications for initial teacher education will be more fully examined under individual differences and diversity later in this chapter.

Consequently, for student teachers, the study of psychology in education can be translated into questions about what can be expected from children at a particular age across the key areas of developmental psychology. This chapter will introduce readers to the key concepts in developmental psychology that contribute to educational practice and teacher education. Specifically, it will assist understanding of the key characteristics of adolescent development in the following areas: biological/neurological development; cognition; intelligence; academic motivation; individual differences; social/emotional development; and special issues. It will also help readers to develop an understanding of what is considered to be best practice by exploring the role of the teacher in facilitating student learning through the creation of positive learning environments, and a recognition and respect for individual differences and diversity, and will contribute to exploring the key issues in effective classroom management and communication skills.

In order to assist readers' understanding of human behaviour, it is important to note that several theories of how people learn and develop exist. Consequently, a variety of theoretical perspectives have emerged within psychology which seek to appraise human development and individual differences from several viewpoints, as theories and views of development proposed by a particular psychologist are anchored in subjective understandings of how the world operates (Bornstein and Lamb, 1999). The following sections will introduce you to three key perspectives within developmental psychology which have made significant contributions to our understanding within educational settings of how children develop across social, emotional and cognitive domains.

THEORETICAL PERSPECTIVES ON DEVELOPMENT

Several definitions of learning exist. For example, Hill (2002, quoted in Woolfolk et al., 2009, p. 244) states that we can say that learning has occurred when experience has caused a 'relatively permanent change in an individual's knowledge or behaviour'. Similarly, Rogers (2008, p. 8), defines learning as 'more or less permanent changes and reinforcements brought about voluntarily in one's pattern of acting thinking and feeling'. From these definitions, we see that knowledge and behaviour become interlinked. Consequently learning, within this context, is not only associated with school but includes all aspects of our experience and how that translates into physical, cognitive, social and emotional development.

Behaviourism

Behaviourists observe the way people behave and then seek to give explanations for the occurrence of that behaviour. Early views of learning were proposed by John B. Watson (1878–1958) who believed that children's behaviour could be shaped by controlling their environment, that is, behaviour change occurs as a result of environmental influences. Watson acquired his beliefs from the earlier work of Ivan Pavlov (1849–1936) who, in a key experiment involving a dog, paired a neutral stimulus (a bell) with an unconditioned stimulus (food) which, in turn, led to a conditioned reflex (salivation). This principle, coined as classical conditioning, was achieved as follows. Pavlov noticed that when food was presented to a dog by an attendant this also resulted in the dog salivating. In laboratory conditions, Pavlov immediately presented food to the dog while ringing a bell at the same time (paired stimulus) and repeated this procedure a number of times. He then refined the procedure by removing the food when the bell ringing occurred. Consequently, the bell now elicited the salivation on its own, that is, Pavlov had conditioned the dog to salivate when he heard the bell and not when the food was presented. Pavlov proposed that when the response (salivation) occurred reliably in the presence of a conditioned stimulus (bell ringing) a 'conditioned learned response' had occurred (Boyd and Bee, 2009). Using the principles of classical conditioning, Watson and Rayner (1920) exposed 'Little Albert', an 11-month-old boy, to a white rat (stimulus) which the child enjoyed playing with. Subsequently, Watson paired (recall the bell and food) the presentation of the white rat with loud noises, resulting in 'Little Albert' becoming fearful and generalising his fear not only to the white rat but also to other white fuzzy objects which he had previously been attached to. Modern behaviourists use the term 'generalise' to describe behaviour that occurs across several settings (e.g. home and school community). For example, reflect upon the implications of the idiom 'street angel, house devil'—the child only demonstrates the behaviour in one setting, and therefore is not generalising his/her behaviour. This experiment highlighted the function of classical conditioning in the role of emotional responses and developmental change. More importantly, it showed how it was possible to condition humans to learn to respond in certain ways and that this process was dependent upon particular environmental influences.

Building on these principles, B. F. Skinner (1904–1990) proposed that many of the voluntary responses (e.g. salivation) of animals and humans are strengthened when they are reinforced by a pleasurable or undesirable consequences, thereby facilitating the development of new behaviours which are desirable and rewarded, and extinguishing undesirable behaviours which are punished. In other words, behaviour is guided by many different kinds of stimuli or events that will have certain consequences, and this enables the individual to respond in a certain way. Skinner referred to these as the contingencies of reinforcement (Kearney, 2008): antecedents (what happens before the behaviour occurs); behaviour (the observed behaviour, e.g. aggression/hitting); and consequences (what happens next, e.g. punishment). This process is underpinned further by reinforcement, punishment and extinction (Carlson et al., 2006).

A reinforcer is anything that follows behaviour and increases the chances of that behaviour occurring again (Woolfolk et al., 2009). Two types of reinforcement exist: positive reinforcement and negative reinforcement. Positive reinforcement occurs when the action or behaviour produces a reward, for example, winning a prize for academic excellence. However, in many classrooms, positive reinforcement occurs unintentionally. The 'class clown' is a typical example of how behaviour is unintentionally reinforced. The teacher may not necessarily be pleased with the constant interruptions of funny comments and jokes from a student, but the student's peers will reinforce the behaviour by laughing or other similar responses. The more other students laugh, the more likely the student is to continue his/her behaviour and thus the behaviours are strengthened. In contrast, negative reinforcement from peers and the class teacher, that is, not reacting to the 'class clown', may lead to the student becoming aware that he/she is becoming an irritant to his/her peers, particularly if the student is in a highly motivated group. This, in turn, becomes an aversive (unpleasant) event which will quickly help to diminish the behaviour. Punishment involves reducing the frequency or decreasing behaviour. If behaviour is followed by punishment, it is less likely to occur again. Within a post-primary school context, this may be quite difficult to achieve. Crucially, in order to reduce unwanted behaviour, there must be consistency in how the student's behaviour is managed and what may serve as a punisher for one student may not work for another, because of individual differences.

The principles of behaviourism are present in many contemporary classrooms and form the basis for discipline policies used by schools to manage and promote pupil behaviour, for example, good/bad notes and so forth (for further reference see NEWB, 2008).

SCHOOL-WIDE POSITIVE BEHAVIOUR SUPPORT

More recently, psychologists have been concerned with applying the principles of Applied Behaviour Analysis (ABA) to create positive learning environments while also managing pupil behaviour. The overarching aim of this is to develop individual education/behavioural plans to reduce the amount of time that pupils with challenging behaviour are excluded from the mainstream classrooms. One particular model, School-Wide Positive Behaviour Support (SWPBS), which has a number of critical components which are ABA in origin, is currently being implemented in many public schools across the United States (Sugai and Horner, 2002). SWPBS has been defined as 'the application of positive behavioural intervention and systems to achieve socially important behaviour change' (Sugai et al., 2000, p. 133). In addition, the model also subscribes to the philosophy of inclusion as a means of enabling pupils with special educational needs (SEN) to access the same opportunities as their peers who do not have such difficulties (Carr et al., 2002).

In essence, a three-tiered prevention model addresses the levels of behavioural need within schools that employ this system (See Table 5.2). This structure clarifies expectations for both staff and students, resulting in fewer students engaging in problematic behaviour (Crone et al., 2010).

Table 5.2: Three-tiered prevention model for school-wide positive behaviour support

Universal support (Tier I)	School-wide rules and expectations are taught to all pupils and proactive classroom management procedures must be employed by all teachers.
Targeted group interventions (Tier II)	Systems of reducing problem behaviour must be in place for students who are at risk of developing patterns of problem behaviour over time and early identification and intervention must be in place.
Individualised student interventions (Tier III)	Individualised behaviour support is offered to students with serious behaviour problems.

SOCIAL LEARNING THEORY

Social learning theory arose out of Albert Bandura's challenge to the principles of behaviourism (1997). He suggested that learning does not always require reinforcement, rather, learning occurs as a result of what we observe in our social environments and is also dependent on personal factors, for example, beliefs, expectations and self-perceptions. While Skinner professed that learning is a gradual process where children must act to learn, Bandura questioned the development of complex behaviours that are learned suddenly and suggested that these occur as a result of children watching their peers, in other words that children learn behaviour by observing others. He suggested that the degree of observational learning is also underpinned by how children demonstrate self-regulation (the cognitive ability of the child) and the existence of individual differences in development. This is evident, for example, in how children quickly learn to behave in school. Children learn how to behave by observing the reactions of teachers to those who misbehave. Consequently, they become observers, whereas the child who misbehaves may not have the capability or understanding to observe and learn how to behave in the same context. In other words, the observant child will behave in the presence of a strict teacher, while the unobservant children will not (Boyd and Bee, 2009). However, Bandura stresses that learning from modelling is not simply imitation but is dependent upon the type of modelling involved: for example, 'live model', observing somebody actually demonstrating a particular behaviour; 'symbolic model', watching somebody in a film; or verbal instructions and descriptions of how to behave.

The acquisition of learning is not an automatic process but is dependent on several cognitive elements, attentional process, memory, motivation and motor reproduction. For example, consider the child in the classroom. Children cannot learn unless they pay attention to what is happening around them (i.e. behave in the presence of the teacher and listen to what is being said). Furthermore, the child must not only recognise the observed behaviour but must remember it at some later time (the teacher gives out if you misbehave/don't listen and punishment may follow). Children will engage in good/bad behaviour only if they have some motivation or reason for doing so (i.e. reward or punishment) and they must be physically and intellectually capable of doing so. Consequently, some children who have learning difficulties may not be in the position to understand that their behaviour is inappropriate in a classroom setting. Furthermore, children with attention problems may have difficulty in appraising the teacher's reactions to their behaviour and continue to misbehave which, in turn, will affect their academic engagement.

COGNITIVE THEORIES

One of the most important areas of study for student teachers is cognitive development. Cognitive theorists are concerned with how people think, learn, and develop new ideas or concepts. They assume that mental processes exist and that humans are active participants in their own acts of cognition (the acquisition of knowledge) and that learning facilitates behavioural change (Ashcraft, 2006). From a cognitive perspective, the mind is viewed as an information-processing system that receives information through the senses which is, in turn, processed by various systems in the brain. The principles underlying the information-processing theory are seen to be comparable to the complex workings of a computer. For example, humans store knowledge in their long-term memory which is similar to the hard drive of a computer. This includes factual knowledge, knowledge of how to do things and images of past experiences. Thinking occurs when the information from the long-term memory is activated into short-term memory and then combined with the information being taken in by the senses (similar to RAM in computer terminology). In short, the development of short-term memory capacity, long-term knowledge and the ways humans plan to acquire new knowledge (i.e. strategies) constitutes cognitive development (Pressley and McCormick, 2008). For example, the way in which students learn new information to assist them in complex cognitive tasks is dependent on a number of factors, including perception and attention. Basic perceptual and attention processes occur when new information is presented (Eysneck and Keane, 2010). Perceptual processes include perceiving new information and assigning meaning to it and are underpinned by 'bottom-up' processing or 'top-down' processing. Top-down processing is based on knowledge and experience (i.e. what the learner already knows about the stimulus/information that is being presented), whereas bottom-up processing is based purely on the features of the stimulus presented. For example, the letter 'B'; whenever a child sees 'B' or anything close to it, they will recognise it (Anderson, 2005). Consequently, how this information is learned is guided by prior knowledge, what we need to know and what we would like to know. This information is then transferred to the short-term memory store and will only transfer into the long-term memory store through the process of rehearsal (i.e. the strategies we use to remember the information). However, from a developmental perspective, children learn to think and solve problems in a variety of ways depending on their age and stage of development.

DEVELOPMENTAL PERSPECTIVES ON COGNITIVE DEVELOPMENT

One of the key theorists identified in contributing to teacher knowledge about how children learn from infancy to adulthood was Jean Piaget (1896–1980). Piaget proposed that all children go through the same stages and sequences of development while discovering and learning new information. This development consists of four distinct stages: sensorimotor (birth to two years); preoperational (two to seven years); concrete operational (seven to 11years) and formal operational (11 years plus).

At each stage, the child has qualitatively different capabilities which lay the foundation for the next stage and reflects a period where the child is capable of understanding certain things but not others (see Table 5.3). Transition from one stage to the next is evidenced by two key factors: maturation (i.e. the level of individual biological/neurological development) and the child's interaction with the environment. As intelligence involves adapting to the environment, the child is active in their own development. Piaget suggested that, in order to behave intelligently, children require three mental structures:

1. schemas which are organised patterns of behaviour that guide a child's actions and behaviour;
2. concepts which are classes/categories of objects, events or ideas that have common properties (e.g. all birds have wings); and
3. operations, that is the mental activity that combines schemas and operations.

In particular, schemas play a central role in cognitive development and these schemas are adapted through the processes of accommodation and assimilation.

Table 5.3 Piaget's stages of cognitive development

Sensorimotor	Birth–2 years	Child develops schemes primarily through sense and motor activities.
Preoperational	2–7 years	Child can think symbolically and holds an egocentric view of the world, i.e. the child can only see problems from his/her perspective.
Concrete operational	7–11 years	Child becomes able to manipulate logical relationships among concepts, but only by generalising from concrete experiences.
Formal operational	11 years to adulthood	Child is able to deal with abstractions, form hypotheses and solve problems systematically.

Assimilation involves taking in new information and fitting it into an existing schema. For example, young children have the schema for four-legged animals and label all four-legged animals as cows. Accommodation occurs when the child acquires new information through experience and interacting with their environment whereupon the child begins to perceive that horses are different to dogs, and dogs are different to cats, even though they all have four legs. Consequently, this information is accommodated into their current schema of four-legged animals and learning and understanding is extended. Piaget called this process adaptation.

Assimilation helps to consolidate mental structures and accommodation leads to growth and change, which, in turn, leads to adaptation (i.e. a broader view of four-legged animals). As a result of these experiences, the child reaches the point of cognitive equilibrium, i.e. the balance between the two processes. If there is accommodation in the absence of assimilation, behaviour would be disorganised and unpredictable and would lead to unchanging, rigid patterns of behaviour, for example that all four-legged animals can only be dogs. A good example of applying this principle to child development is the age group guide on toys and books, giving a child either one when they have not reached the level of cognitive maturity required to interact or play with the item can lead to frustration and boredom.

How does Piaget's theory fit within a context? In order for pupils to understand complex mathematics problems, they must have acquired the basic principles of addition, subtraction, multiplication and division. In a similar vein, historical events and their impact on societal change can only be understood within a system based on prior knowledge and understanding. Piaget developed his theory by observing young children and developing a series of key cognitive tasks, including conservation tasks on liquid, mass, number and length, which illustrated and supported his stage-like theory (see Piaget, 1954; Piaget and Inhelder, 1969). In a simple task on the conservation of number, a child is presented with two rows of marbles and it is established by the child that both rows are the same. The marbles, from one of the rows is then moved in front of the child by the adult, and the child is asked if the two rows are still the same. The child's answer will depend on what stage he/she is at; the preoperational child will say that there are more marbles than before, whereas the concrete operational child will say that they are still the same. Further study in this area will enable discovery of the processes underpinning children's answers and will assist understanding about how teachers match curriculum with ability (see also Bee and Boyd, 2010; Snowman et al., 2009; Child, 2007; Pressley and McCormick, 2008; Woolfolk et al., 2009). It is worthwhile noting that although many shortcomings have been identified in his theories (e.g. Bruner, 1983; Donaldson 1978; McGarrigle and Donaldson, 1974), Piaget's stage-like approach to the development of cognitive capacities is currently in favour with developmental psychologists (e.g. Kuhn, 2008; Shayer, 2008; see also Bee and Boyd, 2010). More importantly, Piaget's work has contributed enormously to educational practice by identifying the relationship between how children think and what they can know, enabling educators to develop curricula in accordance with children's abilities.

While Piaget is seen to be one of the most influential theorists within education, Lev Vygotsky and Jerome Bruner have also made significant contributions. Vygotsky's socio-cultural theory of development proposes that higher intellectual functioning, e.g. reasoning, planning understanding and remembering, develops as a result of social experiences with the assistance and help from others. Crucially, parents and teachers guide cognitive development by motivating children, providing instruction and presenting new challenges. Vygotsky developed an important concept known as the Zone of Proximal Development (ZPD) which, he suggested, was the 'distance between the actual developmental level as determined by independent problem solving and the potential level as determined through problem solving under adult guidance or in collaboration with more capable peers' (Vygotsky, 1978, p. 86). This process, which consists of the interaction between the child and their environment, is what defines them as individuals. It is also referred to as scaffolding. From the teacher's perspective, scaffolding involves facilitating attempts to problem solve by providing pupils with a variety of leading questions and hints. Vygotsky suggests that higher ability students, whose zone of ZPD is wider, require more complex questioning while students with a narrower ZPD require more extensive assistance. Consequently, Vygotsky's theory accounts for individual differences in education by encompassing abilities, attitudes and patterns of thinking which are maturing and can only reach full potential with assistance (Snowman et al., 2009). Within educational settings, Vygotsky highlighted the importance of well-designed instruction on an individual level and the role of the adult in facilitating learning, thus drawing attention to the sensitivity to individual differences and diversity in education.

Building on Vygotsky's concept of scaffolding, Jerome Bruner's pioneering work provided the basis for Constructivist Learning Theory which posits that learning becomes autonomous and self-directed for pupils. According to Bruner (1983), true learning involves 'figuring out how to use what you already know in order to go beyond what you already think' (1983, in Snowman et al., 2009, p. 183). This can be achieved by teachers setting problems for children, who then seek solutions either by themselves or with the assistance of their peers. The principles underpinning this approach and how it applies to learning in the classroom include pupils: gaining an understanding of the common characteristics amongst concepts and how to bring them together; using prior knowledge to gain understanding of new information; developing analytic skills; and appraising successful methods used in solving problems. In essence, this approach enables pupils to have some responsibility for their own learning while also encouraging the development of a wide variety of skills. (For further reading on the constructivist approach to teaching see Snowman et al., 2009.)

ADDITIONAL FACTORS FOR CONSIDERATION IN COGNITION

Intelligence

The concept of intelligence requires a more extensive discussion than can be provided in an overview such as this. 'Intelligence' is a term that is used widely within a variety of contexts in everyday life. Skills, such as the ability to remember items from a list, solve problems, or learn and fully understand new words or terminology, tend to be understood as characteristics of intelligence. Extending on this definition, intelligence is also viewed as the ability to modify and adjust behaviours to accomplish tasks successfully, resulting in the overall capacity of an individual to act purposefully, think rationally and deal effectively with the environment. The concept of intelligence has long been one of the most controversial topics in psychology (Block, 1997 in O'Toole and Barnes-Holmes, under submission). The controversy stems, not just from the emphasis on individual differences in cognitive ability, but also from claims concerning gender and race differences. Other issues that engender heated debate relate to issues such as the malleability and the measurement of intelligence. These controversies are all the more pronounced given the evidence suggesting that intelligence (as assessed by intelligence tests) appears to be an important predictor of critical life outcomes such as health, life-expectancy, monetary income and personal status (Ashenfelter and Rouse, 1998, and Patja, Vesla, Ossanen and Ruppila, 2001, in O'Toole and Barnes-Holmes (under submission).

The controversy surrounding intelligence can also be seen to result from the fact that the construct of intelligence is not one that is readily amenable to scientific investigation. As a result, there have been many different perspectives and much disagreement about its nature. Currently, there are a number of different intelligence theories dominating the literature. These can be loosely classified as biological models, hierarchical models and complex-systems models.

The biological models are based on the premise that highly intelligent people have brains that operate more accurately and efficiently (i.e. have greater neural efficiency) than less intelligent individuals (e.g. Haier et al., 1988; Hendrickson, 1982; Vernon and Mori, 1992). Hierarchical models of intelligence are based on psychometric analyses. The assumption underlying these models is that the structure of intelligence can be discovered by analysing the interrelationship of scores on cognitive abilities tests (e.g. Spearman, 1904; Thurstone, 1924). Current models proposed by Horn and Catell (1966) make the distinction between two types of ability: fluid intelligence, or gf, and crystallised intelligence, or gc. Fluid intelligence is viewed as the biologically influenced dimension of g, a kind of capacity or potential, which is most clearly manifested in novel, complex or challenging environments. Crystallised intelligence, on the other hand, is believed to be influenced by education and culture.

Complex-system models view intelligence as a complex system that includes interactions between mental processes, contextual factors and multiple abilities. According to these models, intelligence is dynamic and can change when contextual conditions change. Most notable of these models is Howard Gardner's multiple intelligences (2010) theory, which focuses on domains of ability rather than processes. Gardner rejects the notion of intelligence as a unitary ability. He suggests that there are at least eight fairly independent, equally important types of intelligence. Three of these intelligences—linguistic, logical-mathematical and spatial—are related to abilities measured by conventional intelligence tests. The remaining five—musical, bodily-kinaesthetic, intrapersonal, interpersonal and naturalist—are valued in most cultures but are not measured in tests of ability. Psychometric testing has already been addressed briefly earlier in this chapter with regard to the work of educational psychologists in supporting children with learning difficulties. Normal intelligence is deemed to be between the ranges of 90–110 with gifted children falling in the range of 140–170 (Lovecky, 2004) (the range of intelligence with regard to students with special educational needs will be briefly addressed later in the chapter). However, a note of caution, intelligence testing is not without its critics and these criticisms are an important area for teachers to consider. For further reading about intelligence and intelligence testing/assessment please refer to Child, 2007; Griffin and Shevlin, 2007; Pressley and McCormick, 2008: Woolfolk et al., 2009.

Memory and learning

Memory plays an important part in learning and remembering new information. It enables individuals to learn from experience and adapt to changing environments while also connecting them to family, friends, places and events which have been experienced individually or shared with others. There are three basic stages involved in the process of learning and memory: encoding, storage and retrieval.

Encoding occurs when new information is presented which, in turn, determines that some information will be stored within the memory system, retrieval occurs when information needs to extracted (Eysneck and Keane, 2010). A three-stage model of memory proposed by Atkinson and Shiffrin (1968) known as the 'multi-store model' has seen to be useful for teachers because of the notion of short-term memory (STM) and long-term memory stores (LTM). For example, when information is presented, it is held very briefly in the STM. Some of the information processed in the STM is transferred to the LTM. How well the information is retained in the LTM is dependent upon rehearsal (i.e. how much effort an individual expends in learning new material). Short-term memory (also referred to as working memory) is viewed as a temporary store for information, e.g. telephone numbers, which has a limited capacity and which can only facilitate a limited amount of information (up to seven items). However, Miller (1956) suggests that while our 'span of absolute judgement' is about seven objects, recall of information can be improved through a process called 'chunking'. This involves grouping items into chunks of seven and is used in learning subjects such as chemistry, by bringing letters and symbols together and learning them in a group (Child, 2007). In contrast, important information is stored in the LTM system which has an unlimited capacity and where information can be potentially retrieved. Recall of information from the LTM is facilitated by the presentation of cues (e.g. a question in a test) and is returned to the STM or working memory. While several theories exist with regard to forgetting information (see Child, 2007) retrieval problems can occur as a result of poor organisation in learning the material or not developing effective strategies to promote storage. Therefore, as a teacher, it is important to assist students in developing strategies for learning, such as 'mind maps' (Buzan, 2000) which are particularly useful for students who have short-term and long-term memory problems.

Motivation

While motivation is a crucial area of study for teachers, it is a very broad subject developed as a result of diverse theories which reflect a variety of approaches in attempting to understand how humans think and behave (Child, 2007; Woolfolk et al., 2009). Motivation can be defined as 'an internal state that arouses, directs and maintains behaviour' (Woolfolk et al., 2009 p. 438). In order to understand what motivates students to learn, psychologists have proposed several questions: Why does it take some learners longer than others to get on task (e.g. homework)? Why do some students give up while others do not? What influences the choices students make about their behaviour around school? How focused are students when they are engaged in academic activities (Woolfolk et al., 2009)? The need to achieve may, partly, explain motivation (i.e. motivation occurs as a result of individual characteristics) or, alternatively, motivation can be viewed as a temporary state. While other explanations exist (e.g. rewards, punishment and social rewards), a basic distinction can be found between intrinsic and extrinsic motivation. Intrinsic motivation is associated with activities that have their own reward, such as playing on the school team. In contrast, extrinsic motivation is governed by rewards and punishments ('If I don't do my homework, I will be punished.'). The difference between both is derived from the notion of the student's reason for acting or participating and is referred to as the 'locus of causality', i.e. students who enter freely into activities have an internal locus of causality, in contrast to those who do not and have an external locus of causality (Woolfolk et al., 2009). This will also have major implications for students with special educational needs who may find it hard to be motivated to tackle academic tasks that they find extremely difficult. Accordingly, it is crucial for teachers to understand the concept of motivation, in order to encourage learning by being sensitive to their students' needs and interests and creating positive learning environments (Child, 2007; Woolfolk et al., 2009).

The sections above provide an insight into some of the most important developmental areas that contribute to teacher education, including learning, behaviour, cognitive development and individual differences. All of these theories have a direct impact on the teaching approaches that are currently employed in schools. However, since the implementation of the 2004 Education for Persons with Special Educational Needs Act (EPSEN) (Government of Ireland, 2004b), children with special educational needs (SEN) are entitled to be educated in mainstream schools alongside their peers who do not have such needs.

Many children with SEN have cognitive difficulties that may impair their ability to learn and remember information, or they have attentional difficulties that impact on their ability to concentrate for long periods of time. Therefore, teachers will meet many challenges in the classroom trying to accommodate individual differences and learning styles. However, it is not only students with special needs who may require specialised teaching methods as many children have other challenges in their lives, including poverty and poor family support, or come from marginalised groups. In order to assist your understanding of how individual differences in human development emerge, the next section will concentrate on what makes us different and unique from each other.

INDIVIDUAL DIFFERENCES

Developmental changes do not occur in a vacuum; rather they are the result of the interplay between genetics (biology) and environment (experience). What it is that makes us different has been central to the nature–nurture debate. Traditionally, infants were viewed as 'empty vessels'. However, it is now acknowledged that children are not 'blank slates' (Pinker, 2000), but are born with a wide range of emotional and cognitive capacities for learning. Between the dynamic interplay of nature and nurture, personality takes shape and the developing child becomes unique within the social world. In addition, temperamental dispositions also contribute to the development of individual differences and the child's temperamental profile may influence the quality of the child's interactions with his/her parents and significant others. Research suggests that people are more likely to react to a happy smiley baby, thereby increasing the likelihood of positive interactions, as opposed to a baby who is cranky and difficult thereby decreasing the same likelihood (Thomas and Chess, 1977). Temperament will also influence how children experience, interpret and think about life events. In short, their responses may have broader consequences for the growth of social skills, friendships and intellectual development. Consequently, children enter schools with predispositions or abilities for music, language, sport, mathematics and science. Whether or not these predispositions are realised is dependent upon their environment, which includes family, peers, community and school.

Behaviour genetics

The notion of predisposition may be explained by the concept of intelligence. A child does not inherit genes that will result in a specific level of intelligence; rather, the extent to which their intelligence develops is dependent on the quality of the environment provided (Pressley and McCormick, 2008). For example, children who inherit high IQ genes from their parents are most likely to live in rich and stimulating environments (Bee and Boyd, 2010). Similarly, children who inherit aggressive tendencies are likely to live in a hostile and aggressive environment, thus reinforcing aggressive tendencies (Reiss 1998, in Boyd and Bee, 2010). Consequently, both environments are accommodating the expression of the genetic make-up of the child's parents. In order to determine the effects of genetics on individual development, behavioural geneticists have used research and adoption studies to compare the degree of similarity between the adopted child and birth parents (shared genetics) and the degree of similarity between the adopted child and adoptive parents (shared environment). The assumption that underpins this approach is questioned by several researchers who suggest that if identical twins grow up to be more similar in certain respects than fraternal twins, this can be explained by heredity or genetic factors (see Bee and Boyd, 2010, for a full review). Pinker (2000) suggests that individual differences in cognitive and emotional disorders have been found to be more prevalent in identical than fraternal twins and that this is better predicted by their biological inheritance rather than their environment. For example, research has confirmed that whether separated at birth or raised together, identical twins are alike in verbal and cognitive abilities (Alexandra et al., 2002); intelligence (Bouchard et al., 1990); emotional disorders (Cardino and Gottesman, 2000); and have similar behaviour with regard to gambling and their potential to engage in crime (Slutske et al., 2000; Eley et al., 1998).

The inheritability of intelligence (IQ) is one such area that has been widely researched and that has experienced significant controversy since the nature–nurture debate began. A study conducted by Bouchard et al., in 1990 traced twins at 40 years of age who had been separated before they were six months old. The results found that twins separated earlier were more alike in IQ than those children who were separated later and that there was a significant correlation between their birth family's IQ scores, with no evidence of IQ scores being affected by their environment.

The degree of similarity in adopted children (not twins) to their parents is based on the notion that similarity is measured between the birth parents and the adopted child, who share genes, and the adoptive parents and child, who share environment. Traditionally, children were adopted into middle-class homes, therefore it could be suggested that adoption studies provide empirical support for the effects of context on IQ scores (Bee and Boyd, 2010). However, a large-scale French study assessed the IQ scores of adolescents who had been adopted as babies from both middle- and working-class groups into both upper- and working-class families. The results found that children who had been raised in upper-class homes had IQ scores approximately 11 points above the others. However, children who had been born to upper-class parents had higher IQs despite the context in which they were raised (Capron and Duyme, 1989). The effects of the environment in adoption studies on IQ have also been shown to decrease over time (Bouchard et al., 1990).

The importance of context

In contrast, other researchers have highlighted the importance of context (i.e. environment) on development. From a theoretical perspective, Brofenbrenner's (1979) theory of the ecology of development stresses that the environment in which children grow up and develop is more complex than previously believed. The ecological environment consists of four nested systems: the microsystem, the mesosystem, the exosystem and the macrosystem (See Figure 5.1).

Figure 5.1: Broffenbrenner's model of the ecology of development

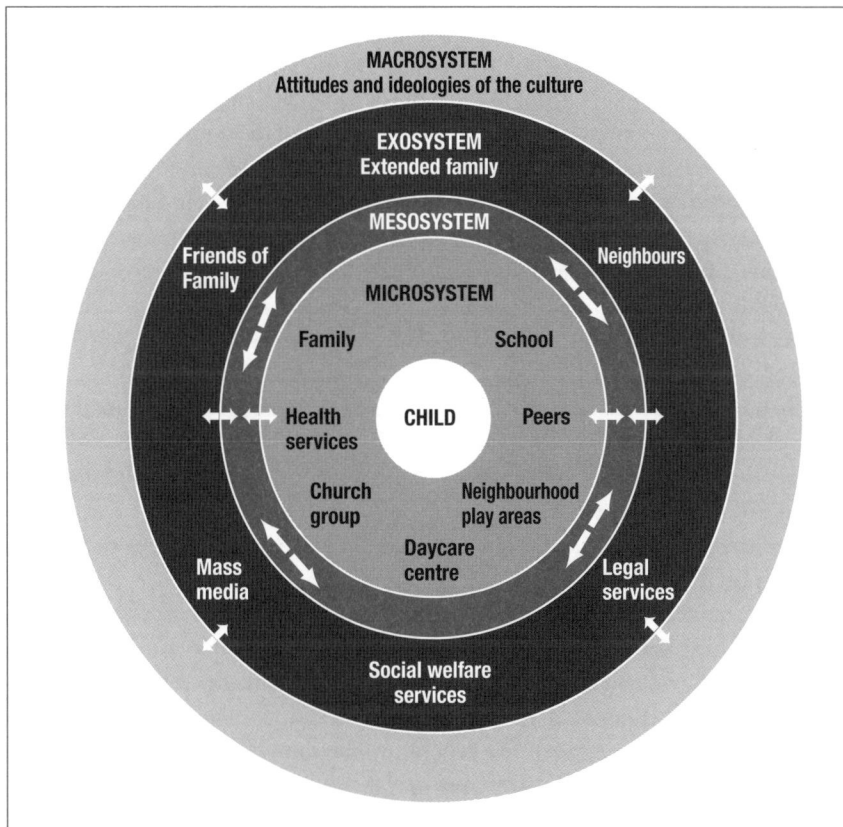

The basic premise of this theory is that these interrelated systems interact with the child's biological make-up. As the child develops, interactions between the levels of the environment become more complex with systems having a psychological impact on the individual through the availability of resources, choices and opportunities. This view is supported by Boyd and Bee (2009) who suggest that explaining the effects of environments on human development is complex. Consequently, psychologists have begun to use the concepts of resilience and vulnerability to explain individual differences. This view is based on the notion that children are born with certain vulnerabilities (e.g. disability) but also come equipped with protective factors, for example, high intelligence or an easy-going temperament, that assist them in the face of stress. Both of these factors then interact with the environment, but crucially the same environment can have different effects on individual children. To develop a further understanding of the complexities inherent within the nature–nurture debate see Pinker (2000).

The contribution of prenatal development to individual differences

Although an important component, it is not possible to review prenatal development in this chapter (for full review see Chapter 2 in Bee and Boyd, 2010). While the prenatal environment is relatively constant, there are many features of the external environment that are influential to development. For example, the term 'teratogen' is used to describe any agent that can damage the fetus, including cigarettes, drugs, alcohol, radiation and diseases, and which can cause physical and/or psychological damage that may not be observed until long after birth. For example, high caffeine intake is associated with low birth weight, miscarriage and newborn withdrawal (e.g. irritability and vomiting) while babies prenatally exposed to cocaine have lasting difficulties that persist through infancy and childhood (Delaney-Black et al., 2000; Mayes et al., 2006), including inattention and behavioural problems, coupled with a high incidence of health and brain defects. Smoking during pregnancy can cause low birth weight and increase the risk of prematurity which can result in serious physical problems and lasting behavioural or psychological problems, including frequent illness, over-activity, language delay and deficits in motor co-ordination.

Birth complications can also have implications for individual development (see Bee and Boyd, 2010) and can result in health and learning difficulties. As a result, it is clear that some children are born with specific difficulties that will impinge on their ability to learn and behave appropriately in school. The child's difficulties may be further compounded by the lack of intervention or in the case of learning disabilities, delayed assessment. A large proportion of the profiles of the children described above are now educated in mainstream settings.

Special educational needs and inclusive education

Worldwide, legislative and policy changes have recently played significant roles in recognising the entitlements of pupils with special educational needs (SEN). In the Irish context, the entitlement of these pupils to gain access to, and benefit from, education has been addressed by a framework of government policies that include: the Education Act (Government of Ireland, 1998); the Education (Welfare) Act (Government of Ireland, 2000a); the Equal Status Acts (Government of Ireland, 2000b) and the Equality Act (Government of Ireland, 2004a); the Education for Persons with Disabilities Bill (Government of Ireland, 2003); and the Education for Persons with Special Educational Needs Act (EPSEN) (Government of Ireland, 2004b).

The EPSEN Act defines SEN as:

> ... a restriction in the capacity of the person to participate in and benefit from education on account of an enduring physical, sensory, mental health or learning disability, or any other condition which results in a person learning differently from a person without that condition (p. 6).

Consequently, the term 'special educational needs' covers a broad spectrum of conditions, ranging from mild general learning disability (MGLD) to severe emotional disturbance and/or behavioural problems (SED/BP) and profound general learning disability (PGLD) (NCSE, 2006). There is limited data on the prevalence of SEN in Ireland. According to the National Council for Special Education (2006), the rate for 2004 was approximately 18 per cent, a figure that includes: physical and sensory disabilities (1.2 per cent); intellectual/general learning difficulties (mild, 1.5 per cent; moderate, severe and profound, 0.41 per cent); specific learning disabilities (SLD, 6 per cent); autistic spectrum disorder (ASD, 0.56 per cent); and mental health difficulties (8 per cent). As outlined, the term 'special educational needs' covers a broad spectrum of needs and therefore it would be impossible to address all of the individual needs of these pupils within this context. As a result, for the purposes of this chapter, the context of students with SEN and its implication for teaching will be addressed. Table 5.4 outlines the main categories of SEN as stated in a Department of Education and Science circular (Department of Education and Science, 2005). It should be remembered that normal IQ is deemed to be between 90 and 110.

The specific difficulties that students with SEN will have in mainstream education have been found to be dependent upon their type of disability and a multitude of other factors, including socio-economic status and family type and race (Griffin and Shevlin, 2007). A key area of challenge for these pupils is the relationship between their disability and their ability to learn and access the curriculum. For example, it has been established that ADHD is a disorder that involves deficiencies in the executive functions of the brain. This system is located

Table 5.4 Overview of categories of special educational needs

Category	Example of Disability
Physical disability	Cerebral palsy; Dyspraxia
Hearing impairment	Partially or completely deaf
Visual impairment	Partially or completely blind
Emotional disturbance	Attention deficit/hyperactivity disorder; Obsessive compulsive disorder; Oppositional defiant disorder
Severe emotional disturbance	As above but can be more extreme and as a result of other factors
Borderline mild general learning disability	IQ range 70–80, may have difficulties in one or more areas of cognition and learning
Mild general learning disability	IQ range 50–70
Moderate general learning disability	IQ range 20–50
Severe/Profound general learning disability	IQ range below 20
Autism/Autistic spectrum disorders	Asperger's syndrome
Specific learning disability	Dyslexia; Dyscalculia; Dysgraphia
Assessed syndromes	Down syndrome; Tourette syndrome; William's syndrome
Specific speech and language disorder	Verbal dyspraxia
Multiple disabilities	A combination of two or more of the above

in the pre-frontal cortex and is a central management system that is crucial in the organisation and integration of cognitive processes over time. As these skills are crucial to enabling students to learn how to learn, students with ADHD can have profound difficulties in mainstream education (Denckla, 2000). Accordingly, they require short, stimulating tasks which demand a higher level reasoning skills and creativity rather than step-by-step learning (Lovecky, 2004). What is important to note is that while students may fall on the continuum of, for example, dyslexia or Asperger's syndrome, they all have individual and specific needs. Therefore, what might work with one student will not necessarily apply to another. In order for teachers to facilitate pupils with SEN in their classroom, they will need to read broadly and attend additional training when possible. It is also essential that teachers become actively engaged in accessing the multitude of resources and reading material to enhance their knowledge and understanding of this cohort of students.

Policy versus practice

The definition of inclusion varies greatly across Europe (EADSNE, 2009). However, within the Irish context, when we refer to inclusionary practices in mainstream education, it is usually associated with accommodating students with SEN. Although inclusion is strongly advocated by legislation and policies at both national and international level, concerns have been raised about whether the process in Ireland has occurred too quickly and without adequate preparation (Department of Education and Science, 2006; Travers, 2006). For example, while generally in favour of inclusive practices for children with SEN (Lawless and Colfer, 1990; Kearns, 1997), teachers appear to have mixed feelings about the delivery of these practices. Specifically, 60 per cent of teachers are unhappy with their school's policy on inclusion (Stevens and O'Moore, 2009) and believe that much depends upon the provision of appropriate supports (Butler and Shevlin, 2001). In short, there is potential for confusion between written policy on inclusion at a national level and experiences in the classroom (Glashan et al., 2004). A number of authors have proposed that a key feature of this chasm between policy and practice for the inclusion of pupils with SEN rests with the organisation of the Irish system of education (Griffin and Shevlin, 2007; Lynch, 2007; White, 2007), however, at a more local level, it can be suggested that attitudes to including pupils with SEN may also be partly dependent on teachers' experiences outside of education.

Curriculum and pedagogy

As a result of the inclusion of students with SEN in mainstream education, schools have discussed the question of how curriculum and pedagogy can be adapted to the needs of specific learners (Tangen, 2005). The National Centre for Curriculum and Assessment (NCCA) is also currently discussing a modified approach to the senior cycle for pupils with learning disabilities. The two programmes at the centre of curriculum reform for the secondary sector are the Junior Certificate School Programme (JCSP) and the Leaving Certificate Applied Programme (LCAP), now taken by 3 per cent and 7 per cent of the school cohort respectively. Although both programmes already emphasise cross-curricular work, tasks and projects, along with personal and social development, there is a further move towards more vocationally oriented alternatives. The National Council for Curriculum and Assessment (NCCA, 2009) is working closely with schools and teachers to develop a sample JCSP for pupils with general learning disabilities. The aim of the programme is to focus on core learning skills, such as communication, literacy, numeracy, personal effectiveness and social skills. In addition, the NCCA is working towards an award system that would enable these pupils to gain qualifications parallel to a FETAC 2 award in mainstream schools.

In summary, from birth, children experience rapid growth and reach what can be described as developmental milestones across all areas of development. These changes, as already highlighted, occur within an environmental and biological context providing the basis for healthy growth and development which, in turn, requires a stimulating and caring environment. A variety of theories, some of which have already been reviewed, assist our understanding of how these factors influence individual development. The following section will examine how, specifically, developmental psychology contributes to our understanding of adolescent development.

THE CONTEXT OF ADOLESCENCE

The transition from primary to secondary school is a significant educational and psychological milestone in the lives of all children. In a context of considerable biological, social, cognitive and emotional change, primary-school pupils quickly face adaptation demands on many levels which might promote or impede psychological and intellectual development. In short, adolescence is considered to be the most challenging developmental stage of human development. While the biological changes of puberty are universal, their particular expression, timing and extent varies enormously and are dependent upon sex, genes and nutrition (Lalor et al., 2007). Diversity also exists in cognitive development. Many adolescents are as egocentric as pre-school children (see Piaget, 1954) while others think logically, hypothetically and theoretically as well as, or better than, many adults (Donaldson, 1978). Psychosocial changes involve the adolescents developing their own identity and choosing from a vast number of sexual, moral, political and educational paths (Erikson, 1968). While complex individual differences exist, a commonality in the adolescent experience is evident, for example, many adolescents are preoccupied with their bodies and self-image (McCabe and Riccardelli, 2003; McSharry, 2008). Gender differences exist, with young males generally evaluating their growing body more in terms of body efficiency and physical ability. Conversely, young women evaluate themselves more in terms of physical attractiveness and the reactions of others (Trew et al., 2006).

PSYCHOSOCIAL DEVELOPMENT

The emergence of self

The development of the self appears to run consistently in parallel with an understanding of others (i.e. understanding what is and is not the self). The earliest signs of a sense of self appear to emerge in infancy, when toddlers begin to recognise themselves visually and can readily differentiate themselves from others (Rathus, 2006). Although a more composite sense of self and others emerges around eight to 11 years of age, these attributions are primarily of an external, rather than internal, nature. Children at this age, for example, are popular because they are extroverted or academically talented.

In contrast, attributions regarding psychological traits do not emerge until late childhood or early teens when personality characteristics begin to demonstrate both stability and integration (Wenar and Kerig, 2005). At this developmental stage, a global sense of self comprises an array of competencies that are academic, physical, social and even psychological (Harter, 1990). These global evaluations are also referred to as self-esteem (Boyd and Bee, 2010). As attributions become increasingly based on psychological traits, it becomes more likely that one's sense of self incorporates weaknesses and negativity than was previously the case (Wiegfield and Karpathian, 1991). These changes are consistent with changes to parenting style (e.g. greater parental willingness to discipline and criticise) and increased academic experiences (that will involve weaknesses relative to others in one area or another). The considerable fluctuations in self-esteem across the teenage years, therefore, are not surprising (Harter, 1990). For example, research has indicated that self-esteem drops at the onset of adolescence and that this has been a consistent finding especially in the context of transition from primary to post-primary school (Evangleous et al., 2008). Although one's sense of self becomes increasingly integrated and psychological in the teenage years, academic attainment continues to be a critical feature in evaluations of the self and others. Indeed, researchers in this area have argued that the relationship between self-esteem and attainment is bi-directional (Lawrence, 1996); that is, perceived academic weakness results in the attribution of negative self-evaluation, while self-esteem in turn exerts control over academic attainment. For students, the varied challenges of the educational environment require some ego resilience, especially in the mastery of new concepts and tasks (Wenar and Kerig, 2005). This is, of course, amplified by the inherently social nature of education, where peers can accurately identify who is best or worst in the class at particular subjects. As self-esteem is seen to be integral to the development of well-being, teachers should be aware of a student's strengths and weakness. In turn, this should facilitate good communication between staff and is a necessary prerequisite in developing positive learning environments to support the psychological well-being of all students, but particularly those who may be less resilient than their peers.

Adolescent identity

A fundamental feature of adolescent development involves self-identity. Goswick and Jones (1982) suggest that one reason why friendships are crucial at this stage is that adolescents are insecure about themselves, and that building an intimate social network with others with common interests may help the individual to prepare for the wider world. Consequently, psychosocial development in adolescence involves developing a sense of identity, dealing with emotions and relating to parents and peers. Erik Erikson (1968) described the adolescent's development during this period as one of defining his or her own identity versus existing in a state of role confusion. Each adolescent has a choice of many 'possible selves' and they quickly realise that their own repertoires consist of a number of roles, enacted in different social and psychological contexts. For example, adolescents play different roles with different people in different circumstances, indeed their behaviour can range from rowdy and overbearing to withdrawn; from vindictive to intimate. The inconsistencies and contradictions felt as a result of these changing roles and new environments bring problems of their own and adolescents learn that hard choices have to be made resulting in a state of role confusion. Marcia (1966) argued that the formation of adolescent identity consisted of two key parts, crisis and commitment, i.e. the adolescent has to experience crisis in order to commit to their future.

Newcomer or minority students also face the dual task of developing not only an individual identity but also an ethnic one. Ethnic identity involves the young person identifying themselves as a member of a specific group and being committed to the values and attitudes of that group, both positive and negative. Research has found that family support in ethnic identity formation is crucial by teaching the teenager the language of their home country and by providing specific information about how their ethnic group differs from the broader group within their current society (Boyd and Bee, 2010).

Parent/Child relationships

While problems of confusion and turbulence exist throughout a person's life span, some adolescents may make fateful choices that might impede or destroy their future. However, seriously troubled adolescents are in the minority. Indeed, many of the so-called problems of adolescence are actually problems more for parents and society than for teenagers themselves. For example, many adults measure their current perceptions of adolescents by their memories of their own youth and view them as being more troubled, less respectful, more self-centred, more assertive and more adventurous than they were (Feldman and Elliott, 1990). Furthermore, conflicts with parents revolve predominantly around minor physical arrangements such as tidiness or helping around the house. However, a significant feature of these conflicts arises from the many changes fundamental to adolescence. Specifically, parents observe changes in the adolescent and increase their expectations accordingly. Similarly, adolescents begin to evaluate parents as other human beings, and make judgments and often criticisms on this basis (Boyd and Bee, 2010).

Peers

From 14 or 15 years of age, adolescents spend more time with friends outside the parental home in comparison with children and early adolescents. It is essential for young people to establish contact with new friends to strengthen existing affiliations. This enables them to reflect on their own ideas and opinions (Johnson and Johnson, 1999). Some leisure-time activities take place in settings, such as bars, discos and parties, in which certain risk behaviours and the development of peer relations come together (Træen and Nordlund, 1993). It can therefore be assumed that some risk behaviours facilitate peer group integration (Engels, 2003). For example, findings from longitudinal studies suggest that abstaining late adolescents and young adults are less likely to develop steady intimate relationships than drinkers (Engels and Knibbe, 2000). Interestingly, when adolescents are asked what motives they endorse for their drinking or smoking behaviour, they often mention the social aspects of substance use, i.e. it makes parties more fun, they feel more relaxed and find it easier to approach others (Engels et al., 2008).

Social groups have an identity that is shared by all members, and conformity to the group norms and values is felt to be important. Bergin (1989) found that the desire to belong was the most important motive for participating in out-of-school activities. In ranking the most important aspects of popularity for boys: participation in athletics; being in the leading crowd; being a leader in activities; getting high grades; and coming from the right family was considered to be important. Similarly for girls: being in the leading crowd; being a leader in activities; getting high grades; and coming from the right family were deemed to be important (Crockett et al., 2010). Given the importance of interpersonal attributes, it is not surprising that adolescents find group acceptance by developing and exhibiting personal qualities that will ensure group acceptance.

The idea that the norms of the peer group force adolescents to act in ways that they otherwise would not is often exaggerated. Because teenagers associate most readily with those who are similar along many dimensions, it is rarely the case that they get 'led astray'. Social pressure to conform to peers is short-lived, peaking around the age of 14. These influences may be neither dysfunctional nor negative. For example, Brown (1990) reported examples of discouragement of smoking amongst peers. During later adolescence, individuals exhibit greater resistance to peer pressure and a greater capacity for autonomous behaviour. Consequently, the monitoring of adolescents' behaviour is the responsibility of parents, teachers and other responsible adults. Decreasing monitoring too early leaves adolescents to cope with tempting situations alone or with friends and peers (Xiaoming et al., 2000). Lack of adult supervision increases an adolescent's inclination to engage in risk-taking behaviour which, when combined with their lack of self-regulatory skills, increases their vulnerability to a host of negative outcomes.

Cognitive changes

When children enter adolescence, they can engage in more abstract reasoning processes. They are now capable of speculating, hypothesising and fantasising more readily than younger children. The distinguishing feature is the ability to think in terms of possibility instead of concrete reality. Basic cognitive skills continue to emerge, the speed of processing increases (guided by brain growth) and they continue to master language and develop the ability to think logically about abstract ideas. They become increasingly aware of world concerns and personal needs by becoming more mature in their use of analysis logic and reason. At this stage, for example, they become involved in activities for human or animal rights become vegetarian or change their religion (see Piaget, 1954, in Boyd and Bee, 2009). Another characteristic of adolescent thought is egocentrism where they believe that their thoughts and feelings are unique (Eklind, 1967). This is similar to the notion that adolescents are self-centred where the world revolves only around them. Other components of egocentrism include the 'invincibility fable' where adolescents feel immune to the laws of mortality and probability and, therefore, take risks, and the 'personal fable' where they imagine their own lives as mythical or heroic and see themselves destined for fame or fortune (e.g. being a celebrity). Eklind also suggested that adolescent egocentrism provides teenagers with the drive to engage and try out various attitudes and behaviours in front of an 'imaginary audience'. This is characterised by the adolescent's preoccupation of how others will react to them and where they do not feel at ease with the social world. According to Boyd and Bee (2009), Eklind's theoretical perspective has been helpful in explaining much of the everyday behaviour of adolescents evident in school and home settings.

How brain development might explain behaviour changes in adolescence

A teacher prepares for her class and starts her lesson by asking students to take out the books and worksheets that they were working on the previous week. The students groan in dismay and respond with 'I forgot' or 'Do you have any spare sheets?' The teacher may despair while reiterating to the students yet again that they should have their books with them at all times and remember their worksheets from week to week. This is a common scenario, familiar to most teachers during their teaching practice. How can this behaviour be explained? Recent research has indicated that the adolescent brain is far less developed than was previously believed (Weinberger et al., 2005; Casey et al., 2008). The dynamic nature of the teen brain is emerging from MRI studies that have enabled researchers at the Harvard Medical School to scan children safely over many years, thus enabling them to track the development of the brain (Weinberger, et al., 2005). The implications of this discovery may explain why adolescents are prone to making poor decisions and also why it places them at an elevated risk to the harmful effects of drugs and other risk-taking behaviours. For example, the pre-frontal cortex (recall the executive functions from the SEN section above) located just behind the forehead, which is sometimes referred to as 'the seat of sober second thought', is responsible for the complex processing of information, ranging from making judgments, to controlling impulses, foreseeing consequences, and setting goals and plans. As it is also the last part of the brain to develop, from a behavioural perspective, this may explain why teenagers show poor judgment and too often act before they think (Weinberger et al., 2005).

In addition, the nucleus accumbens directs motivated behaviour and is responsible for how much effort an individual will expend in order to see rewards. In adolescents, an immature accumbens results in preferences for activities that require low effort yet produce high excitement (e.g. playing video games, skateboarding and substance abuse). This area of the brain has been found to be highly associated with risk-taking behaviour (Casey et al., 2008). The increases and capacity in cognitive ability is thought to be related to regions of the cortex which manages abstract information (recall Piaget's cognitive stages) which are crucial for acquiring concepts such as rules, laws and social conduct that seem to mirror developing adult-like behaviours (Weinberger et al., 2005). Another brain structure, the amygdala, is the structure responsible for integrating emotional reactions to pleasurable and aversive experiences. Theorists believe that a developing amygdala contributes to two behavioural effects: the tendency for adolescents to react explosively to situations rather than with more controlled responses; and the propensity for teenagers to misread neutral or inquisitive facial expressions of others as a sign of anger. Research such as this contributes to the debate about the psychological changes that occur during adolescence but more is required to appreciate and understand how brain development affects individual development during adolescence (Boyd and Bee, 2010; Casey et al., 2008; Weinberger et al., 2005).

School climate

Schools are elaborate, multilevel institutions that influence childhood and adolescent development in ways that extend well beyond educational attainment. In short, they can promote generic developmental competencies and/or reinforce developmental weaknesses (Eccles and Roeser, 1999). Psychological research has indicated that the school climate and the academic environment are crucial variables in supporting and nurturing young adolescents (Booth and Sheehan, 2008). A variety of features have been identified as crucial to the development of a positive school climate, including school size (Kuziembo, 2006), perceived school order (Mijanovich and Weitzman, 2003) and, in particular, teacher support (Rhodes and Mulhall, 2003). How adolescents cope in school is dependent on a number of factors: their individual developmental stage (i.e. not all 14 year olds act like 14 year olds); their cognitive strengths and weakness; their learning style; societal traditions; their educational expectations; and their future needs.

The developmental needs and the challenges of adolescence as described above are often in conflict with the demands of the school environment. For example, it has been found that peers are the primary focus of student attention when in school, providing both positive and negative influences on the individual, while fear of bullying and fighting features as one of the reasons for not liking school (Booth and Sheehan, 2008). The problems associated with bullying in schools are well documented and constitute an international problem (Smith et al., 1999). Indeed, adverse peer relations are thought to contribute to the suicides of young people in England (Marr and Field, 2001), Ireland (O'Moore, 2000), Japan (Morita et al., 1999) and Norway (Olweus, 1993). Bullying can be defined as occurring when 'a student … is exposed, repeatedly and over time, to negative actions on the part of one or more other students' (Olweus, 1994, p. 9). Gender differences exist with girls engaging in more social forms of aggression (e.g. excluding or marginalising the victim from peers and/or activities), while boys employ physical and often violent means (Smith et al., 2004). A representative sample of 819 16-year-olds in Northern Ireland reported victimisation rates of 30.4 per cent (n = 244), while an additional 64.7 per cent reported being stressed in a response to the statement: 'I was bullied at school' (McGuckin et al., 2010). Impaired psychological health and general well-being was found to be associated with bully/victim behaviours. McGuckin and Lewis (2003) stress that adults are central to establishing supportive and inclusive environments and a whole-school approach is required to ensure that low-level aggression and bullying is not tolerated in schools. Indeed, O'Moore (2000) highlighted the necessity for incorporating in-service training programmes for teachers on bullying and victimisation in schools as result of the tragic death of a student in the Ireland who had been the victim of prolonged bullying at school. However, McGuckin et al. (2010) caution that the emergence of cyber bullying is increasingly becoming an issue for students and schools should re-evaluate and update their policies and procedures relating to this phenomenon.

Teachers

The role of the teacher is crucial in supporting students through these vast developmental changes. In particular, high teacher expectations tend to increase student interest and aspirations (Wentzel, 2002), while good teachers push students to do well and make it easier for them to understand material (Tatar, 1998a ;1998b) Several theoretical models have attempted to address the processes by which teachers' expectations are communicated to students (Cooper, 1979; Cooper and Good, 1983). In short, teachers' expectations influence overt (what can be seen) and covert (what cannot be seen) behaviour, which, in turn, is communicated to students and ultimately affects academic self-efficacy and/or performance.

Relationships with teachers are also highly correlated with school satisfaction in contrast to teachers who are hostile and over controlling and who, in turn, are seen to have a negative impact on school climates and students' well-being (Booth and Sheehan, 2008). Within the Irish educational system, school climate has been identified as the key factor in engaging and retaining students in formal education (Byrne and Smyth, 2010). Students cited negative interactions with teachers, not being listened to, and not receiving help and support as the main contributory factors to their decisions to 'drop out' of school. While the authors acknowledge that a multitude of interrelated factors contribute to the phenomena of 'school dropout', negative school experiences are central to young people's decision-making with regard to their future in education. Consequently, creating a positive classroom environment is crucial in promoting learning, sustaining attention and enabling students to experience success. While the task of teaching is 'to teach', in order to be an effective teacher, it is useful to know what expectations should be placed on pupils and how individual needs can be catered for in the classroom. In a similar vein, it is also appropriate for teachers to support their students' learning and assist them in their everyday tasks and challenges, which will be greater for some students.

The key areas of developmental and educational psychology presented in this chapter are only some of the components that will contribute to teachers' development and understanding of human development from a psychological perspective.

RECOMMENDED READING

Alexandra, T., Sponath, F. and Plomin, R. (2002). 'Twins early development study (TEDS): A Multivariate Longitudianal genetic investigations of language cognition and behaviour problems in childhood'. *Twins Research*, vol. 5, no. 5, 444–8.

Anderson, J. R. (2005). *Cognitive Psychology and its Implications* (6th edition). New York: Worth.

Ashcraft, M. H. (2006). *Cognition* (3rd edition). Upper Saddle River, NJ: Prentice Hall.

Atkinson, R. C. and Shriffin, R.M. (1968). 'Human memory: A proposed system and its control processes'. In K. W. Spence and J. T. Spence (eds), *The Psychology of Learning and Motivation: Advances in Research and Theory, Vol. 2*. New York: Academic Press.

Bandura, A. (1997). *Self-efficacy: The exercise of control*. New York: Freeman.

Bee, H. and Boyd, D. (2010). *The Developing Child* (12th edition). USA: Pearson.

Benton, D. (2008). 'A fishy tale? What impact does diet have on behaviour and intelligence?'. *Psychologist*, 21, 850–53.

Bergin, D. A. (1989). 'Student goals for out of school learning activity'. *Journal of Adolescent Research*, 4, 92–109.

Booth, Z. and Sheehan, H. (2008). 'Perceptions of people and place'. *Journal of Adolescent Research*, 23, 722–44.

Bornstein, M. and Lamb, M. (1999). *Developmental Psychology: An advanced textbook* (4th edition). Mahwah, NJ: Lawrence Erlbaum Associates.

Bouchard, T. J., Lykken, D. T., McGue, M., Segal, N. L. and Tellegen, A. (1990). 'Sources of human psychological differences: The Minnesota Study of Twins Reared Apart'. *Science*, 250, 223–8.

Boyd, D. and Bee, H. (2009). *Lifespan Development* (5th edition). USA: Pearson.

Boyd, D. and Bee, H. (2010). *The Growing Child*. USA: Pearson.

Brofenbrenner, U. (1979). *The Ecology of Human Development*. Cambridge, MA: Harvard University Press.

Brown, B. B. (1990). 'Peer groups and peer cultures'. In S. Feldman and G. Elliott (eds), *At the Threshold: The Developing Adolescent*. Cambridge, MA: Harvard University Press.

Bruner, J. S. (1983). *In search of mind: Essays in autobiography*. New York: Harper & Row.

Butler, S. and Shevlin, M. (2001). 'Creating an inclusive school: The influence of teachers' attitudes'. *Irish Educational Studies*, 1, 125–35.

Buzan, T. (2000). *The Mind Map Book*. London: BBC.

Byrne, D. and Smyth, E. (2010). *No way back: The dynamics of early school leaving*. Dublin: The Economics and Social Research Institute.

Capron, C. and Duyme, M. (1989). 'Assessment of Effects of Socioeconomic Status on IQ in a Full Cross-Fostering Study'. *Nature*, 8, 552–3.

Cardino, A. G. and Gottesman, I. I. (2000). 'Twin studies of schizophrenia: from bow and arrow concordances to star wars Max and functional genomics'. *American Journal of Human Genetics*, 97, 12–17.

Carlson, N., Buskist, W. and Martin, G. (2006). *Psychology: The Science of Human Behaviour*. United Kingdom: Allyn & Bacon.

Carr, E., Dunlap, G., Horner, R., Koegel, R., Turnbull, P., Sailor, W., et al. (2002). 'Positive behaviour support: Evolution of an applied science'. *Journal of Positive Behaviour Interventions*, 4, 4–20.

Casey, B., Getz, S. and Galvan, A. (2008). 'The adolescent brain'. *Developmental Review*, 28, 62–77.

Child, D. (2007). *Psychology and the Teacher*. United Kingdom: Continuum.

Cooper, H. (1979). 'Pygmalion grows up: A model for teacher expectation communication and performance influence'. *Review of Educational Research*, 49, 389–410.

Cooper, H. and Good, T. (1983). *Pygmalion grows up: Studies in the expectation communication process*. New York: Longman.

Cooper, J., Allen, A., Pattall, E. and Dent, L. (2010). 'Effects of full day kindergarten on academic achievement and social development'. *Review of Educational Research*, 1, 34–7.

Crocket, L., Loseff, M. and Petersen, A. C. (2010). 'Perceptions of the peer group and friendships in early adolescence'. *Journal of Early Adolescence*, 4, 155–81.

Crone, D., Hawken, L. and Horner, R. (2010). *Responding to problem behaviour in schools*. London: Guilford Press.

Delaney-Black, V., Covington, C., Templin, T., Ager, J., Nordstrom-Klee, B., Martier, S., Leddick, L., Czerwinski, H. R. and Sokol, R. (2000). 'Teacher-assessed behaviour of children prenatally exposed to cocaine'. *Paediatrics*, 105, 4, 782–91.

Denckla, M. B. (2000). 'Learning disabilities and attention deficit/hyperactivity disorder in adults. Overlap with executive dysfunction'. In T. E. Brown (ed.), *Attention-deficit disorders and comorbities in children, adolescents and adults* (pp. 431–51) Washington DC: American Psychiatric Press.

Department of Education and Science (2005). *Circular SP/ED 02/05: Organisation of Teaching Resources for Pupils who Need Additional Support in Mainstream Primary Schools*. Dublin: The Stationery Office.

Department of Education and Science (2006). *School Matters: The report of the task force on student behaviour in second level schools*. Dublin: The Stationery Office.

Donaldson, M. (1978). *Children's Minds*. London: Fontana.

EADSNE (European Agency for Development in Special Needs Education) (2009). *Development of a set of indicators – for inclusive education in Europe*. Brussels: EADSNE.

Eccles, K. and Roeser, R. (1999). 'School and community influences on human development'. In M. J. Bornstein and M. D. Lamb (eds), *Developmental psychology: An advanced textbook* (4th edition) (pp 503–54) Mahwah, NJ: Lawrence Erlbaum Associates.

Eklind, D. (1967). 'Egocentrism in adolescence'. *Child Development*, 38, 1025–34.

Eley, T. C., Lichtenstein, P. and Stevenson, J. (1998). 'Sex differences in the etiology of aggressive and nonaggressive antisocial behavior: Results from two twin studies'. *Child Development*, 70, 155–68.

Engels, R. (2003). 'Beneficial functions of alcohol use for adolescents: Theory and implications for prevention'. *Nutrition Today*, 38, 25–30.

Engels, R. and Knibbe, R. A. (2000). 'Alcohol use and intimate relationships in adolescence: When love comes to town'. *Addictive Behaviors*, 25, 435–9.

Engels, R., Kerr, M. and Stattin, H. (2008). *Friends, Lovers and Groups*. Chichester: Wiley & Sons.

Erikson, E. H. (1968). *Childhood and Society*. New York: W.W. Norton.

Evangelous, M., Taggart, B., Sylva, K., Melhuish, M., Sammons, P. and Siraj-Blatchford, I. (2008). *Effective pre-school, primary and post-primary education 3-14 project. What makes a successful transition from primary to post-primary school?* London: HMSO.

Eysneck, M. and Keane, T. (2010). *Cognitive Psychology: A Students Handbook* (6th edition). London: Psychology Press.

Feldman, S. and Elliott, G. (1990). 'Adolescence: Path to a productive life or a diminished future?'. *Carnegie Quarterly*, 35, 1–13.

Gardner, H. (2010). *Five Minds for the Future*. Cambridge, MA: Harvard Business School Press.

Glashan, L., Mackay, G. and Grieve, A. (2004). 'Teachers experience of support in the mainstream education of pupils'. *Improving Schools*, 7, 49–60.

Goswick, R. A. and Jones, W. H. (1982). 'Components of loneliness during adolescence'. *Journal of Youth and Adolescence*, 2, 373–83.

Government of Ireland (1998). *The Education Act*. Dublin: The Stationery Office.

Government of Ireland (2000a). *The Education (Welfare) Act*. Dublin: The Stationery Office.

Government of Ireland (2000b). *The Equal Status Acts*. Dublin: The Stationery Office.

Government of Ireland (2003). *The Education of Persons with Disabilities Bill*. Dublin: The Stationery Office.

Government of Ireland (2004a). *The Equality Act*. Dublin: The Stationery Office.

Government of Ireland (2004b). *Education for Persons with Special Educational Needs Act (EPSEN)*. Dublin: The Stationery Office.

Griffin, S. and Shevlin, M. (2007). *Responding to Special Educational Needs*. Dublin: Gill & Macmillan.

Haier, R. J., Siegel, B. V., Nuechterlein, K. H., Hazlett, E., Wu, J. C., Paek, J., Browning, H. L. and Buchsbaum, M. S. (1988). 'Cortical glucose metabolicrate correlates of abstract reasoning. Attention studied with positron emission tomography'. *Intelligence*, 12 (2), 199–217.

Harter, S. (1990). 'Issues in the assessment of the self-concept of children and adolescents'. In A. LaGreca (ed.), *Through the eyes of a child*. Boston: Ally & Bacon.

Hendrickson, A. E. (1982). 'The biological basis of intelligence. Part 1: Theory'. In H. J. Eysneck (ed.), *A Model for Intelligence* (pp. 151–96). New York: Springer Verlag.

Horn, J. L. and Catell, R. B. (1966). 'Refinement and test of the theory of fluid and crystallized intelligence'. *Journal of Educational Psychology*, 57, 253–70.

Johnson, P. B. and Johnson, H. L. (1999). 'Cultural and familial influences that maintain the negative meaning of alcohol'. *Journal of Studies on Alcohol*, 13, 79–83.

Kearney, J. A. (2008). *Understanding Applied Behaviour Analysis: An Introduction to ABA for Parents, Teachers and Other Professionals*. London: Jessica Kingsley.

Kearns, H. (1997). 'Initial teacher education with pupils with Special Educational Needs'. *REACH Journal of Special Needs Education in Ireland*, 11, 13–21.

Kuhn, D. (2008). 'Formal operations from a twenty-first century perspective'. *Human Development*, 51, 48–55.

Kuziembo, I. (2006). 'Using shocks to school enrolment to estimate the effect of school size on student achievement'. *Economics of Education Review*, 25, 63–75.

Lalor, K., de Róiste, A. and Devlin, M. (2007). *Young People in Contemporary Ireland*. Dublin: Gill & Macmillan.

Lawless, A. and Colfer, J. (1990). 'Integration: Attitudes and experiences of primary school teachers'. *REACH Journal of Research in Special Educational Needs*, 5, 7–11.

Lawrence, D. (1996). *Enhancing Self-Esteem in the Classroom*. London: Paul Chapman.

Lovecky, D. (2004). *Different Minds: Gifted Children with AD/HD, Asperger Syndrome and other Learning Deficits*. London: Jessica Kinglsey.

Lynch, P. (2007). 'Inclusion provision practice and curriculum: Time for a closer look'. *REACH Journal of Special Needs Education in Ireland*, 4, 7–11.

MacKay, T. (2010). 'Can psychology change the world?'. *The Psychologist*, vol. 21, 11, 928–31.

Marcia. J. E. (1966). 'Development and validation of ego identity status'. *Journal of Personality and Social Psychology*, 3, 551–8.

Marr, N. and Field, T. (2001). *Bullycide: Death at Playtime*. Didcot, Oxfordshire: Success Unlimited.

Mayes, C., Grillon, C., Granger, R. and Schottenfeld, R. (2006). 'Regulation of arousal and attention in preschool children exposed to cocaine prenatally'. *Annals of the New York Academy of Sciences*, 846, 126–43.

McCabe, M. and Riccardelli, L. (2003). 'A longitudinal study of body change strategies'. *Journal of Youth and Adolescence*, 32, 105–13.

McGarrigle, J. and Donaldson, M. (1974). 'Conversations and accidents'. *Cognition*, 3, 341–50.

McGuckin, C. and Lewis, C. A. (2003). 'Youth aggression and bullying: challenges for pastoral care workers'. In D. Herl and M. L. Berman (eds), *Building bridges over troubled waters: enhancing pastoral care and guidance* (pp. 215–42). Ohio: Wyndham Hall Press.

McGuckin, C., Cummins, P. and Lewis, C. (2010). 'Fef and cyberbullying among children in Northern Ireland: Data from the kids life and times surveys'. *Psychology, Society and Education*, 2, 67–78.

McSharry, M. (2008). *Schooled Bodies*. Stoke-on-Trent: Trentham Books.

Mijanovich, T. and Weitzman, B. C. (2003). 'Which 'broken windows' matter? School, neighborhood, and family characteristics associated with youths' feelings of unsafety'. *Journal of Urban Health: Bulletin of the New York Academy of Medicine*, 80, 400–415.

Miller, G. (1956). 'The magic number seven plus or minus two some limits on our capacity for processing information'. *Psychology Reviews*, 63, 81–97.

Morita, Y., Soeda, H., Soeda, K. and Taki, M. (1999). 'Japan'. In P. K. Smith, Y. Morita, J. Junger-Tas, D. Olweus, R. Catalano and P. Slee (eds), *The Nature of School Bullying: A Cross-National Perspective* (pp. 309–23). London and New York: Routledge.

NCCA (National Council for Curriculum and Assessment) (2009). *Special Educational Issues: Curriculum Issues Discussion Paper*. Dublin: NCCA.

NCSE (National Council for Special Education) (2006). *Implementation Report: Plan for the phased implementation of the EPSEN Act (2004)*. Dublin: The Stationery Office.

NEWB (National Educational Welfare Board) (2008). *Developing a code of behaviour: Guidelines for schools*. Dublin: The Stationery Office.

Olweus, D. (1993). *Bullying at school. What we know and what we can do.* Cambridge, MA: Blackwall Ed.

Olweus, D. (1994). 'Annotation: Bullying at school: Basic facts and effects of a school based intervention program'. *Journal of Child Psychology and Psychiatry*, 35, 1171–90.

O'Moore, M. (2000). 'Critical issues for teacher training to counter bullying and victimisation in Ireland'. *Aggressive Behaviour*, 26, 99–111.

O'Toole. C. and Barnes-Holmes, D. (under submission). 'The role of relational responding and relational flexibility in human intelligence: An investigation using the Implicit Relational Assessment Procedure (IRAP)'.

Parrott, A., Morinam, A., Moss, M. and Scoholey, A. (2004). *Understanding Drugs and Behaviour*. Chichester: Wiley & Sons.

Piaget, J. (1954). *Intelligence and affectivity: Their relationship during child development*. Palo Alto, CA: Annual Review, Inc.

Piaget, J. and Inhelder, B. (1969). *The Psychology of the Child*. New York: Basic Books.

Pinker, S. (2000). *The Blank Slate*. London: Penguin.

Pressley, M. and McCormick, C. (2008). *Child and Adolescent Development for Educators*. London: Guildford Press.

Putnam, S. and Stifter, C. (2008). 'Reactivity and regulation: The impact of Mary Rothbard on the study of temperament'. *Infant and Child Development*, 17, 311–20.

Rathus, Spencer A. (2006). *Childhood Voyages in Development* (2nd edition). USA: Thomson.

Rhodes, J. E. and Mulhall, P. (2003). 'The influence of teacher support on student adjustment in the middle school years: A latent growth curve study'. *Development & Psychopathology*, 15, 119–38.

Rogers, A. (2008). *Teaching Adults* (3rd edition). Milton Keynes: Open University Press.

Scanlon, G. and McGilloway, S. (2005). 'Managing children with special needs in the Irish education system: A professional perspective'. *REACH Journal of the Irish Association of Teachers in Special Education*, 19, 81–94.

Scanlon, G., Barnes-Holmes, Y. and Lodge, A. (2010). 'Promoting inclusion for students with emotional and behavioural difficulties (EBD): Interventions to support change in teacher attitudes and practices'. Ireland: The National Council for Special Education.

Shayer, M. (2008). 'Intelligence for education as described by Piaget and measured by psychometrics'. *British Journal of Educational Psychology*, 1, 1–29.

Slutske, W. S., Eisen, S., True, W. R., Lyons, M. J., Goldberg, J. and Tsuang, M. (2000). 'Common Genetic Vulnerability for Pathological Gambling and Alcohol Dependence in Men', *Archives of General Psychiatry*, 57, 666–73.

Smith, P. K., Morita, Y., Junger-Tas, J., Olweus, D., Catalano, R. and Slee, P. (eds) (1999). *The Nature of School Bullying: A Cross-National Perspective*. London and New York: Routledge.

Smith, P. K., Pepler, D. J. and Rigby, K. (eds) (2004). *Bullying in schools: How successful can interventions be?* Cambridge: Cambridge University Press.

Snowman, J., McCown, R. and Biehler, R. (2009). *Psychology Applied to Teaching* (12th edition). USA: Wadsworth Cengage Learning.

Spearman, C. M. (1904). 'The proof and measurement of association between two things'. *The American Journal of Psychology*, 15, 201–93.

Stevens, P. and O'Moore, M. (2009). *Inclusion or illusion? educational provision for primary school children with mild general learning disabilities*. Dublin: Blackhall Publishing.

Sugai, G. and Horner, R. H. (2002). 'The evolution of discipline practices: School-wide positive behavior supports'. *Child and Family Behavior Therapy*, 24, 23–50.

Sugai, G., Horner, R. H., Dunlap, G., Heineman, M., Lowis, T. J., Nelson, D. M., et al. (2000). 'Applying positive behaviour support and functional behavioural assessment in schools'. *Journal of Positive Behaviour Interventions*, 2, 131–43.

Tan, E. and Goldberg, A. (2009). 'Parental school involvement in relation to children's grades and adaptation to school'. *Journal of Applied Developmental Psychology*, 30, 442–53.

Tangen, R. (2005). 'Promoting inclusive education in secondary school in Norway: A national programme for teachers' development'. *European Journal of Special Needs Education*, 24, 103–107.

Tatar, M. (1998a). 'Extent and source of parents' school-related information'. *The Journal of Educational Research*, 92, 101–106.

Tatar, M. (1998b). 'Significant individuals in adolescence: Adolescent and adult perspectives'. *Journal of Adolescence*, 21, 691–702.

Thomas, A. and Chess, S. (1977). *Temperament and Development*. New York: Brunner/Mazel.

Thurstone, L. L. (1924/1973). *The Nature of Intelligence*. London: Routledge.

Træen, B. and Nordlund, S. (1993). 'Visiting public drinking places in Oslo: An application of the theory of planned behaviour'. *Addiction*, 88, 1215–24

Travers, J. (2006). 'Perceptions of learning-support teachers and resource teachers of each other's role in Irish primary schools'. *Irish Educational Studies*, 25, 155–69.

Trew, K., Barnett, J., Stevenson, C., Muldoon, O., Breakwall, G., Brown, K., Doherty, G. and Clark, C. (2006). *Young people and food – Adolescents dietary beliefs and understandings*. Dublin: Safefood (Food Safety Promotion Board).

Tschanned-Moran, M. and Woolfolk-Hoy, A. (2001). 'Teacher efficacy: Capturing the elusive construct'. *Teaching and Teacher Education*, 17, 783–805.

Vernon, P. A. and Mori, M. (1992). 'Intelligence reaction times and peripheral nerve conduction velocity'. *Intelligence*, 16, 273–88.

Vygotsky, L. (1978). *Interaction between Learning and Development*. In M. Cole (trans.), *Mind in Society* (pp. 79–91). Cambridge, MA: Harvard University Press.

Watson, J. B. and Rayner, R. (1920). 'Conditioned emotional reactions'. *Journal of Experimental Psychology*, 3, 45–56.

Weinberger, D., Elvevåg, B. and Giedd, J. (2005). *The Adolescent brain: A work in progress*. Washington, DC: The National Company to Prevent Teen Pregnancy.

Wenar, C. and Kerig, P. (2005). *Developmental Psychopathology: From infancy through adolescence* (5th edition). New York: McGraw Hill.

Wentzel, K. R. (2002). 'Are effective teachers like good parents? Teaching styles and student adjustment in early adolescence'. *Child Development*, 73, 287–301.

White, L. (2007). 'Principal teachers' perceptions of inclusive provisions in mainstream and transfer to the special school for students with Moderate General Learning Disabilities'. *REACH Journal of Special Needs Education in Ireland*, 21.

Wiegfield, A. and Karpathian, M. (1991). 'Who am I and what can I do? Children's self-concepts and motivation in achievement situations'. *Educational Psychologist*, 26, 233–61.

Wilkinson, R. B. (2009). 'Adolescent best friends as attachment figures: Implications for psychological health and adjustment'. In J. C. Toller (ed.), *Friendships: Types, cultural, psychological and social aspects* (pp. 1–37). Hauppauge, NY: Nova Science Publishers.

Woolfolk, M., Hughes, M. and Walkup, V. (2009). *Psychology in Education*. England: Pearson Longman.

Xiaoming, K., Feigeleman, S. and Stanton, B. (2000). 'Perceived parental monitoring and health risk behaviours among urban low income African-American children and adolescents'. *Journal of Adolescent Health*, 27, 43–8.

FURTHER READING

Bee, H. and Boyd, D. (2010). *The Developing Child* (12th edition). USA: Pearson.

Boyd, D. and Bee. H. (2009). *Lifespan Development* (5th edition). USA: Pearson.

Boyd, D. & Bee, H. (2010). *The Growing Child*. USA: Pearson..

Brofenbrenner, U. (1979). *The Ecology of Human Development*. Cambridge, MA: Harvard University Press.

Bruner, J. (1982). 'Models of the learner'. *Educational Researcher*, 4, 5–8.

Carr, E., Dunlap, G., Horner, R., Koegel, R., Turnbull, P., Sailor, W., et al. (2002). 'Positive behaviour support: Evolution of an applied science'. *Journal of Positive Behaviour Interventions*, 4, 4–20.

Child, D. (2004). *Psychology and the Teacher*. UK: Continuum.

Crone, D. and Horner, R. (2003). *Building Positive Behaviour Support Systems in Schools: Functional Behavioural Assessment.* London: Guilford Press.

Crone, D., Hawken, L. and Horner, R. (2010). *Responding to problem behaviour in schools.* London: Guilford Press.

Department of Education and Science (2001). *Report of the task force on dyslexia.* Dublin: The Stationery Office.

Department of Education and Science (2001). *The report of the task force on autism: Educational provision and support for persons with autistic spectrum disorders.* Dublin: The Stationery Office.

Department of Education and Science (2005). *Circular SP/ED 02/05: Organisation of Teaching Resources for Pupils who Need Additional Support in Mainstream Primary.* Dublin: The Stationery Office.

Department of Education and Science (2006). *School Matters: The report of the task force on student behaviour in second level schools.* Dublin: The Stationery Office.

Frederickson, N. and Cline, T. (2009). *Special Educational Needs, Inclusion and Diversity.* Milton Keynes: Open University Press.

HADD Family Support Group (2005). *Attention Deficit Hyperactivity Disorder. ADHD and Education: A Resource for Teachers.* Dublin.

Lovecky, D. (2004). *Different Minds: Gifted Children with AD/HD, Asperger Syndrome and other Learning Deficits.* London: Jessica Kingsley.

McGuckin, C., Cummins, P. and Lewis, C. (2010). 'Fef and cyberbullying among children in Northern Ireland: Data from the kids life and times surveys'. *Psychology, Society and Education, 2,* 67–78.

Pinker, S. (1994). *The Language Instinct.* London: Penguin.

Pinker, S. (2000). *The Blank Slate.* London: Penguin.

Pressley, M. & McCormick, C. (2008). *Child and Adolescent Development for Educators.* London: Guilford Press.

Rathus, Spencer A. (2006). *Childhood. Voyages in Development* (2nd edition). USA: Thomson.

Santrock, J. (2009). *Adolescence.* USA: McGraw Hill.

Scanlon, G. and McGilloway, S. (2006). 'Managing children with special needs in the Irish education system: A professional perspective'. *REACH Journal of the Irish Association of Teachers in Special Education, 19,* 81–94.

Scanlon, G., Barnes-Holmes, Y. and Lodge, A. (2010). 'Promoting inclusion for students with emotional and behavioural difficulties (EBD): Interventions to support change in teacher attitudes and practices'. Ireland: The National Council for Special Education.

Snowman, J., McCown, R. and Biehler, R. (2009). *Psychology Applied to Teaching* (12th edition). USA: Wadsworth Cengage Learning.

Vygotsky, L. (1978). *Interaction between Learning and Development.* In M. Cole (trans.), *Mind in Society* (pp. 79–91). Cambridge, MA: Harvard University Press.

Wilkinson, W. K. (2003). *Straight Talk about AD/HD. A Guide to Attention Deficit/Hyperactivity Disorder for Irish Parents and Professionals.* Ireland: Collins Press.

Woolfolk, M., Hughes, M. and Walkup, V. (2009). *Psychology in Education.* England: Pearson Longman.

Index

ABA (Applied Behaviour Analysis), 138
ABAS (Adaptive Behaviour Assessment
    System), 135
ability grouping, 81, 83, 84
access to education, 58
accommodation, 142
accountability, 63, 65, 119
Achenbach Child Behaviour Checklist,
    135
Act to Restrain Foreign Education
    (1695), 39
adaptation, 142
Adaptive Behaviour Assessment System
    (ABAS), 135
adequation, 9
ADHD, 151–4
adolescence, 154–61
adopted children, 148–9
aims of education, 18–26, 64
    in curriculum, 72–3
    in Education Act, 64
    junior cycle, 74–7, 78–9
    senior cycle, 91, 92–3
Aldhelm, Bishop of Malmsburg, 35
alienation and violence, 113
anti-social expressive behaviour, 113
Applied Behaviour Analysis (ABA),
    138
aretaic view, 28
aristocracy, and equality, 113–14
Aristotle, 7–8, 9, 16, 18, 19–20, 28
assessment, 73
    behavioural, 135
    cognitive ability, 134–5
    intelligence, 134–5, 144
    Junior Certificate, 77–8
    Leaving Certificate, 94–5
assimilation, 142

Association of Management of Catholic
    Secondary Schools, 61
asylum seekers, 117
Atkinson, R. and Shiffrin, R., 145
attendance, compulsory, 53
attitudes to school, 82–3, 84
autonomy, 21–2

Bandura, Albert, 139
Bauman, Z., 112, 113
behaviour, 132–40
    assessment, 135
    behaviourism, 136–8, 139
    genetics and, 133, 148–9
    School-Wide Positive Behaviour
        Support, 138
beliefs, personal, 27
    and cultural heritage, 116–17
beliefs, societal, 109–11
Belmore Commission (1897), 49
Belvedere College, 50
Bentham, Jeremy, 27
Bergin, D., 157
Bhreathnach, Niamh, 61, 120–1
bi-directional dynamic, 7
birth complications, 150
Blackrock College, 50
boards of management (BOM), 60, 63–5
    duty defined, 65
Bouchard, T. et al., 148
Boulter, Archbishop Hugh, 39
Bourdieu, Pierre, 114–16, 118
bourgeois, 112, 115
Boyd, D. and Bee, H., 150, 158
brain functioning, 132
    in adolescence, 158–9
Brennan, Séamus, 60, 65
Broadfoot, P., 77

Brofenbrenner, U., 149–50
Brown, B., 157
Bruner, Jerome, 143
bullying, 87, 160
Butler, J., 123

Cameron, D., 122–3
Campion, Edmund, 34
capital, 115
    cultural capital, 114–17, 118
Cardwell, Lord, 46
Carlson, N. et al., 132
categorical imperative, 27
Catholic Relief Act 1783, 40
Catholicism and education, 110, 117–22
    historically, 36, 37, 38–46, 49–50,
        52, 53–4, 118
    paternalistic concept of ethos,
        118–19, 122
    present loss of influence, 120, 122
    sexuality and, 125
    sexuality education, 120–2
    statistics (2008), 118
charity schools, 39–40
charter schools, 39–40
Charter on Fundamental Rights of the
    European Union, 120
Charting our Education Future (1995),
    62–4, 72
chemistry, 58
child-centred education, 23–5
Christian Brothers, 44, 50
Christian existentialism, 26
Christianity, 35
chunking, 146
Church Education Society (CES), 44
citizenship, 76, 91
civil society, 108
classical conditioning, 136–7
clinical psychology, 133
Clongowes Wood College, 50
Codes of Professional Conduct for
    Teachers, 28–9
cognitive ability assessment, 134–5
cognitive development, 139–47
    adolescence, 158
    stages, 140–3

cognitive equilibrium, 142
cognitive psychology, 133
collective conscience, 109–11, 114
Collingwood, R., 12
Commission on Education in Ireland
    (1806–12), 40–1
Commission on Technical Education, 53
Commission on the Points System, 61
community, 108
    and social cohesion, 108–11
community schools, 57
complex-system models, 145
comprehensive schools, 55
computer studies, 97
Comte, Auguste, 109
concept of education, 7–11
concrete operational stage of
    development, 141
conditioning, 136–7
conduct, professional, 28–9, 66
conformity, 9
Connell, R., 123
CONNERS-3 assessment, 135
conscience, collective, 109–11, 114
Constitution of Ireland, 119
constructivism, 10, 82
constructivist learning theory, 143
Council of Education, 54
critical pedagogy, 25–6
Croce, B., 12
Cromwell, Oliver, 38
cronyism, 113–14
Cullen, Cardinal, 46
Culliton, J., 95
cultural capital, 114–17, 118
cultural heritage, 116–17
cultural relativism, 27
Cumann na nGaedheal, 53
curriculum, 72–102
    definition of, 72–3
    curriculum as experience, 73
        junior, 84–9
        senior, 100–2
    curriculum as intention, 73
        junior, 74–7
        senior, 91–9
    curriculum as interaction, 73

junior, 80–4
    senior, 98–100
historical development, 48–9, 51,
        52–3, 54, 57, 63
informal (para-curriculum), 73–4
    case study, 87
Junior Certificate, 74–90
Leaving Certificate, 93–102
'null curriculum', 74
SEN, 153–4
senior cycle, 90–102

Dáil Commission on Secondary
        Education (1921–2), 52–3
Dale and Stephens Report (1905), 51
Day Vocational (Group) Certificate, 75
DEIS (Delivering Equality of opportunity
        In Schools), 80
democracy, 23–5, 112
deontology, 27
Department of Education, 53
depression, 132
Derrig, Tómas, 54
Descartes, René, 16, 17
developmental psychology, 133, 134,
        136–54
    cognitive development, 139–47
        adolescence, 158
        stages, 140–3
    development theories, 136–47
    ecology of development model,
            149–50
    individual differences, 147–54
    nature–nurture debate, 147–50
Dewey, John, 10–11, 19, 23–5
Dilthey, W., 12
diocesan schools, 37
discrimination, sexual, 58–9, 60, 64
diversity, teachers' beliefs, 117
Dublin Model School, 42, 44
Dunne, J., 11
Durkheim, Émile, 108–11, 117
dyslexia/dyspraxia, 152–3
    case study, 86–8

Early School Leavers' Programme, 79
ecology of development model, 149–50

economy, and education, 56–7, 58, 60
    youth unemployment, 94
education
    concept of, 7–11
    distinct from schooling, 108
Education Act 1998, 64–5, 151
Education For a Changing World (1992),
        60–1
Education for Persons with Disabilities
        Bill 2003, 151
Education for Persons with Special
    Educational Needs Act 2004 (EPSEN),
        147, 151
Education (Welfare) Act 2000, 151
educational psychology, 133, 134
egocentrism, 158
Eisner, E. and Vallance, E., 74
Eklind, D., 158
emotivism, 27
empirical knowledge, 12
empiricism, 109
encoding, 145
Enlightenment, 21, 22
Epstein, D. and Johnson, R., 124
equality, 63, 111–14
    gender equality, 58–9, 60, 64
Equal Status Act 2000, 151
Equality Act 2004, 151
Erikson, Erik, 156
ethics, 26–8
ethnic identity, 156
European Convention, 120
European Union, 94, 95, 120
existentialism, 17, 26
extracurricular activities, 74

femininity, 122–3
feminist thought, 22–3, 122
Feyerabend, P., 14
Fianna Fáil, 54–5, 59
filid, 34–5
Fine Gael, 54, 58
formal operational stage of development,
        141
Foucault, M., 17, 123–5
Frankfurt School, 26
free schools, 37–8

Freire, Paolo, 25–6
functionalist model, 16–17

Gadamer, Hans-Georg, 11
Gaelic League, 51, 52
Gallagher, R., 125
Gardner, Howard, 17, 145
Gearing Up for the Exam, 80, 83–4
Gemeinschaft, 108
gender and sexuality, 122–5
gender equality, 58–9, 60, 64
generalising, 137
genetics and behaviour, 133, 148–9
Gesellschaft, 108
Gleeson, J. and Granville, G., 100
Goswick, R. and Jones, W., 155
Gray, John, 122
Green Paper: Education For a Changing
        World (1992), 60–1
Greenwood, Hamar, 52
grinds, 83
growth, 19

Habermas, J., 10
Hargreaves, A., 77
hedge schools, 39
Henry II, King, 36
Henry VIII, King, 34, 36
hermeneutical view of truth, 11
Hill, W. F., 136
Hillery, Patrick, 54–5
history (as a subject), 12–13
history of education in Ireland, 34–71
    ancient and medieval, 34–6
    16th century, 36–7
    17th century, 37–9
    18th century, 39–40
    19th century, 40–51
    20th century, 49, 51–65
Hogan, P., 8, 11, 15, 19, 82
holism, 16, 28, 62
Holy Ghost Fathers, 50
Home/School/Community Liaison
        Scheme, 79
homogeneity, 111
homosexuality, 123–5
Horn, J. and Catell, R., 144

Horowitz, Irving Louis, 114
Howard, John, 40
Hume, David, 109
Hussey, Gemma, 58
hylomorphism, 16
hypotheses, deductive method, 14

ICT studies, 97
idealism, 10
identity, 154, 155–6
identity, learners-models of self, 15–18
inclusion, 138, 153–4
Incorporated Society for Promoting
English Protestant Schools in Ireland,
        39–40
Individual Education Plan (IEP), 135
individualism, 24, 109, 110
inductive reasoning, 14
information-processing, 140
Inglis, Tom, 120
'Innovation and Identity: Ideas for a New
        Junior Cert', 90
inspectorate, 64
instrumental goals of schools, 112–13
instrumental learning, 8
integrity, 8
intelligence, 144–5
    genetics and, 148–9
    multiple intelligences theory, 17, 145
    testing, 134–5, 144
Intermediate Certificate, 75
intermediate education *see* secondary
        education
Intermediate Education (Amendment)
        Act 1924, 53
Intermediate Education (Ireland) Act
        1878, 50
intersubjectivity, 10
Investment in Education Report (1965),
        55–7
invincibility fable, 158
IQ, 134–5
Irish language teaching, 49, 51, 52, 53,
        54, 95

James, William, 10
Jeffers, G., 92, 98

Jefferson, Thomas, 111–12
Jesuit schools, 20, 50
Junior Certificate, 74–90
    aims of, 74–7, 78–9
    curriculum and assessment, 77–8
    curriculum as experience, 84–9
    curriculum as intention, 74–7
    curriculum as interaction, 80–4
    evaluation and future of, 89–90
    historical development, 51, 53, 61,
        62, 63
Junior Certificate School Programme
    (JCSP), 78–80, 153–4

Kant, Immanuel, 10, 21–2, 27
Kelly, A., 73
Kildare Place Society (KPS), 41
kindergartens, 49
knowledge, 7–18
    empirical, 12
    knowledge of knowledge, 8–9
    learners-models of self, 15–18
    pragmatic tradition, 10
    subject areas, 11–15
    truth theories, 9–11
Kuhn, Thomas, 14

league tables, 65
learners-models of self, 15–18
learning, 136–50
    cognitive development, 139–47
    defining, 136
    genetics and, 148–9
    observational learning, 139
    social learning theory, 139
learning difficulties see special
    educational needs
Learning Support Department, 135
Leaving Certificate, 92, 93–102
    case studies, 100–2
    historical development, 51, 53, 57,
        61, 63
Leaving Certificate Applied (LCA), 63,
    93–5, 98–9, 153–4
    case study, 101
Leaving Certificate Established, 95–6,
    99–100

case study, 102
Leaving Certificate Vocational
    Programme (LCVP), 63, 96–8, 100
Leavy, A., 117
Lenihan, Brian, 57
liberation, 25–6
literacy, 25, 79, 99
local education authorities (LEAs), 52
Locke, John, 24
logic, 158
Lord Lieutenant's Fund, 41
Loreto Order, 50
Lynch, Jack, 54
Lyotard, J.-F., 17

McGuckin, C. and Lewis, C., 160
Macionis, J. and Plummer, K., 107
MacPherson Education Bill (1919–20),
    52
magnetic resonance imaging (MRI), 132
Marcia, J., 156
Martin, Archbishop Diarmuid, 119
Martin, Jane Roland, 22
Marx, Karl, 112, 113
masculinity, 122–3
maturation, 141
memory, 140, 145–6
meritocracy, 111–14
methodology, 5
Miller, G., 146
Mills, C. and Gale, T., 117
mind and body, 15–18, 132
mind maps, 146
model schools, 42–5, 46
modelling, 139
Molony Inquiry (1919), 51–2
monasteries, 35–6
moral action, 7–8
morality and ethics, 26–8
Morrison, K., 109
motivation, 146–7
Moving Up, 80–2
Moylan, Seán, 54
MRI (magnetic resonance imaging), 132
Mulcahy, Richard, 54
multiple intelligences theory, 17, 145

National Education Convention (1993), 61–2, 64, 66
national schools, 42–9
  conditions (19th century), 47–8
native schools, 34–5, 36
naturalism, 20–1
nature–nurture debate, 147–50
negative reinforcement, 137
neo-conservatism, 107
nepotism, 113–14
neuroscience, 133
Noddings, Nel, 8, 23
normative questions, 6
numeracy, 79

Oakeshott, Michael, 1, 12
observational learning, 139
O'Connell, Daniel, 41
O'Connor, Joseph, 50–1
O'Moore, M., 160
organisational goals of schools, 112–13
O'Rourke, Mary, 59–60, 64

Palles Commission (1899), 51
parental rights and roles, 60–1, 64
parish schools, 36–7
Parliamentary Review of Irish Education (1824–7), 41–2
partnership, 63, 64
Pathways through the Junior Cycle, 80, 82–3
Patrick, Saint, 35
Pavlov, Ivan, 136
pedagogy, 25–6, 73
  SEN, 153–4
Peel, Robert, 45
peer groups, 157
perceptual processes, 140
personality, 147, 155
philosophy of education, 5–29
physiological psychology, 133
Piaget, Jean, 140–3
Pierce, C. S., 10
Pinker, S., 148
Plato, 15, 19, 111
pluralism, 63
Popper, Karl, 14

positive reinforcement, 137, 138
postmodernism, 119
power and sexuality, 125
powerlessness, 113
Powis Report (1870), 46–8
prenatal development, 150
preoperational stage of development, 141
Presbyterian Church, 43–4
prescriptivism, 27
Presentation Sisters, 50
principal, role of, 65
Pring, R., 8
process adaptation, 142
processing of information, 140
professional conduct, 28–9, 66
Programme for Education (1984–7), 58–9
proletariat, 112
Protestantism, 37, 39–40, 42–3, 44–5
  suicide rates, 117
psyche, 16
psychology of education, 132–61
  branches of, 133
  research and application, 133–6
psychometric analyses, 144
psychotherapy, 133

quality, 63, 76
Queen's College Belfast, 45

Ranelagh School, Athlone, 50
rationality, 20
reasoning, inductive, 14
refugees, 117
reinforcement, 137–9
relationships and sexuality education (RSE), 120–2
relativism, 27
religion, and education, 117–22
  choice of school, 119–20
  historically, 36, 37, 38–46, 49–50, 52, 53–4, 118
  statistics, 118
religious education, 39, 41–6, 121
religious orders, 50, 118
Renehan, C., 123
Revised Programme for National Schools (1900), 49

rights, 120
risk-taking behaviour, 158, 159
Rockwell College, Cork, 50
Rogers, A., 136
role confusion, 156
Rousseau, Jean-Jacques, 20–1, 22
Royal School, Cavan, 50
RSE (relationships and sexuality
     education), 120–2

St Andrews College, Dublin, 50
Saint Germans, Earl of, 46
scaffolding, 143
schemas, 141–2
School Attendance Act 1926, 53
school climate, and adolescence, 159–61
School Completion Programme, 79
school principal, role of, 65
School-Wide Positive Behaviour Support
     (SWPBS), 138
schooling, distinct from education, 108
science (as a subject), 13–14
Second Level Support Service (SLSS),
     93
secondary education, 90–102
     aims of, 91, 92–3
     curriculum as experience, 100–2
     curriculum as intention, 91–9
     curriculum as interaction, 98–100
     historical development, 49–52, 54–5,
          56–7, 59
self, 154–5
self, learners-models, 15–18
self-esteem, 155
self-estrangement, 113
self-identity, 154, 155–6
self-image, 154–5
self-regulation, 139
SEN see special educational needs
Senior Certificate, 93
sensorimotor stage of development, 141
sexual equality, 58–9, 60, 64
sexuality, 123–5
sexuality education, 120–2
Sidney, Sir Henry, 37
Sisters of Mercy, 50
skills, 144

Skinner, B.F., 137, 139
Smyth, E. et al., 80–1, 98
social capital, 115, 118
social cohesion, and education, 108–11
social contract, 20
social groups, and acceptance, 157
social learning theory, 139
social mobility, 114, 116
social psychology, 133
social realism, 109
social solidarity, 110
socialisation, 111
sociology of education, 107–25
soul, 15–16
special educational needs (SEN), 151–4
     categories of, 152
     definition, 151
     inclusion, 138, 153–4
     legislation, 147, 151
     School-Wide Positive Behaviour
          Support, 138
Special Educational Needs Team, 135
Stanley, Edward, 42–5
stereotyping, gender, 123
storytelling tradition, 34
streaming, 81, 83, 84
structuring activities, 82
student teacher, case studies, 88–9, 100–1
suicide rates, and religion, 117–18
Sullivan, Thomas, 34
SWPBS (School-Wide Positive
     Behaviour Support), 138
syllabus, 73
Synod of Thurles (1850), 45

TALIS report, 82
teachers
     beliefs and cultural heritage, 116–17
     career expectations, 61
     codes of professional conduct, 28–9
     conditions and salary (19th century),
          47–8
     expectations of students, 160–1
     knowledge of knowledge, 8–9
     sexual culture and, 124
     students' concept of good teachers,
          83, 84

students' relationships with, 161
Teaching Council Act 2001, 66
Teaching Council of Ireland, 65–6
   proposed, 61, 62
technical education *see* vocational
   education
temperament, 147
teratogen, 150
testing *see* assessment
Thatcher, Margaret, 107
theory, 5
Thayer-Bacon, 22
Tönnies, Ferdinand, 108, 110
Transition Year (TY), 92–3
   case study, 98
Travelling Community, 117
Trinity College Dublin, 37, 38
truth and truth theories, 9–11
twins, 148

understanding, 11
unemployment, youth, 94
Universal Declaration of Human Rights,
   120
universities, 37, 45
University College Cork, 45
University College Galway, 45
Ursuline Order, 50
utilitarianism, 27

values, personal, 27
   and cultural heritage, 116–17
values, social, 109–11
Vienna Circle, 12

violence, 113
virtues, 20, 27
vocational education, 93–4, 96–8
   historical development, 53–4, 55, 57,
      59, 63
Vocational Education Act 1930, 53–4
Vocational Preparation and Training
   Programme (VPT1), 93
Vygotsky, Lev, 143

Wain, K., 18
Watson, John B., 136
   and Rayner, R., 136–7
Weber, Max, 108
Wechsler Individual Achievement
   Test-111 (WIAT-111), 135
Wechsler Intelligence Scale for Children
   (WISC), 134–5
Whately, Archbishop, 45
White Paper: Charting our Education
   Future (1995), 62–4, 72
wisdom, 20
Wittgenstein, Ludwig, 9
women in society, 122–3
   equality, 58–9, 60, 64
Woolfolk, M. et al., 146
Wundt, Wilhelm, 12

Young, Michael, 113–14
Youthreach, 93

Zone of Proximal Development (ZPD),
   143